By his will, Mr. Thomas Spencer Jerome endowed the lectureship that bears his name. It is jointly administered by the University of Michigan and the American Academy in Rome, and the lectures for which it provides are delivered at both institutions. They deal with phases of the history or culture of the Romans or of peoples included in the Roman Empire.

F. E. Adcock, *Roman Political Ideas and Practice*

G. W. Bowersock, *Hellenism in Late Antiquity*

Frank E. Brown, *Cosa: The Making of a Roman Town*

Jacqueline de Romilly, *The Rise and Fall of States According to Greek Authors*

Anthony Grafton, *Commerce with the Classics: Ancient Books and Renaissance Readers*

Fergus Millar, *The Crowd in Rome in the Late Republic*

Claude Nicolet, *Space, Geography, and Politics in the Early Roman Empire*

Massimo Pallottino, *A History of Earliest Italy*

Jaroslav Pelikan, *What Has Athens to Do with Jerusalem?* Timaeus *and* Genesis *in Counterpoint*

Brunilde S. Ridgway, *Roman Copies of Greek Sculpture: The Problem of the Originals*

Lily Ross Taylor, *Roman Voting Assemblies: From the Hannibalic War to the Dictatorship of Caesar*

Mario Torelli, *Typology and Structure of Roman Historical Reliefs*

Paul Zanker, *The Power of Images in the Age of Augustus*

The Crowd in Rome in the Late Republic

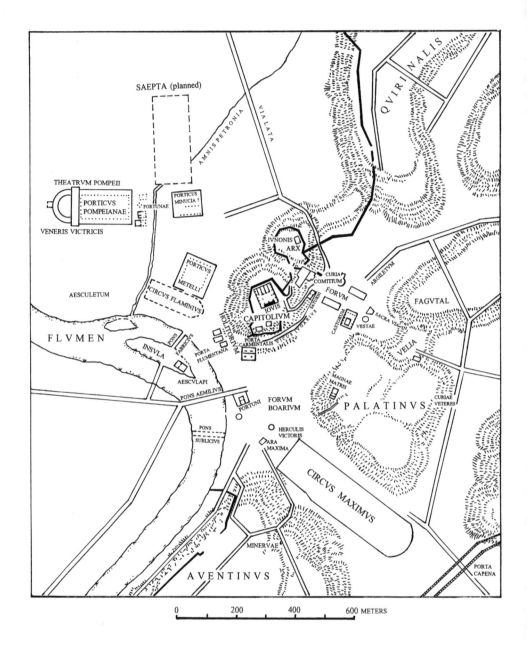

The Center of Rome in 53 B.C. Adapted from L.R. Taylor, *Roman Voting Assemblies: From the Hannibalic War to the Dictatorship of Caesar* (Ann Arbor: University of Michigan Press, 1966). Reprinted by permission of the publisher. Drawn by Jenny Graham.

JEROME LECTURES, 22

The Crowd in Rome
in the
Late Republic

Fergus Millar

Ann Arbor

THE UNIVERSITY OF MICHIGAN PRESS

First paperback edition 2002
Copyright © by the University of Michigan 1998
All rights reserved
Published in the United States of America by
The University of Michigan Press
Manufactured in the United States of America
⊚ Printed on acid-free paper

2005   2004   2003   2002   5   4   3

A CIP catalog record for this book is available from the British Library.

Library of Congress Cataloging-in-Publication Data

Millar, Fergus.
    The crowd in Rome in the late Republic / Fergus Millar.
      p.   cm. —(Jerome lectures ; ??)
    Slightly expanded version of the five Jerome lectures given at the
  University of Michigan at Ann Arbor in 1993 and at the American
  Academy in Rome in 1994.
    Includes bibliographical references and index.
    ISBN 0-472-10892-1 (alk. paper)
      1. Rome—Politics and government—265–30 B.C.   2. Crowds—Rome—
  History. 3. Collective behavior.   I. Title. II. Series: Jerome
  lectures ; 22nd ser.
  DG254.2.M55   1998
  937'.05—dc21   97-50351
                                                                   CIP

ISBN 0-472-08878-5 (pbk : alk. paper)

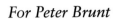

For Peter Brunt

Preface

This book represents a slightly expanded version of the five Jerome Lectures that I had the honor and pleasure of giving at the University of Michigan at Ann Arbor in the autumn of 1993 and at the American Academy in Rome in the spring of 1994. Anyone who is acquainted with either institution will appreciate what a privilege it was for my wife and myself to spend a period in each. Our stay in Ann Arbor represented the culmination of a world tour that took in Moscow, St. Petersburg, Beijing, Tianjin, and California, and it was made particularly rewarding by the responsiveness of the audience for the lectures, the warm hospitality of the members of the Department of Classical Studies, and the helpfulness of the Rackham Graduate School. Our stay in Rome in the following spring followed directly on the reopening of the Academy after a period of refurbishment. We look back with pleasure on the magnificent apartment that we occupied, on the splendid setting of the Villa Aurelia, where the lectures were given, and on the welcome we received from Malcolm Bell and from the director of the Academy, Caroline Bruzelius. It was a particular pleasure that the last of the five lectures could be attended by a large number of Italian colleagues, among them Emilio Gabba, acknowledged by all as the doyen of Republican studies today.

In conception, however, the book goes back to another stay in Rome, when I spent a month at the British School as a Baldson Fellow in the spring of 1983. That, I have to confess, was the first time that I came to appreciate the topography of Rome and to understand something of the significance of its public spaces. A historian of the Roman Empire by origin and training, and always located intellectually more in the Greek-speaking than in the Latin-speaking part of it, I had not at that time written anything on the Republic. The immense impact of the physical reality of the city, ancient and modern, stimulated a number of preliminary studies of popular participation and also resulted in a much earlier, and shorter, draft of the Jerome Lectures, and of this book, in the form of the three lectures given in 1987 in the course of an extremely enjoyable stay at the University of Victoria, British Columbia, as a Lansdowne visitor.

Though the stimulus gained elsewhere has been essential, I would like to put on record again that all the work directed toward this book, and all of the writing of it, has been carried out, as always, in the Ashmolean Library in Oxford, with the help of Brian McGregor and his staff. As always also, the task of translating my uniquely illegible handwriting into a finished text has fallen to Priscilla Lange. I am grateful to her, and to Jenny Graham for preparing the two plans and the indexes.

I would not have ventured into Republican history if I had not felt that I had something to contribute, or, to put it another way, that there was an extraordinary gap between the way the political life of the Republic seemed often to be portrayed and analyzed in the modern world and what appeared to present itself in the sources. Nonetheless, I have been throughout preparation of this book, and remain now, painfully conscious that I do not possess the weight of learning in the complex institutions, history, and historiography of the Republic that is needed for a real understanding of our evidence. If I have made any progress in understanding, it is almost entirely due to what I learned during eight deeply rewarding years at University College, London, from John North and later from Tim Cornell. The former's classic articles and chapters on the Republic and the latter's book *The Beginnings of Rome,* published in 1995, will illustrate what I mean. This acknowledgment, which is very deeply felt, should not be taken as implying that either of them would not view much in this book with deep skepticism. The same is true of Michael Crawford, from whom I have also learned continuously, and whose two volumes entitled *Roman Statutes* published in 1996 represent a major landmark in Roman studies.

Nonetheless, the figure who must be overwhelmingly present to the mind of anyone who ventures to offer a series of Jerome Lectures on any aspect of the Republic must be Lily Ross Taylor. I never met her in person, though I vividly recall hearing as a graduate student the lecture "Forerunners of the Gracchi" that she gave at the Triennial Conference of the Greek and Roman Societies in 1961 and then published in the *Journal of Roman Studies* in 1962. But to me *Party Politics in the Age of Caesar* (1949) still remains the best book on the political life of the late Republic, and I hardly need to stress the fundamental importance for my topic of *The Voting Districts of the Roman Republic* (1960) and, above all, of course, of *Roman Voting Assemblies* (1966), the Jerome Lectures of 1964.

I have taken this latter work as a basis and could not in any case come anywhere near rivaling Lily Ross Taylor's learning as regards Republican institutions, the topography of Rome, or the history of its public buildings and public spaces. More generally, since the purpose of this book is merely to try to feed into our attempts to understand Republican Rome a sense of the possible significance of a series of images of political meetings that are to be found in our literary sources, I have not made any attempt to do justice to the vast legacy of detailed scholarship on the period. The work does indeed represent an implicit dialogue, or argument, with what I take to be the ruling presuppositions about Roman society and politics that have characterized historical writing in this century. But it is a deliberately chosen feature of the literary character of the text, as a somewhat expanded version of a series of five lectures, that it does not argue directly and continuously with any of the major interpretations of this period that conceive of it in rather different terms. So the reader will not find the text engaging, for instance, with Christian Meier's *Res Publica Amissa* (1966), his *Caesar* (1982; translated by D. McLintock in 1995), or Erich Gruen's *The Last Generation of the Roman Republic* (1974; 2d ed., 1995). I am well aware that, partly for that reason, the views and conceptions expressed here may well seem partial, superficial, and inadequate. So indeed they are; they are intended as a one-sided contribution to an ongoing dialogue.

One particularly valuable contribution to this dialogue appeared just when my text was all but ready to be sent off to Michigan and too late for any real account to be taken of it. I refer to Francisco Pina Polo's *Contra Arma Verbis: Der Redner vor dem Volk in der späten römischen Republik* (Heidelberger Althistorische Beiträge und Epigraphische Studien, vol. 22 [Stuttgart: Franz Steiner Verlag, 1996]). Pursuing many comparable themes, if with a different political interpretation, it offers a further and more systematic treatment of a number of topics—for instance, of the identity and status of those who presented themselves as orators before the people.

One effect of the fact that this book, by virtue of its nature as a slight essay, does not engage seriously and directly with the great mass of modern literature on its topic is that, in terms of footnote references, it also makes little or no allusion to precisely those books from which I have actually learned most and which have offered the essential starting point for my own views. This preface is therefore the place to put on record, for a start, the fundamental debt I owe to two books by Claude Nicolet: first,

Le métier du citoyen dans la Rome républicaine (1976), translated as *The World of the Citizen in Republican Rome* (1980); and second, *Rome et la conquête du monde méditerranéen,* vol. 1, *Les structures de l'Italie romaine* (1977). But the book that most decisively reasserted that we must read the political history of the Republic as a story of real politics involving major social and constitutional issues, not as the sterile interplay of "factions" or *clientelae,* was of course Peter Brunt's *Social Conflicts in the Roman Republic* (1971). The categorical disproof of the idea that the evidence would support the interpretation of Republican politics in terms of these two concepts was to be reserved for two masterly chapters in his *The Fall of the Roman Republic and Related Essays* (1988). But it was still *Social Conflicts* that opened up the path to a new and better way of understanding Republican history—or perhaps to the renewal of an older way, from which the approaches that have been dominant throughout most of the twentieth century have been a diversion.

But for the dilatoriness of the author, and his preoccupation with other duties, it might have been possible to bring out this book in time to honor the eightieth birthday of Peter Brunt, on June 23, 1997. It is in any case not to be supposed that, when he does see it, he will not perceive in it many fundamental weaknesses. But I will still allow myself the privilege of dedicating this small volume to a great historian of Rome.

Brasenose College, Oxford
September 1996

Postscript. I would like to offer sincere thanks to the three readers appointed by the University of Michigan Press, whose comments—received, it is true, after a considerable delay—have been of the greatest value in revising the book. To one of these readers in particular, Professor D.R. Shackleton Bailey, I owe a real debt for many salutary observations on my translations from Latin and on matters of prosopography and nomenclature. Many valuable observations and corrections on such matters were also supplied by David Phillips. It would be agreeable to pretend to oneself that all the defects in the text were the result of the pressures on one's time felt in the modern university. But I fear that this is not so, and it is no mere form of words to say that all three readers have saved me from a host of errors, and that those remaining are my responsibility.

June 1997

Contents

Illustrations   xiii

Conventions and Abbreviations   xiii

I. Approaches and Interpretations   1

II. The Roman Crowd in Perspective: Historical Background and Contemporary Setting   13

III. Popular Politics in the 70s: The Demand for the Restoration of Sovereignty   49

IV. The Crowd, Oratory, and Imperialism, 69–65   73

V. Oratory, Disorder, and Social Problems, 64–60   94

VI. Empire, Legislation, and Political Violence, 59–56   124

VII. Popular Politics in Decline, 55–50   167

VIII. The Crowd in Rome: What Sort of Democracy?   197

Subject Index   227

Index of Literary Sources   231

Illustrations

The Center of Rome in 53 B.C.   frontispiece

The Forum in 53 B.C.   40

Conventions and Abbreviations

Standard abbreviations of collections of inscriptions, works of reference, and so forth occur throughout this book and are not included here. Numbers in brackets after references to the letters of Cicero refer to the numbering in the editions by D.R. Shackleton Bailey. Asconius is cited by page numbers in the Oxford text by A.C. Clark. The translations of these and other sources are my own unless otherwise indicated.

Unless marked as A.D., all dates are B.C.

Alexander, *Trials*	Alexander, Michael C. *Trials in the Late Republic, 149 B.C. to 50 B.C.* Toronto: University of Toronto Press, 1990.
Broughton, *MRR*	Broughton, T.R.S. *The Magistrates of the Roman Republic.* Vol. 2, 99 B.C.–31 B.C. New York: American Philological Association, 1952.
Coarelli, *Foro*	Coarelli, F. *Il foro romano.* Vol. 1, *Periodo arcaico,* and Vol. 2, *Periodo repubblicano e augusteo.* Rome: Edizioni Quasar, 1983–85.
Crawford, *Fragmentary Speeches*	Crawford, Jane W. *M. Tullius Cicero, the Fragmentary Speeches: An Edition with Commentary.* Atlanta, Ga.: Scholars Press, 1994.
Crawford, *Roman Statutes*	Crawford, M.H., ed. *Roman Statutes.* 2 vols. London: Institute of Classical Studies, School of Advanced Studies, University of London, 1996.
David, *Patronat judiciaire*	David, J.M. *Le patronat judiciaire au dernier siècle de la République romaine.* Rome: École française de Rome, 1992.

LTUR	Steinby, E.M., ed. *Lexicon Topographicum Urbis Romae.* Vols. 1–3. Rome: Edizioni Quasar, 1993–96.
Malcovati, *ORF*	Malcovati, H. *Oratorum Romanorum Fragmenta Liberae Rei Publicae.* 4th ed. Turin: I.B. Paraviae, 1976.
Peter, *HRR*	Peter, H. *Historicorum Romanorum Reliquiae.* 2d ed. Vol. 1. Leipzig: Teubner, 1914.
Platner-Ashby, *Topographical Dictionary*	Platner, S.B., and T. Ashby. *Topographical Dictionary of Ancient Rome.* London: Oxford University Press, 1929.
Rotondi, *Leges Publicae*	Rotondi, G. *Leges Publicae Populi Romani.* Hildersheim: G. Olms, 1912. Reprint, 1966.
Taylor, *Party Politics*	Taylor, L.R. *Party Politics in the Age of Caesar.* Berkeley: University of California Press, 1949.
Taylor, *Voting Assemblies*	Taylor, L.R. *Roman Voting Assemblies: From the Hannibalic War to the Dictatorship of Caesar.* Ann Arbor: University of Michigan Press, 1966.
Taylor, *Voting Districts*	Taylor, L.R. *Voting Districts of the Roman Republic: The Thirty-five Urban and Rural Tribes.* Rome: American Academy, 1960.

I

Approaches and Interpretations

The first purpose of this book is to present a series of images of the Roman people: assembling in the Forum, listening to orations there, and responding to them; sometimes engaging in violence aimed at physical control of their traditional public space; and dividing into their thirty-five voting groups to vote on laws.

The second purpose is to argue strongly that our whole conception of the Roman Republic has been distorted by theories that have allowed us not to see these open-air meetings *(contiones)* of the *populus Romanus* as central to Roman politics. This book is thus the last in a series of studies that have been designed to place the *populus Romanus*—or the crowd that represented it—at the center of our picture of the Roman system.[1]

The third aim is to relate the first two objectives to the last three decades of the Republic proper, from the resignation of Sulla as dictator in 80 to Julius Caesar's crossing of the Rubicon in January 49. In terms of the concentration both of contemporary evidence, very largely from Cicero (letters, speeches, political and oratorical treatises), and of later narrative evidence in the form of histories and biographies, the political life of these three decades is more fully recorded than that of any other period of the ancient world.

What marks out this period, however, are three features that require us to do more than simply present images drawn from a profusion of evidence. First, there is the successful reassertion of the people's long-established right to legislate. Second, there is the very close connection between the exercise of popular sovereignty and the quickening pace of

---

1. These studies, ordered here in terms of their chronological coverage, are "Political Power in Mid-Republican Rome: Curia or Comitium," *JRS* 79 (1989): 138; "The Political Character of the Classical Roman Republic, 200–151 B.C.," *JRS* 74 (1984): 1; "Politics, Persuasion, and the People before the Social War (150–90 B.C.)," *JRS* 76 (1986): 1; and "Popular Politics at Rome in the Late Republic," in I. Malkin and Z. Rubinsohn, eds., *Leaders and Masses in the Roman World: Studies in Honor of Zvi Yavetz* (New York: E. Brill, 1995), 91 (an essay covering the themes of the present book).

Roman imperialism; in that sense this book takes up again a theme brilliantly argued some years ago by Ernst Badian.[2] Third, there is the equally close connection between popular sovereignty as expressed through the laws that the people passed, the concentration of unprecedented military power in the hands of individuals, and the origins of a monarchical system in which successive dynasties, all using the Republican cognomen *Caesar,* were to be superimposed on the institutions of the ancient Republic.

If we look forward, the emergence of monarchy from within the Republican system had immense consequences, whether we think of the conversion to Christianity of a single individual, the emperor Constantine; of the establishment of an empire of *Rōmaioi* based on Constantinople; of Charlemagne and the long history of the Holy Roman Empire to its end in 1806; or of the fall, in the second decade of the twentieth century, of the last kaiser and the last czar.

Contemporaries living in the last three decades of the Republic were acutely aware of the possibility that so much power might come to be concentrated in one pair of hands that the Republic, with its extremely complex division of powers, would not survive. Precisely one of the purposes of this book is to show that awareness of this possibility, like awareness of many other complex issues, was not confined to theoretical treatises or to debates within the walls of the Senate; it was also expressed in speeches before the people in the open-air theater of the Forum. The most common vehicle for debate, however, was not prediction about the future but reinterpretation of the past. The Roman past, which public speeches assumed to be generally familiar to their audiences, was itself a complex story involving a series of kings eventually deposed, the creation of Republican institutions, struggles between groups with different formal statuses, and a long process of gradual evolution and growing complexity. The system was marked, in a very general sense, by a balance, subdivision, and limitation of powers; more specifically, it exhibited a remarkable degree of incoherence and built-in friction, or opposition of powers, in which voting bodies that were structured in quite different ways elected annual magistrates whose respective rights were not fully defined and who in no sense formed a unified government or administration.

One effect of this is extreme difficulty for the modern reader in understanding the workings of the Roman system, even at the most factual or antiquarian level. Our evidence comes from contemporary (late-

---

2. E. Badian, *Roman Imperialism in the Late Republic,* 2d ed. (Oxford: Blackwell, 1968).

Republican) representations of the past and of the creation and evolution of institutions, from assertions and interpretations offered in the course of contemporary late-Republican debates, or from narratives and biographical works that in effect portray in their own terms incidents in which we seem to see the system working, or that record the system and its values in the forms of assertion or interpretation that the main figures had put forward at the time.

Nowhere in our evidence is there anything resembling the analysis of the fourth-century Athenian system provided by the Aristotelian *Athēnaiōn Politeia (Constitution of the Athenians)*. All the evidence we have to use in analyzing the constitution of the Roman Republic is narrative, persuasive, allusive, or all three. Nonetheless, it remains extraordinary that the student of today cannot turn to any textbook that sets out in comprehensible terms the key features of the system: what public offices there were and how a person was appointed to one, what the Senate did or did not do, how elections were conducted and who the electors were, and what types of communal decision making counted as legislation, and who had the power to legislate. Any such textbook would have to be structured so as to set everything in the two dimensions of space and time—space because political life was conducted almost entirely in the open air, and hence nothing in the Roman system can be understood except against the framework of the topography of the city, time because the Roman year itself dictated the division of power. Precisely the most important step toward monarchy taken in this period was that the people, who alone could legislate, were persuaded to break the normal restrictions of time (and indeed of space, in the provincial context) in giving powers to individuals. Such a textbook would also have to see the whole system in the framework of the communal relation to the gods and of the conduct of the *sacra* and the taking of *auspicia*,[3] emphasize the quite widespread use of the lot (for instance, in the annual allocation of consular and praetorian *provinciae*),[4] and give proper place to the very important role of public oath taking.

---

3. See, for examples of what needs to be done and how to do it, J. Linderski, "The Augural Law," *ANRW* II.16.3 (1986): 2146; J.A. North, "Religion in Republican Rome," in *CAH²* 7.2, *The Rise of Rome to 220 B.C.,* ed. F.W. Walbank, A.E. Astin, M.W. Frederiksen, and R.M. Ogilvie (Cambridge: Cambridge University Press, 1989), 573; M. Beard, "Religion," in *CAH²* 9, *The Last Age of the Roman Republic, 146–43 B.C.,* ed. J.A. Crook, A. Lintott, and E. Rawson (Cambridge: Cambridge University Press, 1994), 729.

4. See now the excellent treatment by N. Rosenstein, "Sorting Out the Lot in Republican Rome," *AJPh* 116 (1995): 43.

Such a basic guide will not be provided here, though I have attempted, as far as I can, to make intelligible all those institutions that come into the story. Also, in the last chapter, I will return to discuss, in somewhat greater detail, how we should understand the political system of the late Republic. This book is not, however, intended to be either a complete constitutional analysis of the Roman system in the late Republic or a balanced interpretation of its political character. It is, specifically and deliberately, an assertion of the centrality—to any construction of the political character of the Republic—of persuasion addressed to the people through the medium of speeches and of voting by them.

It thus represents an unambiguous assertion that in a formal sense the sovereign body in the Republican constitution was the *populus Romanus,* as represented by the various forms of voting assembly, and that, at the level of interpretation, the fact of this sovereignty has to be central to any analysis of the late Republic as a political system. The book is, and is intended to be, a one-sided contribution to a future—and, one may hope, more satisfactory—political analysis by someone else. Before such an analysis can be achieved, however, various other major topics would also have had to be analyzed more adequately than they have been so far.

The first of these topics is that of what terminology, and what conceptions, we should apply to the study of those who held elective office in Rome. Was there a "governing class," an "aristocracy," or an "elite"? Was it defined by descent, and if so, in what way? For instance, patricians were by definition the descendants of earlier generations of patricians (until the emperor gained the right to make new ones). But nothing guaranteed a patrician a public office, a priesthood, or a seat in the Senate. It remains extraordinary that there is no modern study of the role of *patricii* in the late Republic. Alternatively, the Romans themselves very consciously spoke of some persons in public life as being *nobiles,* while others were not. The term referred to those whose ancestors (or at least one ancestor, who could be many generations in the past) had held a major public office.[5] But the expression was social or political, not constitutional; to be described as a *nobilis* was in no way like being a peer with inherited constitutional rights. Even a person who was both a *patricius* and a *nobilis* still had to compete for office.

It is therefore entirely circular to say that whoever played a political role belonged to the aristocracy and that whoever belonged to the aristoc-

---

5. See P.A. Brunt, "*Nobilitas* and *Novitas,*" JRS 72 (1982): 1.

racy played a political role.[6] But if the term *aristocrat* here is to mean more than (circularly) "officeholder," it must imply that birth (and specifically birth rather than, for instance, the current possession of a certain level of wealth) gave some persons a markedly enhanced expectation of election to office. In that case, however, the question becomes empirical: precisely *what* difference did birth make and in relation to which offices? That it did indeed make a great difference in relation to the consulship has always been assumed and has recently been demonstrated in detail by Ernst Badian in relation to the late Republic.[7] But at the other end of the scale of prestige, every year there were, for instance, twenty-four elected *tribuni militum,* twenty *quaestores,* and ten *tribuni plebis.* It is very significant that Keith Hopkins and Graham Burton were able to demonstrate that the effects of "nobility" on the expectation of gaining office were strongest at the very top and were less dominant at each of the more junior stages.[8] Entry to the Senate, even in the earlier period, when it was secured by enrollment by the censors every five years, had always been closely dependent on election to some public office. After Sulla's reforms of the late 80s, and hence in the period covered by this book, it seems that entry to the Senate followed automatically on election to the quaestorship.

To what extent the Senate as a whole, with three hundred members before Sulla and six hundred after his reforms, represented a descent-group or, in some loose sense, an aristocracy is thus an open question, to which our evidence would allow something resembling an empirical answer. But neither *aristocracy* nor any other term can be applied to the Senate as if it represented some simple, unproblematic truth. The one concrete and certain fact, however, is that no one became a member of the Senate by right of birth, or without gaining some annual office that was filled by popular election.

That said, it is unmistakable—and vividly illustrated in many examples of public discourse in the Forum, the subject of this book—that distinguished ancestry (or its absence) played a very important and perhaps even increasing part in the ideology of public life in the late Republic. We need think only of the funeral orations of prominent Romans,

---

6. Chr. Meier, *Res Publica Amissa* (Wiesbaden: F. Steiner, 1966), 47, writes, "Wer Politik trieb, gehörte zum Adel, und wer zum Adel gehörte, trieb Politik." He is quoted by K.J. Hölkeskamp in *Die Entstehung der Nobilität: Studien zur sozialen und politischen Geschichte der römischen Republik im 4. Jhdt. v. Chr.* (Stuttgart: F. Steiner, 1987), 248.

7. E. Badian, "The Consuls, 179–49 B.C.," *Chiron* 20 (1990): 371.

8. K. Hopkins and G.P. Burton, *Death and Renewal* (Cambridge: Cambridge University Press, 1983), chap. 2, "Political Succession in the Late Roman Republic."

which by a long-established custom were delivered from the Rostra to the crowd in the Forum;[9] the *imagines* of ancestors that decorated the houses of prominent Romans and were carried at their funerals;[10] the laudatory or reproachful references to the historic role of the ancestors of other participants in debates in the Forum which we find in contemporary political and forensic speeches; or the (apparently) novel tendency of the late Republic for the construction of family histories, whose earlier phases were often of a legendary kind.[11] That the elaboration of full-scale narrative histories of early Rome was also heavily influenced by the need to represent an appropriate role for one's own or others' alleged ancestors was no secret at the time and has never been doubted since.

Thus modern scholars who have seen late-Republican Rome as a society and a political system dominated by an "aristocracy" of "noble" families have of course not done so without reason. But the functional importance of descent as affecting the ability of an individual to attain office is a complex question. And whatever place we give to "aristocratic" descent as the key to prominence in the present, the question of a *collective* dominance by the "elite" is wholly separate. If we look at elections, their primary characteristic is that they were competitive, and Cicero's reflections on future elections show perfectly clearly that the results were unpredictable. The notion that the class-structured assembly known as the *comitia centuriata* (see further chap. 8), which elected the consuls and praetors of each year, was subject to a collective dominance by the elite has been challenged in a major article by A. Yakobson.[12] A secure collective dominance in terms of policy and legislation might certainly have characterized the system, if there had been unity of principle and attitude among officeholders. But the history of every one of the last thirty years of the Republic shows conclusively, as we will see, that this was not the case. Far from being a tightly controlled, "top-down" system,

---

9. See already Polybius 6.53.1–54.3, with H. Kierdorf, *Laudatio funebris: Interpretationen und Untersuchungen zur Entwicklung der römischen Leichenrede* (Meisenheim am Glan: Hain, 1980).

10. See now H. Flower, *Ancestor Masks and Aristocratic Power in Roman Culture* (Oxford: Oxford University Press, 1996).

11. See esp. the classic article by T.P. Wiseman, "Legendary Genealogies in late-Republican Rome," *Greece and Rome* 21 (1974): 153 = *Roman Studies, Literary and Historical* (Liverpool: F. Cairns, 1987), 207; note also O. Wikander, "Senators and Equites," part 5, "Ancestral Pride and Genealogical Studies in Late Republican Rome," *Opuscula Romana* 19 (1993): 77.

12. A. Yakobson, "*Petitio et Largitio:* Popular Participation in the Centuriate Assembly of the Late Republic," *JRS* 82 (1992): 32.

the late Republic was on the contrary a very striking example of a political system in which rival conceptions of state and society, and rival policies as regards both internal structures and external relations, were openly debated before the crowd in the Forum.

It would be of some relevance, nonetheless, if we could achieve a better and more nuanced conception of lateral connections and alliances between members of the Senate, whether based on ties of family or marriage; on mutual obligations *(officia)*, arising, for instance, from support in legal proceedings; or even on community of political principle. But given that simple assertions that political life was dominated by "factions" *(factiones)* have now been abandoned,[13] we remain strangely far from having evolved any adequate alternative models for the nature of political groupings within the Senate. Even if a better model were on offer, however, it would hardly be of decisive importance. For a crucial fact cannot be repeated too often: the Senate was not a parliament, cannot be seen as an example of "representative" government, and could not legislate. There were indeed quite important political or administrative decisions which it did take, such as the determination of which would be the consular and praetorian *provinciae* for the coming year. But it was not a legislature. That role belonged to the *populus Romanus* itself, or rather to those citizens who were present in the Forum when the moment came for them to form themselves into the thirty-five voting units, or *tribus,* that constituted the normal form of legislative assembly, the *comitia tributa.*

This fact, the formal and exclusive right of the popular assemblies to pass legislation, has never been denied. But its importance has been profoundly obscured by two features of modern conceptions of the late Republic. First, there has not been sufficient emphasis on just how fundamental a role was played in this period by decisions taken in the form of laws *(leges),* voted on by the people in the Forum. Second and more important, much (though of course not all) historical writing on the Republic for the last eighty years has been dominated by the notion that we know that vertical links of dependence were sufficiently strong, and sufficiently pervasive of the whole of Roman society, to mean that popular voting was itself simply an expression of "elite" control. To put it another way, the dominant theory has been that the key to Roman political life was the operation of *clientela.*

---

13. See R. Seager, "*Factio:* Some Observations," *JRS* 62 (1972): 53; P.A. Brunt, *The Fall of the Roman Republic and Related Essays* (Oxford: Clarendon, 1988), chap. 9, "Factions."

This theory is of course the one set out in the brilliant and extremely illuminating monograph of 1912 by Matthias Gelzer. The work remains one of the finest and most stimulating of all modern studies on Republican history. But, curiously, it ends with a conclusion of a sweeping kind that is not borne out in the slightest by the detailed evidence cited earlier. It is worth quoting this conclusion, as it appears in the valuable English translation of 1969 by R. Seager.

> The entire Roman people, both the ruling circle and the mass of voters whom they ruled, was, as a society, permeated by multifarious relationships based on *fides* and on personal connections, the principal forms of which were *patrocinium* in the courts and over communities, together with political friendship and financial obligation. These relationships determined the distribution of political power. To maintain their rights citizens and subjects alike were constrained to seek the protection of powerful men, and the beginner in politics had need of a powerful protector to secure advancement. Political power was based on membership of the senate, which was composed of the magistrates elected by the people. Thus the most powerful man was he who by virtue of his clients and friends could mobilise the greatest number of voters. From the character of the nobility (the descendants of the most successful politicians) arose the hereditary nature of political power in the great aristocratic families. The forces of political life were concentrated in them, and political struggles were fought out by the *nobiles* at the head of their dependents. It made no difference in what way these dependents had been acquired, or with what means and in what field the struggle was being conducted, and if from time to time in the course of events a new man was brought to the fore, the overall picture did not change.[14]

It would in principle, as a matter of logic, be formally impossible to prove the negative of this conclusion—that is, to prove that the narrative representations of oratorical persuasion addressed to crowds, of apparent conflicts of principle and policy, and of violent clashes aimed at securing domination of the traditional space, the Forum, in which voting had to be conducted, are *not* to be explained by the unseen operation of "cli-

---

14. M. Gelzer, *Die Nobilität der römischen Republik* (Leipzig: Teubner, 1912), 134–35 = *Kleine Schriften*, vol. 1 (Wiesbaden: F. Steiner, 1962): 17, as translated in *The Roman Nobility*, trans. R. Seager (Oxford: Blackwell, 1969), 139.

entage," namely, the systematic dependence of voters on members of the elite. What can be asserted categorically, however, is that a rigorous examination by P.A. Brunt of the evidence for the operations of *clientela* has shown that the evidence available to us contains no valid support for the notion that the key to Roman politics lies here.[15] In the future, someone else may successfully reinterpret the evidence and reestablish *clientela* as a fundamental feature not only of Roman social relations but of the functioning of politics and of voting in elections and in the passing of *leges*. For the moment, however, this book will operate on the assumption that no such universal clue is at hand.

Instead, it will give priority to the patterns of events as they present themselves in our narrative sources and to the implications of the arguments presented before the people in speeches. These two categories of evidence of course overlap. Our narrative sources present many examples of "speeches" by individuals delivered in political contexts; and the surviving speeches of this period, all of them by Cicero (other than a quite large number known from fragmentary quotations), contain long sections of narrative, concerning both contemporary and past events. Except for a few examples of contemporary legislation preserved on inscriptions,[16] these sources are all that we have to go on. We are thus dealing, in essence, with an indirect literary reflection, produced by a rather small number of members of the office-holding group, of political events that potentially involved a now vast and widely dispersed electorate, and that at crucial moments did genuinely and directly involve many thousands of people who were present in the Forum for major debates and for voting on important issues. We cannot even be in the least sure that those texts of political and forensic speeches that have survived in manuscripts accurately represent—in scale, in structure of argument, or in their use of historical examples—even what their authors had intended to say, let alone what they actually had managed to say, often in circumstances of violent disturbance. Our sources themselves make it quite explicit that there could be a real difference between a speech as delivered and the text of it as subsequently disseminated (or *edita*—to use the word *published* implies more than the facts of literary diffusion in the Roman context warrant).[17]

---

15. Brunt, *Fall of the Roman Republic*, chap. 8, "*Clientela.*"

16. See now the major new work edited by Michael Crawford, *Roman Statutes.*

17. E.g., Valerius Maximus (5.9.2) writes, "hac scilicet sententia, quam etiam editae orationi inseruit . . ." on a forensic speech by the famous orator Q. Hortensius (Malcovati, *ORF*, no. 92, xxiv/52).

If there is any way to get behind the speech as preserved in manuscript and to go back to the actual speech as spoken before the crowd, I have not found it. Once again, therefore, we have no option but to use as surrogates for the real orations, of which we have no record, the written versions that were composed, or at least edited (in the modern sense), afterward. As we will see, however, it is very important to note not only that rumors and reports circulated about what was being or had recently been said in the Forum (and within the Curia) but that written versions might on occasion be available within a day or two and might reach places in Italy at a considerable distance from Rome.[18] The slight and indirect evidence we have for the types of attention paid by the public to the content of *contiones* in the Forum, inadequate as it is, is nonetheless extremely important.

It goes without saying that we have no real evidence that in any detailed way even offers any representation of the political awareness or political reactions of the ordinary people in Rome or of the large population in Italy who were in principle entitled to come to Rome and vote, and who sometimes did so. Still less do we have any personal reports or reminiscences from within the *plebs urbana* (just as we have no evidence comparable to the police reports which reveal the social composition of the crowds in Paris during the French Revolution).[19] Any impression we can gain of the voters themselves comes, once again, from narratives and speeches, which themselves often offer tendentious interpretations of recent politically significant episodes. These sources do, however, provide extremely vivid representations of crowd reactions, of interchanges between orators and crowds, and of actual dialogues between speakers and audiences.

The barriers to any real understanding of the political life of the late Republic are therefore formidable, and they are certainly not surmounted in this book. We do not yet understand whether we should categorize those who held public office as a "class," an "elite," or an "aristocracy." Nor do we know how to assess the relative contributions of "noble" descent, wealth, oratorical ability, and military reputation to electoral success; how family and marriage connections, personal obligations, or local networks of support really worked in the context of public life; or whether (as was long assumed without question) vertical links of obliga-

---

18. See pp. 29, 194–96 below.

19. See esp. G. Rudé, *The Crowd in the French Revolution* (Oxford: Clarendon, 1959); *The Crowd in History: A Study of Popular Disturbances in France and England, 1730–1848* (London: Lawrence and Wishart, 1981).

tion and dependence, tying the broad masses of the population to the "elite," really were prevalent enough and strong enough to be a determining factor in the political process. It also remains very difficult, as we will see, to assess the significance of participation in the political process by voters from outside Rome, in the novel circumstances, characteristic of this precise period, of the extension of Roman citizenship to most of Italy.[20]

For these reasons and others, no simple categorization of the Roman political system of the late Republic will be offered here. I reiterate, however, that in this system, public office could be gained only by direct election in which all (adult male) citizens, including freed slaves, had the right to vote, and all legislation was by definition the subject of direct popular voting. That being so, it is difficult to see why the Roman Republic should not deserve serious consideration, not just as one type of ancient city-state, but as one of a relatively small group of historical examples of political systems that might deserve the label "democracy."[21]

These considerations will recur later in this book, especially in the second and final chapters. For the moment, all that is necessary is to assert that, however hard it is to understand the wider context, our very full literary evidence for the last three decades of the Republic, if read without misleading presuppositions as to what we know about the political context, does revert again and again to representing images of oratory in the Forum and the reactions of the crowd. In so doing, this literary evidence, which includes texts that are themselves versions of speeches delivered before the crowd, embodies a wide range of argument about historical precedents, constitutional rights, public malpractice, social measures, personal honor or disgrace, the exploitation of the profits of empire, the needs of the empire in terms of provincial commands, and the current military and strategic situation. We will also see, from these very representations of orations, counterorations, and popular reactions, that

---

20. See pp. 19–34, 210–11 below.

21. For a recent, and very valuable, response to the problem of how far we might see Republican Rome as a democracy, see M. Jehne, ed., *Demokratie in Rom? Die Rolle des Volkes in der Politik der römischen Republik* (Stuttgart: F. Steiner, 1995). See now also G. Laser, *Populo et scaenae serviendum est: Die Bedeutung der städtischen Masse in der Spaten Römischen Republik* (Trier: Wissenschaftlichen Verlag, 1997), an excellent contribution to the debate. I discuss various ways in which the Republic has been analyzed as a political system, including the question of the (rather rare) interpretations of it as a democracy, in the Jerusalem Lectures in History in Memory of Menahem Stern delivered in spring 1997, under the title "The Roman Republic in Political Thought."

precisely the sovereign power of the people, inherited from the city-state of the early Republic, was the subject of the most acute controversy. The essence of popular sovereignty, namely, the right of the *tribuni plebis* to propose laws to the people without prior senatorial approval, had indeed been lost in Sulla's reforms of the late 80s; was regained as a result of popular pressure over the next decade; was exercised to the full, in conditions of increasing violence, over the next two decades; and in the end contributed strongly to the installation of monarchy. In this brief period, we can catch the echoes of a level of open public debate that is not common in human history.

II

The Roman Crowd in Perspective: Historical Background and Contemporary Setting

Our primary means of access to the political life of the late Republic is through the surviving written word, in the form of those letters, narratives, and speeches that happen to have been preserved. This limitation is crucial and must serve to place restraints on the conclusions we can draw about the "reality" of the political process. That being so, it may be salutary to begin the discussion of the historical and geographical framework of popular politics with a literary image presented in a speech that might have been delivered in the Forum but never was, and that looks forward to an event that never in fact took place.

The context is the year 70, when Cicero was prosecuting Verres for extortion as governor of Sicily in 73 to 71. In the speech against Verres that he did deliver (*Verr.* 1), Cicero had been addressing a *quaestio* or *iudicium publicum* of thirty-two jurors, or *iudices*, drawn from the Senate, which sat in the open air, surrounded by interested bystanders, somewhere toward the western end of the Forum. I will come back later in this chapter to the ways in which a forensic speech such as this, primarily addressed to a restricted group of *iudices*, both resembled and differed from a political speech *(contio)* addressed directly to the crowd. But it is essential to emphasize that forensic speeches not only took place within the same broad physical setting as political ones, but could have recourse to the same range of emotive political considerations and historical references, and depended for much of their effect on the reactions of the circle *(corona)* of bystanders. This was all the more so in the year 70, when, after a decade of protest, major changes in the constitution were under way. When Cicero was speaking, the rights of the *tribuni plebis* to put legislation directly to the assembly of the thirty-five tribes *(comitia tributa)* had already been restored, and changes in the composition of the *quaestiones* themselves—namely, the removal of Sulla's provision that only senators could serve as jurors—were expected at any moment. Cicero's *First Verrine,* delivered in August, constituted his first great oratorical triumph, after which Verres abandoned his defense and went into exile.[1] Cicero, however, had either already written or went on to write the five further speeches that would have been required; as we shall see in chapter 3, (paradoxically) these undelivered speeches evoking the atmosphere of the year 70 suggest, more than any other evidence we have, the force of popular opinion as mobilized in the Forum and the way in which *quaestiones* functioned both as representatives of the *populus* and, quite literally, under its gaze.

Standing jury courts of this type, with a restricted number of jurors, drawn from the senatorial or equestrian orders, were a relatively new feature of the Roman constitution, going back only some eight decades, to the middle of the second century B.C. Alongside them, there survived an older, more primitive and more cumbersome form of court, directly involving the people, in which a *tribunus plebis* or *aedilis* could bring an accusation before the whole body of the thirty-five *tribus,* the *comitia tributa.*[2] As it happened, Cicero himself had been elected to the relatively modest and junior office of aedile for the following year, 69, and could therefore anticipate (or imagine himself anticipating) that if Verres were, disgracefully, acquitted, he himself would be able to bring a case against him next year. His words deserve extensive quotation.

> Suppose that he escapes from this court too; I will embark on that course to which the *populus Romanus* has already been calling me. For as regards the rights of citizenship and of liberty, it considers that the right of judgment is its own, and rightly so. Let him by his use of force break his own senatorial councils and force his way through the *quaestiones* that represent us all; let him escape your [the jurors'] severity. Believe me, when he is before the *populus Romanus,* he will be held in tighter snares. The *populus Romanus* will believe those *equites Romani* who, when produced earlier as witnesses before you [the jurors], testified that by that man, while they themselves looked on *[ipsis inspectantibus],* a Roman citizen who could offer respectable men as guarantors had been hoisted on

1. For the context, see the remarkable chapter in a much underestimated work, Taylor, *Party Politics,* chap. 5, "The Criminal Courts and the Rise of a New Man."

2. Much remains controversial as regards the nature of such trials and their procedures. For a succinct treatment, see A.H.M. Jones, *The Criminal Courts of the Roman Republic and Principate* (Oxford: Blackwell, 1992), chap. 1, *"Iudicia Populi."*

a cross. All thirty-five *tribus* will believe a man of exceptional gravity and distinction, M. Annius, who declared that in his presence a Roman citizen had been executed with an ax. . . . When I, by the *beneficium* of the *populus Romanus,* am able to conduct this case from a higher seat [the magistrate's tribunal], I do not fear either that any force will be able to save him from the votes *[suffragia]* of the *populus Romanus* or that on my part any gift *[munus]* of my aedileship can be more magnificent or more welcome to the *populus Romanus.*[3]

Nothing could express more clearly the principle that the senatorial jurors, functioning in the open Forum before the eyes of the people, were supposed to be there as the people's delegates or representatives. As the late A.N. Sherwin-White showed in a masterly article, exactly the same principle informs the text of the inscribed copy of a law setting up an extortion court, almost certainly that which had been passed in the tribunate of Gaius Gracchus in 123.[4] The praetor selecting the (then) equestrian jurors had to have their names read out in a *contio* ("facito recitentur in contione") and to take an oath concerning his selection (line 15). The names were also to be written up where anyone who wished could copy them down (line 18). The law also laid down every detail of the voting procedure, and the provision that each voting tablet had to be shown to the people (lines 50–54). Precisely the same presuppositions are reflected in Cicero's words in the *Verrines.* It should be stressed that Cicero, whose later utterances represent our best evidence for hostility to popular sovereignty and its ideological basis, in his earlier speeches offers the best evidence for the opposite. In this particular case, he is stressing that if (or rather when) the senatorial jurors fail in their public duty, the *populus,* which so far has merely been observing *(ipsis inspectantibus),* has the right, and the constitutional machinery, to fulfill the jurors' functions itself.

That constitutional machinery consisted, as Cicero indicates, of the *populus* divided into thirty-five *tribus* or voting units, the *comitia tributa.* He does not need to indicate that the place of meeting of the *comitia*

---

3. Cicero *Verr.* 2.1.5/12–14.

4. A.N. Sherwin-White, "The Lex Repetundarum and the Political Ideas of Gaius Gracchus," *JRS* 72 (1982): 18, esp. 21. For the text of the law and a translation, see A.W. Lintott, *Judicial Reform and Land Reform in the Roman Republic* (Cambridge: Cambridge University Press, 1992), 73ff.; Crawford, *Roman Statutes,* 1: no. 1.

tributa would have been the same as for the *quaestio,* namely, the Forum itself, and thus also the same as for most *contiones* (speeches to informal meetings of the people) and the same again for the *comitia tributa* when it was meeting to pass *leges.*

The *comitia tributa* also had another function, with which this book will be very little concerned, the election of *quaestores, aediles,* and *tribuni plebis.* In the later Republic, electoral meetings of this body were held not in the Forum but, as a general rule, outside the city, in the Campus Martius, beside the Tiber.[5] This transfer of function had taken place because the Campus Martius had from the beginning been the site for meetings of the other established popular assembly, the *comitia centuriata.* According to tradition this assembly was even older, going back even to the regal period, and it was certainly always marked by strongly archaic features. It met outside the ritual boundary of the city, the *pomerium,* because in structure it reflected—and in essence it was (or originally had been)—the Roman army. Its meetings preserved, not merely until the late Republic, but well into the empire—at least until the third century A.D.—the convention that a flag would be flown from the crest of the Janiculum, which rose up on the opposite, western bank of the river. If the flag were struck, it signified that enemy forces (presumably Etruscans) were approaching, and the assembly would be dissolved.[6] The structure of the *comitia centuriata* was based on that of the archaic army, with eighteen *centuriae* of cavalrymen voting first, followed by the *centuriae* of infantry (assumed, like the hoplites of early Greek city-states, to be wealthy enough to provide their own armor); then followed the poorer groups in order, their limited military roles reflecting their progressively lower economic status and equally determining their place in the voting order. The details, which are extremely complex and difficult, are not worth pursuing here, primarily because the structure of the archaic *comitia centuriata* (the only phase described in detail by our sources),[7] was subsequently altered, probably in the third century B.C. Whatever else is uncertain about the *comitia centuriata* of the later Republic, it is clear that the later structure represented an assertion of power by the broader group of infantrymen, as against the richer cavalrymen. The cen-

---

5. In what follows, I am of course simply summarizing the irreplaceable work of Taylor, *Voting Assemblies,* chap. 3, based on the Jerome Lectures of 1964. See also Coarelli, *Foro,* 2:164–65.

6. This convention is set out with great clarity by Cassius Dio at 37.27.3–37.28.3, referring to the trial of Rabirius before the *comitia centuriata* in 63; see also chap. 5.

7. See Cicero *De re pub.* 2.22/39–40; Livy 1.43; Dionysius *Ant.* 4.20–21. See chap. 8.

turies of *equites* no longer voted first. This change, which in the context of early- or middle-Republican society may well have seemed quite revolutionary, may be the justification for the remark by Dionysius of Halicarnassus, writing under Augustus, that the assembly had subsequently "changed to a more democratic form."[8]

What is significant in this context about the *comitia centuriata* is, first, that its meetings were uncharacteristic of the public, open-air functioning of the *res publica* in not taking place in the Forum. (Presumably it was because this alternative meeting place was a long-established feature of the *res publica* that elections by the *comitia tributa* could later move there also.) Second, it was characterized by social stratification, which was fundamental to its procedures. The centuries voted in order of socioeconomic status and ceased to vote when an overall majority had been achieved. From time to time proposals were made for rearranging in some way the established order of the centuries. Gaius Gracchus is alleged to have promulgated a tribunician law by which the centuries of all five of the *classes* into which it was divided would have voted in an order determined by lot.[9] If such a proposal had gone through, it would have subverted the entire structure of this assembly. A comparable proposal is reflected in Cicero's *Pro Murena*, a speech delivered toward the end of 63. Addressing Servius Sulpicius, a defeated candidate in the consular elections for 62, Cicero says, in the course of illustrating Servius' capacity to give offense and hence his failure:

> You have demanded a mingling of the votes . . . the leveling of influence, dignity, and voting. It was badly received by distinguished men, and ones who were of influence in their neighborhoods and local towns [*municipia*], that such a man [as you] should fight for the abolition of all distinctions of dignity and influence.[10]

I will come back later in this chapter to the very significant reference to respectable men from local towns in Italy. What matters at this point is

---

8. Dionysius (*Ant.* 4.21.3) writes, μεταβέβληκεν εἰς τὸ δημοτικώτερον. See L.J. Grieve, "The Reform of the *Comitia Centuriata*," *Historia* 34 (1985): 278; A. Yakobson, "Dionysius of Halicarnassus on a Democratic Change in the Centuriate Assembly," *SCI* 12 (1993): 139.

9. [Sallust] *Ad Caes. Sen.* 2.8 reads, "Magistratibus creandis haud mihi quidem absurde placet lex quam C. Gracchus in tribunatu promulgaverat, ut ex confusis quinque classibus sorte centuriae vocarentur."

10. Cicero *Mur.* 23/47.

that the archaic structure of *classes* of *centuriae* based on wealth, which had long lost all practical connection with the Roman army, did—despite occasional proposals for reform—survive the Republic and could still be in operation in the third century A.D. But it needs to be stressed that in the late Republic the only normal and regular function of this form of assembly was the annual election of consuls and praetors. The voting structure that produced these annual elected magistrates was indeed systematically class structured. But the elections were competitive, and their results were visibly uncertain and unpredictable. As mentioned earlier, it has been shown quite clearly that such elections would have produced a simple class dominance only in a case where there was a consensus among the richer voters. This was very often not the case, and the results of the elections were often not decided until a large proportion of the total number of *centuriae,* thus reaching as far as the poorer voters, had been able to vote.[11]

On rare occasions, such as the trial of Rabirius for *perduellio* (treason) in 63 (see chap. 5), the *comitia centuriata* also acted, in a way analogous to the *comitia tributa,* as a court to hear capital charges. It also had the right to pass *leges,* proposed by consuls or praetors, the only annual officials with the power to convene this assembly. But this right of legislation was rarely exercised in the late Republic; the most notable case, to which we will return more than once, was the *lex* to legislate for the return of Cicero from exile in 57.[12]

The *comitia centuriata* demonstrated in very visible and concrete form how the structure of the Roman *res publica* of the first century B.C. was still fundamentally determined by that of the small nuclear city-state of the archaic period, some of whose institutions may even have gone back to the regal period. In electing consuls and praetors, who then coexisted with ten annual tribunes of the plebs, elected by the *comitia tributa,* it thus contributed to the balance of powers—or, to describe it differently, to the built-in friction and opposition of powers—that marked the political stage of the late Republic.

But in this respect too we are in a new phase in the post-Sullan period. One reason why *consules* (and indeed *praetores*) had always been elected by the *comitia centuriata* was that, as Cicero explicitly recalls in his *Pro*

---

11. See Yakobson *JRS* 82 (1992): 32. See more fully chap. 8.

12. See the discussions later in this chapter and in chap. 6. Another example was a *lex* for the removal of the Roman citizenship from some *municipia,* proposed by Sulla as dictator in 81 and put through the *comitia centuriata* (Cicero *Dom.* 30/79).

Murena, in electing consuls the people had in the past specifically been electing generals *(imperatores).*[13] It had also been normal in the second century B.C. that both consuls, and all but two of the six or eight praetors, had been allocated *provinciae* at the beginning of their year of office, and had gone off to them after a short interval in Rome. Military and provincial command was thus the primary role for which they had been elected. But after Sulla's reforms of the late 80s, praetors first drew lots for urban responsibilities (also called *provinciae*)—mainly, the presidency of *quaestiones*—to be held during their year of office; then they submitted to a second sortition for provincial commands as propraetors *(propraetore).*[14] All the praetors were now, therefore, present in Rome for their year of office. In practice the same applied to consuls, even though they still received a *provincia* outside Rome from the beginning. The normal pattern was now that they stayed in Rome for all or most of their year of office, before going out to their provinces.[15] The effect therefore was a very literal collision and conflict of powers, rights, and statuses, in which more office-holding actors than before were present in Rome, and which was played out on the public stage of the Forum.

The formal process of election, in both types of *comitia,* now took place outside the city, on the Campus Martius. But campaigning for office, the process of "going around" *(ambitio)* and gathering up support, also took place primarily in the Forum and led to the delivery of speeches by the candidates and to speeches by others recommending them (the common notion that there were no election campaigns in Rome is wholly false).

If we are to understand the structure of politics at Rome, it is impossible to overstress the centrality, in all senses, of the Forum, or the fundamental role of the other archaic form of assembly, the *comitia tributa,* namely, the voting assembly divided (eventually) into thirty-five "tribes" *(tribus).* As with the *centuriae* of the *comitia centuriata,* each voting unit, or *tribus,* voted by majority, and the resultant vote counted as one (in this case one of thirty-five). If the votes of eighteen *tribus* were in agreement, the procedure stopped there, for a majority had been reached. Here

---

13. Cicero (*Mur.* 17/38) writes, "imperatores enim comitiis consularibus, non verborum interpretes, deliguntur."

14. See the case of Verres: Cicero Verr. 2.1.40/104 (*sortitio* for *urbana provincia*); 2.2.6/17 (for propraetorian province).

15. See J.P.V.D. Balsdon, "Consular Provinces under the Late Republic," *JRS* 29 (1939): 57; A. Giovannini, *Consulare Imperium* (Basel: F. Reinhardt, 1983).

again, it is impossible to understand the system as it was in the first century B.C. without following at least the broad lines of developments since the period of the archaic, nuclear city-state of the early Republic.[16] For that period there is of course no direct Roman evidence, and there happen also to be no reports by Greek observers. There might have been: Herodotus, in the fifth century B.C., refers in some detail to Agylla (Caere), which lies a mere thirty kilometers away from Rome.[17] But the institutions and customs of this small city-state and its surrounding territory were to mark the public life of Rome for centuries. Thus, in the fifth century B.C., the *tribus* into which the citizens were divided had numbered twenty-one, and had been both geographical and social units: four of the *tribus* were "urban," representing four sections of the city, and the other seventeen (the *tribus rusticae*) occupied the surrounding territory. There may have been some thirty-five thousand adult male citizens. The procedure for the passing of laws continued always to reflect this world, now only very indirectly accessible to us, an urban center with a surrounding agricultural population. So, for instance, there was the rule that a *lex* had to be posted *(proposita)* over three eight-day periods *(nundinae)* before it could be voted on. In his *Historiae*, Rutilius, the consul of 105, had explained the rationale of this *lex*, and his explanation was quoted later by Macrobius.

> Rutilius writes that the Romans instituted *nundinae,* so that for eight days the *rustici* should do their work in the fields, but on the ninth day, leaving off their agriculture, they should come to Rome for trade and for passing laws, and in order that *[plebi]scita* and *[senatus] consulta* should be put forward before a larger crowd of people.[18]

A fifth-century observer of the early Roman state would have been invaluable for us. But far more valuable would have been any observer of the rapidly expanding and developing Roman state of the fourth and third centuries. For then there was a steady expansion of Roman territory, eventually stretching southeastward into Campania and northward,

---

16. For a full analysis of what can be known of this period, see T.J. Cornell, *The Beginnings of Rome: Rome and Italy c. 1000–264 B.C.* (London: Routledge, 1995).

17. Herodotus 1.167.

18. Macrobius *Sat.* 1.16.34. For Rutilius' text, see Peter, *HRR*, Rutilius frag. 1 (p. 187). Different explanations are offered by other sources.

diagonally across Italy, to the Adriatic. With that there came the step-by-step increase in the number of *tribus,* which reached thirty-five (still four "urban" and now thirty-one "rustic") in 241, and which—for reasons quite unknown—was never exceeded afterward.[19] A Greek observer *might* even have been at hand, for we know that Aristotle referred to the capture of Rome by the Gauls early in the fourth century.[20] But there is no reason to believe that Rome was included in the list of constitutions collected by Aristotle's school. When the Aristotelian *Athēnaiōn Politeia* was being composed in the 320s, giving an analysis of the Athenian system that cannot be paralleled for Rome at any period, Rome was already in a period of dramatic transformation, sending out "Latin" colonies and either absorbing existing communities fully into its own citizenship or offering some of them—for example, Cicero's hometown, Arpinum, in 303—citizenship without the vote *(civitas sine suffragio).*

A Greek observer, if there had been one, would surely have used the word *sympoliteia* of these grants of citizenship to existing communities. Such an observer would indeed have had before him the evolution of what was, in one sense, a quite new political and constitutional system. On the one hand, large areas of Italy became Roman territory, inhabited by Roman citizens, but without (as it seems) the destruction of local self-government. On the other, the central contradiction of the late-Republican system had already come into effect, namely, the fact that the institutions of the enormously expanded Roman *res publica* remained exactly those of the original nuclear city-state. Almost all the crucial features of this expanding *res publica* are revealed conveniently in Livy's report of measures taken in 188 in relation to the extension of full voting rights to three Italian communities that until that time had enjoyed only citizenship without the vote, one of them being Arpinum.

> As regards the inhabitants of the *municipia* of Formiae, Fundi, and Arpinum, C. Valerius Tappo, *tribunus plebis,* promulgated a law to the effect that they should have the right of casting a vote (for until then they had had the *civitas* without the vote). When four *tribuni plebis* vetoed this bill, on the grounds that it was not being put forward on the authority of the Senate, they were informed that it was the right of the *populus,* not the Senate, to grant the vote to whomsoever it wished; so they desisted. The bill *[rogatio]* was

19. See the classic work of L.R. Taylor, *Voting Districts.*
20. See Plutarch *Camillus* 22.

passed, with the effect that the Formiani and Fundani should vote in the *tribus* Aemilia, the Arpinates in the Cornelia. And now, for the first time, on the basis of the *plebiscitum* passed by Valerius, they were enrolled in the census as members of these *tribus*. M. Claudius Marcellus, the censor, having been successful over T. Quinctius [his colleague] in the drawing of lots, completed the lustrum [ritual purification]. There were 258,318 citizens listed in the census. When the lustrum was complete, the consuls set off for their provinces.[21]

We need not review here the complex and highly uncertain stages by which measures proposed by *tribuni plebis* and passed by the plebs *(plebiscita)* had come to have the status of *leges* binding on the whole community. But we may note that the ten tribunes of the year might each act separately and might follow different interpretations of the constitution. No one disputed, however, that each separately had the right of veto (the distinction between positive and negative tribunician powers was to be all-important). More significant still is the clear indication that prior senatorial approval of *plebiscita* was normal but was not a constitutional necessity. Significant again is the expansion of full Roman citizenship to include a group of three communities lying some one hundred kilometers away to the southeast. As we will see, in the late Republic, voters could, and on occasion did, come from such distances to exercise their rights; but inevitably distance must have imposed severe limitations on active participation.

Equally important is the indication that these communities were allotted to different Roman *tribus*. As I noted earlier, the number of *tribus* had reached thirty-five in 241 and was never subsequently expanded. In this period, therefore, membership of a *tribus* was still determined by locality, but the areas allocated to any one *tribus* were no longer geographically coherent. Far from being "primitive," the structure of "tribes" was an artificial construct, and the members of a "tribe" functioned as a group only in the sense that they voted together, each in sequence, and that the majority vote in each counted as one vote among thirty-five.

Finally, the total number of Roman citizens recorded in the census of 189/8 is also of immense significance.[22] No Greek city-state ever ap-

---

21. Livy 38.36.

22. For all related questions, see P.A. Brunt, *Italian Manpower, 225 B.C.–A.D. 14* (Oxford: Clarendon, 1971).

proached a citizen body of a quarter million adult males; and in none of the contemporary Hellenistic monarchies could their inhabitants be thought of as "citizens" in any real sense.

By lateral extension of its citizenship, Rome was thus, in some limited respects, coming to resemble a nation-state rather than a city-state. At least one contemporary observer, however, Philip V, the king of Macedon (221–179), noted another profound difference between Rome and the normal Greek city-state. Writing to the people of the Thessalian city of Larissa in 214, he encouraged them to be generous with their citizenship and drew to their attention the fact that when the Romans freed slaves, they gave them citizenship.[23] That the king misleadingly supported his argument by saying that these freed slaves had given the Romans the manpower to send out "nearly 70 colonies" does not seriously detract from the force of his observation. It was true that Greek cities did not allow freed slaves to become citizens and that Rome did. Moreover, the slave of a Roman citizen, after being formally manumitted, gained not only the negative freedom of release from ownership by another, but the positive freedom to vote as a citizen.[24] Much more clearly than the question of the class-stratified voting procedures of the *comitia centuriata* discussed earlier in this chapter, however, the question of the place which *libertini* should occupy in the *comitia tributa* remained perpetually controversial. Should they, as was the standing rule, be registered only in one of the four "urban" tribes, or might they belong to any tribe? For the moment, we may note, for instance, the radical proposal by Ti. Sempronius Gracchus, as one of the two censors of 169/8, to deprive *liberti* altogether of registration in a *tribus* and hence of the vote. His colleague C. Claudius Pulcher argued that the censors had no right to take such action without a vote of the *populus,* and in the end the rule was established that freedmen should be registered in one of the four *tribus urbanae.*[25] Writing his *De oratore* in the 40s, Cicero declared that, if that measure had not been taken, the *res publica* would long since

---

23. *Syll.*[3], no. 543.

24. See F. Millar, "The Roman *Libertus* and Civic Freedom," *Arethusa* 28 (1995): 99, one of a group of discussions of the issues raised by the interesting study by O. Patterson, *Freedom,* vol. 1, *Freedom in the Making of Western Culture* (London: I.B. Tauris, 1991). For the details, see Taylor, *Voting Districts,* chap. 10, "The Urban Tribes and the Registration of the Freedmen"; S. Treggiari, *Roman Freedmen during the Late Republic* (Oxford: Clarendon, 1969), 37–38; G. Fabre, *Libertus: Recherches sur les rapports patron-affranchi à la fin de la république romaine* (Rome: École Française de Rome, 1981), 5–6.

25. See Livy 45.15.3–7.

have disappeared.[26] As we will see later, the question of allowing freedmen to be registered in the "rustic" tribes also still remained acutely controversial in the 60s and 50s.[27]

Both the vast expansion in numbers and the wide extent of the territory in which Roman citizens lived must profoundly affect our view of the Roman political system, even as it was in the later third and second centuries. But an extremely important analysis of the Roman *politeia* in this period, offered by a Greek observer, Polybius, who was in Rome as a hostage from 167 to 150, does not—so far as it is preserved—take into account the question of numbers or that of geographical extension. In his very fine analysis of the system, as a mixture of the "monarchic" (the consuls), the "aristocratic" (the Senate), and the "democratic" (the people), he takes the "people" *(dēmos)* as a powerful element in the state, which alone has the power to give honor *(timē)* and punishment *(timōria)*, and which tries offenses punishable by a fine, especially on the part of officeholders, as well as capital cases. Moreover, it is the people, Polybius observes, who elect officeholders, have the right to pass laws, declare war, and ratify alliances, peace terms, and treaties.[28] In speaking of the "people" *(dēmos)*, he does not differentiate between the two radically different forms of assembly, and thus does not indicate, for instance, that the *comitia tributa* imposed fines while the *comitia centuriata* tried capital cases, or that the *comitia tributa* normally passed laws while the *comitia centuriata* (it seems) voted for declarations of war.[29]

Polybius' deliberately schematic analysis also tends to leave out of account elected officeholders other than the consuls. So he does not mention the praetors or discuss how many tribunes there were or how they were elected. But he does note that any one tribune could veto proceedings in the Senate, and he offers the view that "the tribunes *[dēmarchoi]* are obliged always to do what seems best to the *dēmos* and above all to seek to carry out its wishes."[30]

The essential characteristic of Polybius' analysis, however, is that it is devoted to the interlocking functions of different elements in the Roman

26. Cicero *De or.* 1.9/38.

27. See chaps. 7 and 8.

28. Polybius 6.14. See now F.W. Walbank, "Polybius' Perception of the One and the Many," in I. Malkin and Z.W. Rubensohn, eds., *Leaders and Masses in the Roman World: Studies in Honor of Zvi Yavetz* (New York: E. Brill, 1995), 201.

29. See J.W. Rich, *Declaring War in the Roman Republic in the Period of Transmarine Expansion* (Brussels: Latomus, 1976).

30. Polybius 6.16.4–5.

res publica, rather than being in any real sense a sociological, or even political, study. He might nonetheless have mentioned the division of both types of assembly into subunits *(tribus* or *centuriae),* the geographical extension of Roman citizenship, and the complex geographical distribution of the *tribus.* Instead, he ignores the geographical aspect, consciously or unconsciously following the logic of the central institutions of the Roman *res publica* itself, which still functioned exactly as if Rome were a nuclear city-state. Within that city-state, the prime location for political action was and always remained the Forum.

Even though in the 140s elections by the *comitia tributa* joined elections (and all other functions) carried out by the *comitia centuriata* in being conducted in the Campus Martius, the place for making oneself known to the people and for actual electoral canvassing was and remained, for all types of post, the Forum itself. Thus Polybius could observe that while Scipio Aemilianus devoted himself to hunting, "the other young men concerned themselves with legal cases and greetings, spending their time in the Forum, and thus tried to recommend themselves to the many."[31]

The Forum was indeed the place where one recommended oneself to the many, even when what was in prospect was an election to the consulship, which would be made by a meeting of the *comitia centuriata* held in the Campus Martius. This function of the Forum was perfectly shown by L. Hostilius Mancinus, who was a candidate for the consulship in the year at which Polybius' great *History* stopped, 146. He had played a prominent role in the assault on Carthage, and he exploited this role by erecting in the Forum a picture representing the topography of the city and the attacks made on it. With the aid of this visual representation, he narrated the events of the siege to the crowd in the Forum, "by which agreeableness *[comitas]* he won the consulship at the next elections."[32]

The face-to-face operation of politics had its disadvantages, however, from the point of view of the citizen, for until this same period, the voter had not only had to appear in person, in the Campus Martius or the Forum, to register his vote but had evidently had to do so by recording his vote out loud. Hence he was clearly open to pressure from others, and especially from his social superiors. So, in the 130s, a series of laws was passed by tribunes that instituted the fundamentally important right to vote by secret ballot. Looking back on this major step (in many ways

31. Polybius 31.29.8.
32. Pliny *NH* 35.7/23.

comparable in importance to anything done by either of the Gracchi), Cicero, in his *De legibus,* puts into the mouth of his brother, Quintus, the view that precisely the removal from the voter of the influence of his betters had been most regrettable.

> Who does not realize that a ballot law *[lex tabellaria]* has removed all the *auctoritas* of the *optimates?* A law that, when it was free, the *populus* never sought, but that it demanded when it was oppressed by the domination and power of the *principes!* Similarly there are on record more severe judgments in cases concerning the most powerful men [when voting was by use] of the voice rather than the ballot. For this reason an excessive freedom in voting in dubious causes should have been removed from the powerful, rather than a hiding place given to the *populus,* in which, without the respectable *[boni]* knowing what opinion each one had, the voting tablet *[tabella]* would hide a mischievous vote. So for such a bill *[rogatio]* no good proposer *[lator]* or supporter *[auctor]* could ever have been found.
>
> There are four *leges tabellariae,* of which the first concerns election to magistracies. That was the *lex Gabinia,* passed by an unknown and disreputable man [139]. There followed two years later [137] the Cassian law about the *iudicia populi,* proposed by L. Cassius, who was a *nobilis* but, if his family will allow me to say so, was at odds with the *boni* and seeking to catch every breath of popular gossip by his *popularis* methods. The third is that of Carbo, a seditious and corrupt citizen, on the passage and rejection of laws [131 or 130].[33]

Cicero then adds a final example, the law of C. Coelius in 107, relating to trials for treason *(perduellio),* the only one which itself will have been passed using the ballot. It is not possible now to estimate how important these new procedures were in the contentious politics of the half century before the Social War, which were notable for the fact that the sphere of tribunician legislation extended (on occasion) to the allocation of provincial commands, to the exploitation of the empire, to strategic dispositions, and to the founding of colonies.[34] All that is clear from Cicero's

33. Cicero *De leg.* 3.15–16/34–35.

34. See F. Millar, "Politics, Persuasion, and the People before the Social War (150–90 B.C.)," *JRS* 76 (1986): 1.

words is how deeply someone who believed that society needed to be guided by its "better" elements felt the loss of control brought about by these laws. The principle of the protection of the ordinary individual from outside pressure contrasts strongly with the provisions of the Gracchan extortion law mentioned earlier in this chapter, insisting on the glare of publicity for the operations of the *quaestio* on extortion, manned by men drawn from a well-off group, the *equites*.

A far more obvious and fundamental change in the nature of the Roman *res publica* was brought about by the Social War of 90–87, when the Italian allies demanded admission to the citizenship, and when the Romans, though militarily victorious, were so (it may be suggested) only because they had almost immediately conceded the basic principle (in the *lex Iulia* of 90).[35] Much remains extremely obscure, not least as regards the northern boundary of the area where citizenship became universal. The northern quarter of the Italian peninsula, Gallia Cisalpina in Roman terms, remained a *provincia,* and it is clear at least that the northernmost part of it, Transpadana, did not receive a general grant of the citizenship until 49. But even here there were many Roman citizen communities already in existence between 80 and 50.

The process of the integration of the Italians into the citizenship is not at all clear; all that is certain is that, despite abortive proposals to increase the number of *tribus,* the number remained at thirty-five, and each of the new citizen communities was registered in one of them. The 80s were a period of acute instability and civil war, and it is in fact only in 70, and through the medium of Cicero's *First Verrine* (the speech actually delivered), that we catch a glimpse of the new political structure. In his speech, Cicero begs the senatorial jurors not to disgrace themselves once again by a corrupt verdict of not guilty, and to be aware of the exceptional degree of publicity attending this case. Cicero is anxious that further hearings should not be put off.

> I will not let it happen that this case might be decided only then, when this great crowd *[frequentia]* from all over Italy has departed from Rome, [this crowd] which has come together at one moment from all directions for the elections and the games and in order to be registered in the census *[censendique causa].*[36]

---

35. The best account of the Social War is now that by E. Gabba, "Rome and Italy: The Social War," *CAH*[2] 9 (Cambridge: Cambridge University Press, 1994), chap. 4.

36. Cicero *Verr.* 1.18/54.

It is possible that those whom Cicero represents as having come for the census were in fact not tens of thousands of individuals but delegations from the Italian towns, bringing locally compiled lists of Roman citizens. Such a system is envisaged in the famous inscription of the 40s from Heraclea in southern Italy, the *Tabula Heracleensis.*[37] But, as we have seen, any people who came specifically for the elections will necessarily have come as individuals, to exercise their rights as citizens in the only way open to them, in person in the Campus Martius.

By a fortunate accident, we have some figures for the census of 70, the first to be completed for a couple of decades.[38] These show at once that the total citizenry had leaped from (it seems) nearly 400,000 in the late second century to 900,000 or 910,000. The number of citizens, already far beyond that found in any Greek city-state, had more than doubled, and the area entirely occupied by citizens now stretched south to the toe of Italy, some five hundred kilometers from Rome, and north to (perhaps) the River Po, over three hundred kilometers away, with considerable blocks of citizens settled further north still.

As Cicero says in a justly famous passage from his *De legibus,* the situation of a person like himself who came from a town *(municipium)* in Italy was that he had two "native cities" *(patriae):* one by nature, in his case Arpinum, and one by citizenship, Rome.[39] In what ways could this citizenship be exercised? All the new citizens, we must presume, were now subject to Roman law. As we will see later, there is also ample evidence that at least many Italians absorbed Roman culture and tradition as their own.[40] All were now also liable to service in the legions. In terms of political rights, all were now to be included in the lists of Roman citizens carried by municipal delegates to Rome. But did they actually vote? For most of Italy, there was no likelihood that peasants would come in from the fields for a day to go to market and participate in political decisions.

One aspect of the situation is that the *municipia* of Italy, still enjoying local self-government, took to intervening in Roman politics as col-

---

37. *CIL* I², no. 593 (with subsequent bibliography in *CIL* I³, p. 916; see now Crawford, *Roman Statutes,* 1: no. 24). The provisions relating to the census and dispatch of *legati* to Rome are contained in lines 142–58.

38. See the table in Brunt, *Italian Manpower,* 13–14, with the discussion in his chaps. 7–8.

39. Cicero *De leg.* 2.2/5.

40. See chap. 8.

lectivities, by sending delegates to speak before the Senate.[41] Another is that we do have some evidence, from both ends of the Italian peninsula, either for interest and involvement in the political process in Rome or for the presumption that the voters there were worth canvassing. The first aspect is illustrated by Cicero's experience in August of 44 when he was at Rhegium, at the very toe of Italy. While he was staying at a villa near Rhegium, he reports, "several townsmen of Rhegium came to me, of whom some had recently been in Rome; from them I for the first time obtained [a text of] the speech *[contio]* of M. Antonius, which pleased me so much that when I had read it I began for the first time to think of returning."[42]

As for Gallia Cisalpina, there are a number of indications that Romans seeking public office thought it worthwhile to canvass there. Cicero, looking ahead in 65 to the consular elections for 63, was already considering the importance of "Gallia" in the voting and was thinking of going there for some time to raise support. From the opposite direction, Hirtius describes how Julius Caesar in 50 traveled at maximum speed from Transalpine Gaul to what he calls "Italia" (Gallia Cisalpina, part of his *provincia*) to collect votes for Antonius, who was a candidate for election to a priesthood in Rome.[43]

It must be stressed that all such efforts would have been purposeless unless some of the persons canvassed then individually made the journey to Rome and voted. The nearer to Rome an area was, clearly the greater the likelihood that this might actually happen. Defending Murena against a charge of having gained the consulship for 62 by corrupt means, Cicero argues that functions performed by him in Umbria and Gallia had won him much support.

Setting out [to his province, Transalpine Gaul, in 64], he held a levy in Umbria; the *res publica* gave him the opportunity for generosity *[liberalitas]*, by exploiting which he attached to himself many *tribus* that are made up of the *municipia* of Umbria.[44]

---

41. See E. Gabba, "Le città italiche del I sec. a.C. e la politica," *Riv. Stor. It.* 93 (1986): 653, reprinted in his *Italia Romana* (Como: New Press, 1994), 123.

42. Cicero *Phil.* 1.3/8.

43. Cicero *Att.* 1.1.2 (10); [Caesar] *Bell. Gall.* 8.50. See Taylor, *Party Politics,* chap. 3, "Delivering the Vote." See further pp. 188–90 below.

44. Cicero *Mur.* 20/42.

The evidence for significant electoral support coming from some distance from Rome is certainly stronger than for comparable involvement in voting on laws. But in 56, for instance, Cicero was expecting, or at least hoping, that a large band *(magna manus)* would arrive from Picenum and Gallia to help to resist the bills *(rogationes)* proposed by the tribune C. Cato.[45] Even in regard to elections, it lay in the nature of the case that it could not be predicted which efforts by which candidates would actually succeed in evoking support, particularly support at a level sufficient to affect the result. Precisely this unpredictability is the point of Cicero's defense of Plancius, a successful candidate for the aedileship of 55. His unsuccessful rival, of more distinguished birth, had not expected defeat, and hence prosecuted Plancius for obtaining election by improper means. But Cicero points out that Plancius, who came from the town of Atina (situated about 110 kilometers southeast of Rome) had actually benefited from coming from this relatively remote and modest origin. The place had a large number of well-off citizens, and support had come also from other places in the neighborhood, such as Arpinum, Sora, Casinum, Aquinum, Venafrum, or Allifae. At Tusculum, near Rome, from where Plancius' opponent came, there was no special interest in the possibility of a local man gaining a modest public office in Rome. But in the region of Atina this possibility had aroused general enthusiasm.[46]

It is best to envisage the demography of Roman voting as a series of zones, beginning at the extremes of the peninsula and moving through central Italian regions like the Atina area or Picenum (from which the effort of voting would still have demanded at least some three days' journey in either direction) to the immediate vicinity of the city. As soon as we come into the zone within which voting might be achieved at the cost of perhaps a single day's journey to Rome and back, we return to something like the archaic context imagined by Rutilius (cited earlier in this chapter). Within that zone, as we shall see shortly, we can envisage the extensive (but very little known) built-up area of the city proper, then the area of popular *tabernae* and prominent houses near the Forum, and finally the Forum itself.

As regards the city of Rome and the zone around it, we do have extremely important evidence that bears directly on the possibility of participation in the political process and on the possible representativeness of the crowds who appeared in the Forum. For example, Dionysius

---

45. Cicero *Q.f.* 2.3.4(7).
46. Cicero *Planc.* 8–9/19–23. See more fully chap. 7.

of Halicarnassus, writing his *Antiquitates Romanae* a few decades after the period with which we are concerned, offers a vivid description of Rome and its suburban area.

> But all the inhabited places round it [Rome], which are many and large, are unprotected and without walls, and very easy to be taken by any enemies who may come. If anyone wishes to estimate the size of Rome by looking at these suburbs he will necessarily be misled for want of a definite clue by which to determine up to which point it is still the city and where it ceases to be the city; so closely is the city connected with the country, giving the beholder the impression of a city stretching out indefinitely.[47]

Dionysius' description makes it quite certain that the eleven-kilometer circuit of the fourth-century wall around Rome (the so-called Servian Wall) no longer marked a sharp break between city and country (indeed, he goes on to say that the wall was in many places obscured by buildings on either side). There was therefore an area of dense, though not necessarily continuous, habitation that stretched well beyond the wall.

For an understanding of the real social context of the open-air functions of the *res publica* in the Forum, nothing would be more important than a conception of habitation patterns and habitation densities, within the fourth-century wall and in the area outside it, as well as in the ring of small places situated around Rome as far, for example, as Ostia in the one direction or Tibur and Tusculum in the other. The nature of the *suburbium* of Rome and the relation to Rome of the towns and villages within, say, a thirty-kilometer radius can hardly be grasped for the late-Republican period.[48] But we catch a glimpse of the traffic to and from the city in the famous incident of 52 when Milo, on his way to the *municipium* of Lanuvium (some thirty kilometers from Rome), encountered Clodius, on his way back from Aricia (a journey of some twenty-two kilometers); as Asconius' narrative of the incident reveals, both places enjoyed local self-government (Clodius had been addressing the town councillors of Aricia).[49]

---

47. Dionysius *Ant.* 4.13.3–4, Loeb trans.

48. See, however, E.J. Champlin, "The *Suburbium* of Rome," *AJAH* 7 (1982): 97; and for the official roles filled in Rome by men from the nearer towns, see N. Purcell, "The *Apparitores*: A Study in Social Mobility," *PBSR* 51 (1983): 125.

49. Asconius 31C.

Many other places in the area around Rome will have been simply villages *(vici),* and we seem also to catch a very significant glimpse of them in Plutarch's report of the dinner provided for the people by Lucullus on the occasion of his triumph in 63: "In addition to this, he feasted the city magnificently and also the surrounding villages, which they call *vici.*"[50] If Plutarch has understood his Latin source correctly, this reference is extremely important; it would indicate clearly that the (undefinable) zone of "surrounding villages" was, or could be, systematically included in the benefits offered to the people of Rome.

Unfortunately, however, there is a chance that he has overinterpreted his Latin source and that what it referred to was *vici* in a different sense, that is, the local subdivisions of the city itself. We do indeed find that distributions of benefits were occasionally made not at one central location but throughout the quarters *(vici)* of the city.[51]

The conclusions to be drawn from this evidence therefore remain uncertain. But far greater significance attaches in any case to the figures which we find for the 50s and 40s for the numbers of recipients of the free monthly corn ration, which was established by the tribunician legislation of Clodius in 58. By 46 the number of recipients is said to have risen to 320,000, a figure reassessed on the orders of Julius Caesar and in some way (it is not known how) reduced to 150,000. We need not pay attention to the details, for those figures belong in the same range (320,000 down to some 200,000) as those for recipients of cash distributions under Augustus.[52] The lower figures certainly represent an artificial closing of the list of entitled persons, rather than any sudden drop in population, though they may also of course reflect the more effective exclusion of fraudulent claims. It is certain at any rate that in the middle and latter part of the first century, corn or cash could be distributed to vast numbers who counted as belonging to the *plebs urbana* of Rome, numbers that at the maximum approximated to one-third of the total number of Roman citizens as listed in the census of 70 mentioned earlier in this chapter. There appears to be no evidence as to on what principle, if at all, a

50. Plutarch *Luc.* 37: ἐπὶ τούτοις τήν τε πόλιν εἱστίασε λαμπρῶς καὶ τὰς περιοικίδας κώμας, ἃς οὐίκους καλοῦσι.

51. E.g., Livy (25.2.8) writes, "congii olei in vicos singulos dati."

52. Suetonius *Div. Iul.* 41.3; Augustus *RG* 15. See D. van Berchem, *Les distributions de blé et d'argent à la plèbe romaine sous l'Empire* (Geneva: Georg Editeur S.A., 1939); G.E. Rickman, *The Corn Supply of Ancient Rome* (Oxford: Clarendon, 1980): 175–76; C. Virlouvet, *Tessera Frumentaria: Les procédures de distribution du blè public à Rome à la fin de la République et au début de l'Empire* (Rome: École française de Rome, 1995).

geographical boundary was set to define who was entitled. All that seems clear is that something like one-third of the total numbers of Roman citizens must have lived either in Rome itself (however defined) or sufficiently near to be able to collect a ration of corn once a month.

To return to a concept used earlier, it may be useful to continue to think of successive zones centering on the Forum: the extremities of Italy, including Gallia Cisalpina (from which some voters were expected to come on some occasions); central Italy, north and south of Rome, from places like Arpinum to regions like Umbria and Picenum; places from which one might, by starting early, get to Rome and back in a day or at the cost of one night's stay; the *vici*, in the sense of actual villages, around the city; the *vici*, or quarters, of the city itself, within the fourth-century wall; the area immediately around the Forum; and finally the Forum itself, which, as many sources indicate, was usually full of idle observers or casual passersby, under whose gaze *(conspectus)* public acts of various kinds took place, from the holding of jury courts *(quaestiones),* to the taking of oaths, to the calling of public meetings *(contiones).*

What is essential about this picture from the point of view of the Roman *res publica* is that absolutely no steps were taken to facilitate voting or any other form of active participation at a distance (by contrast, the levy for the Roman legions certainly was conducted locally, and so, as we have seen, was the census).[53] A mere couple of sentences in Suetonius' *Divus Augustus* report that Augustus allowed the town councillors of his new *coloniae* in Italy to vote locally for magistracies in Rome and to send in their votes under seal, and they also report that the towns (perhaps these *coloniae* only) were allowed to make collective recommendations for the filling of equestrian posts.[54] In the late Republic, however, voting still depended wholly on personal presence. Canvassing, however, as we have seen earlier in this chapter, was carried to the voters in their *municipia*. The *Commentariolum petitionis,* a work that claims to be addressed to Cicero by his brother, Quintus, gives the advice that it is essential for a candidate to know the voting potential of every district of Italy.

Next, make sure that you have all of Italy fixed in your mind and memory, as divided into *tribus,* so that you do not allow there to be

---

53. The census is discussed earlier in this chapter. For levies, see P.A. Brunt, "The Army and the Land in the Roman Revolution," *JRS* 52 (1962): 69, extensively revised in *The Fall of the Roman Republic and Related Essays* (Oxford: Clarendon, 1988), chap. 5.

54. Suetonius *Div. Aug.* 46.

a single *municipium, colonia, praefectura,* or locality of Italy in which you do not have sufficient support. You should inquire about and check on individuals from every area, get to know them, seek them out, make sure of them, and see to it that in their neighborhoods they may canvass for you and act as candidates on your behalf.[55]

Politically, therefore, the Roman system did embrace Italy, as it did also, in some respects, in the administrative and military sphere. The notion that Italy was a sort of nation-state in the late Republic is not entirely misleading. But *constitutionally* the exercise of positive rights could still only take place in Rome. Nonetheless, as we have seen earlier in this chapter, participation by particular groups from particular regions of Italy could have tangible and unpredictable effects on the outcome of voting in Rome.

As I will discuss further later, when we come to reflect on the nature of this curious hybrid system, in which aspects characteristic of a nation-state coexisted with ones appropriate to a small city-state, the fact that Italians were now "Roman" and *could* vote in Rome and hold office there was of immense long-term significance (see chap. 8). But in the immediate short term, active participation must have been overwhelmingly dominated by those who lived in Rome or near it, who seem to have amounted to approximately one-third of the whole citizen body.

It would be of great help if we had a clearer grasp of habitation patterns within the city, of the social character of the different *vici,* and of the shrines and localized festivals that were to be found there.[56] It would be equally valuable to be able to envisage what mechanisms existed for evoking the political involvement of the inhabitants and bringing them *en masse* to the Forum. But again we are almost wholly dependent on Cicero's hostile representations of the middle-rank agents whom he describes as calling out disreputable mobs from the *vici* of Rome.[57] It may be

---

55. *Com. pet.* 8/30.

56. For the city population, see the classic article by Z. Yavetz, "The Living Conditions of the Plebs in Republican Rome," *Latomus* 17 (1958): 500; B. Kühnert, *Die Plebs Urbana der späten römischen Republik,* Abh. Leipz., phil-hist. reih. 73, no. 3 (Berlin: Akademie-Verlag, 1991); N. Purcell, "The City of Rome and the *Plebs Urbana* in the Late Republic," in *CAH²* 9, *The Last Age of the Roman Republic, 146–43 B.C.,* ed. J.A. Crook, A. Lintott, and E. Rawson (Cambridge: Cambridge University Press, 1994), 644.

57. I rely here on the study by P.J.J. Vanderbroek, *Popular Leadership and Collective Behaviour in the Late Roman Republic (ca. 80 B.C.)* (Amsterdam: Gieben, 1987).

sufficient here to recall his picture, in his *Pro Sestio* of 56, of how disorderly groups were recruited throughout the city to achieve physical dominance of the Forum: "when *vicus* by *vicus* men were being enrolled and organized into units."[58]

As regards physical violence, much more fully attested for the 50s than earlier, or as regards the crowds at *contiones,* whose often vivid reactions were a fundamental means of the expression of public opinion, we are dealing with what inevitably remains for us an undifferentiated mob, whose geographical and social origins were and remain indiscernible. But precisely the most significant aspect of the crowd in Rome, and one that entirely differentiates it from the urban crowds studied in other historical societies,[59] is that this crowd was not limited to demonstrations of public opinion, to destructive violence, or to protests against the actions of some sovereign, or of some legislative body. For as soon as it had re-formed into its constituent *tribus,* it *was* the sovereign body in the Roman *res publica,* and it not only could legislate but was, in normal circumstances, the only body that did so.

When it came to voting, therefore, it mattered a great deal which *tribus* a citizen belonged to, or, to put it differently, which *tribus* were represented in the Forum on the day in question and by whom.

One aspect of the background of the tribal registration of freedmen is relatively clear. As we have seen earlier in this chapter, since the second century the established principle had been that each *libertinus* should be enrolled in one of the four *tribus urbanae* and not therefore in any of the other thirty-one *tribus.* It is no surprise that tribunician proposals continued to be made in the first century to allow *libertini* registration in any tribe—in 88 by Sulpicius Rufus, in 67 by Cornelius, and in the next year by Manilius.[60] The issue appears for the last time in 52, as a prospective proposal by Clodius, who at the time of his death was a candidate for the praetorship (a clear indication that candidates might very well already have publicly known political programs). Asconius notes that Clodius had been proposing to allow *libertini* to vote also in the *tribus rusticae,* "which are the preserve of the freeborn." He was commenting on an

---

58. Cicero *Sest.* 15/34: "cum vicatim homines conscriberentur, decuriarentur"; see more fully chap. 6.

59. See, e.g., E.J. Hobsbawm, *Primitive Rebels: Studies in Archaic Forms of Social Movement in the Nineteenth and Twentieth Centuries,* 3d ed. (Manchester: Manchester University Press, 1971), and the works by G. Rudé cited in n. 19 in chap. 1.

60. For Sulpicius, see Livy *Per.* 77; for Cornelius, Asconius 45C (see chap. 4); for Manilius, Asconius 64–65C and Dio 36.42.2.

enigmatic and rhetorical statement by Cicero in his *Pro Milone,* that Clodius had been preparing laws "that would have subjected us to our slaves."[61]

This rule, which was not in fact changed, was thus partly a matter of status and political rights. But it may also have had some greater statistical significance in the 50s, if Dionysius' claim that masters now freed slaves more readily, to allow them to participate in the free distributions of corn, was already applicable to this period.[62] But from the point of view of political "representation," that is, of how many people there were at hand to exercise the votes of each of the thirty-five *tribus,* it would be much more important to know whether, either in principle or in actual practice, freeborn Roman citizens, registered in one of the *tribus rusticae,* who then migrated to live in or near Rome, were as a consequence transferred by the censors into one of the four *tribus urbanae.* Though the censors are reported to have had the right to change tribal registrations,[63] there is in fact no evidence that they systematically reregistered citizens who moved to Rome. In any case the censorship operated only spasmodically in the first century B.C.[64] The probability is, therefore, that large numbers of persons who came originally from places registered in one or another of the thirty-one "rustic" tribes were in fact living in and around Rome, still belonged to those tribes, and could vote in them. If so, the de facto inhabitants of Rome and its suburban area will have been able, in a very significant way, to exercise for their own advantage the voting rights of the whole Roman citizen body, which was in principle distributed across all of Roman territory (and in this period, therefore, across all of Italy).

It should be noted, however, that in a much quoted passage of his *Pro Sestio* of 56, Cicero claims precisely that the *comitia tributa* did *not* properly represent the whole citizen body. On the contrary, he says, there had on occasion been so few people present that people had had to be drafted in from other *tribus* so that the voting role of each tribe could be fulfilled.[65] The report has to be taken seriously, even if it is part of a highly tendentious stretch of argument, designed to prove that other, less formal, types of public assembly better represented the real will of the

61. Asconius 52C; Cicero *Mil.* 32/87 (and 33/89).
62. Dionysius *Ant.* 4.24.5.
63. See Livy 45.15.4 (on the censors of 169/8 B.C.).
64. See, e.g., T.P. Wiseman, "The Census in the First Century B.C.," *JRS* 59 (1969): 59.
65. Cicero *Sest.* 51/109, quoted and discussed in chap. 6.

populus Romanus than did either *contiones* or legislative assemblies. There does not seem to be any way of checking whether Cicero's representation of very low attendance levels corresponded to the facts. It is best to confess that we cannot gain any clear conception of the degree to which those who did come to the Forum to vote represented anything like a fair cross section of the total mass of voters.

It is certain only that those who lived in and near the city must have enjoyed a wholly disproportionate representation among those who came to vote and that at no time can those who voted have amounted to more than a minute proportion of the total of theoretically entitled voters—perhaps, at best, on the most crowded occasions, one in forty-five (see chap. 8). Moreover, those who lived or worked near the Forum had, inevitably, an extra advantage in participation. Although, as we have seen earlier in this chapter, notice of a proposed law needed to be given over a period of three *nundinae* before it was put to the vote, the actual moment of voting could be announced quite suddenly and might be accompanied by an instruction that the *tabernae* (that is, those situated around the Forum) should be closed. Thus the contrast between immediate participation by those in the vicinity, on the one hand, and the potential participation (given sufficient motive and sufficient notice) by citizens from all over Italy, on the other, could hardly escape contemporaries. It is stressed most clearly by Cicero, referring to the law validating his own return from exile in 57, which was, unusually, put through the *comitia centuriata*, meeting in the Campus Martius, rather than the *comitia tributa*, meeting in the Forum. Moreover, as Cicero endlessly emphasizes, support had been gathered from respectable persons from all the towns of Italy, and large numbers had made the journey to Rome to vote.[66] Cicero, addressing the pontifices after his return, exploited the contrast in participation, notionally addressing his opponent Clodius.

> Do you think that that group is the *populus Romanus* which is made up of those who are hired for pay, who are incited to use force against the magistrates, besiege the Senate, and hope every day for slaughter, fire, and devastation—that *populus* whom you could not have got together except by having the *tabernae* closed. . . . But *that* was the beauty of the *populus Romanus*, that its true shape, which you saw in the Campus at the moment when even you had the

66. E.g., Cicero *Post. red. in Sen.* 11.27–28, *Post red. ad Quir.* 8/18, *Dom.* 28/75, *Sest.* 60/128, *Pis.* 15/36. See more fully pp. 152–55 below.

power to speak against the authority and the will of the Senate and of the whole of Italy. *That* is the *populus* which is the master of kings, the victor and commander of all peoples, whom you saw then on that famous day, you criminal, when all the leading men of the state, all of all ranks and ages, believed themselves to be voting on the salvation not of one *civis* but of the *civitas,* when, in short, people came to the Campus after not shops [*tabernae*] but towns [*municipia*] had been closed.[67]

Cicero was of course correct to imply that most votes conducted in Rome did not draw participation from all parts of Italy. He must also be right in his implied contrast between the respectable voters who could (or might) make the journey to Rome from a distance and the more lower-class character of the crowd that could be rapidly assembled in the Forum. Yet, as is shown by a mass of evidence for speeches made there, including his own, the implication that such a crowd was normally assembled simply for pay is plainly false. The Forum was, on the contrary, the place where the conflicting values and traditions shared by Roman citizens were argued out in public and where a very complex, "face-to-face" political system with various diverse components functioned in the open air, with the different elements operating literally in sight of each other and all under the gaze of whatever onlookers were present. It was this crowd that, even at its most passive (that is, when simply functioning as witnesses), represented the wider *populus Romanus.* As Cicero himself says in his *De lege agraria* of 63, "it is not lawful for the censors to lease out the *vectigalia* except under the gaze [*conspectus*] of the *populus Romanus.*"[68]

The traditional, even archaic, character of the Forum and of the various open-air functions that were performed within it and around it symbolized the maintenance of long-established rights, while its restricted area necessarily placed severe limits on the representativeness of those who were present there. Its character as a slowly developing public space, surrounded by monuments with profound historical associations, has been brilliantly explored by Filippo Coarelli, whose analysis has been developed in different ways by Jean-Michel David and by Nicholas Purcell, whose contribution appears as an article in the invaluable *Lexicon*

---

67. Cicero *Dom.* 33/89–90.

68. Cicero *De leg. ag.* 1.3/7: "censoribus vectigalia locare nisi in conspectu populi Romani non licet."

Topographicum Urbis Romae.[69] Only a few essentials, directly relevant
to the public life of the period from 80 to 50, will be touched on here (see
the plan of the Forum in 53 B.C. on p. 40).

The Forum consisted of a roughly oblong open space, from whose east
side the Clivus Capitolinus led up to the Capitol and to the late-sixth-
century temple of Iuppiter Optimus Maximus. On the slope of the Capi-
toline hill lay the fifth-century temple of Saturn, which also functioned as
the treasury of the *res publica,* that is, as a storehouse of both money and
documents. To the north of the temple of Saturn, on a platform overlook-
ing the Forum, was the temple of Concordia, and further north along the
side of the hill was the *carcer,* or prison, a structure with an inner cham-
ber carved out of the rock of the hillside, which played a notable part in
symbolic public conflicts between tribunes of the plebs and consuls.

Close to this eastern end of the Forum lay the archaic jurisdictional
and constitutional center of the *res publica,* the Comitium, or "meeting
place," where voting by the *comitia tributa* had taken place until 145,
when it was transferred to the main open space of the Forum. To its
north, the Comitium was fronted directly by the Curia Hostilia, the
Senate house, a single-chamber building allegedly constructed by one of
the kings. The Senate was unique among all the public institutions of the
Republic in regularly meeting indoors under a roof, most often in the
Curia itself, but quite frequently in various temples, among them that of
Concordia.[70] It was perhaps equally significant that the location of the
Curia exposed meetings of the Senate to the pressures of the crowd
outside, whose shouts could be heard inside, and through whom senators
had to make their way to and from meetings.

Outside the Curia, and around the Comitium, were the established
seats of a number of public officials. Immediately outside the Curia,
indeed, and under the *Tabula Valeria,* a picture representing an episode
from the First Punic War, was the bench of the ten tribunes, placed there
to make them available to give help *(auxilium)* to any citizen who appealed for it and also to allow them to observe and check proceedings
inside the Curia. The most immediate context for such help was juridical.

69. Coarelli, *Foro,* vols. 1 and 2; David, *Patronat judiciaire,* esp. 14–15 and 406–7;
N. Purcell, "Forum Romanum (the Republican Period)," in *LTUR* 2 (1995): 325. See now
also L. Thommen, "Les lieux de la plèbe et de ses tribuns dans la Rome républicaine," *Klio*
77 (1995): 358.

70. See M. Bonnefond-Coudry, *Le sénat de la République romaine* (Rome: École française de Rome, 1989), 25–26.

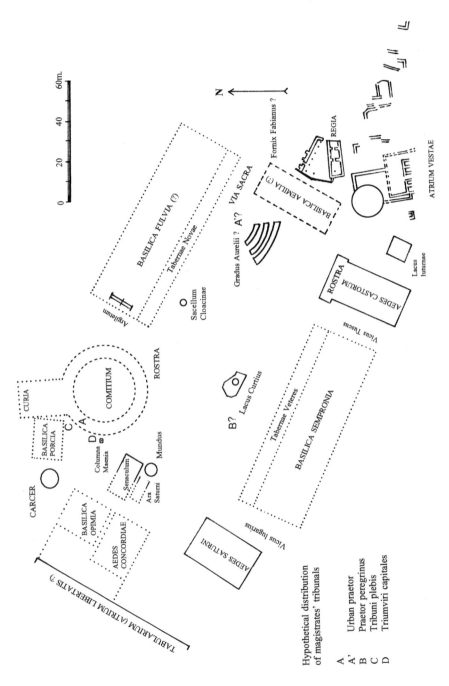

The Forum in 53 B.C. Based on the hypothetical plan of the Forum in J.M. David, *Le patronat judiciaire au dernier siècle de la République romaine* (Rome: École française de Rome, 1992). It should be stressed that there are numerous uncertainties as to the location or identity of many of the buildings. Plan adapted by kind permission of J.M. David. Drawn by Jenny Graham.

Hypothetical distribution
of magistrates' tribunals

A   Urban praetor
A'   Praetor peregrinus
B   Tribuni plebis
C   Triumviri capitales

Labels within the plan:

60m. 0 20 40

N

CURIA
CARCER
BASILICA PORCIA
BASILICA OPIMIA
AEDES CONCORDIAE
TABULARIUM (ATRIUM LIBERTATIS ?)
COMITIUM
ROSTRA
Columna Maenia
Senaculum
Ara Saturni
Mundus
AEDES SATURNI
Vicus Iugarius
BASILICA SEMPRONIA
Tabernae Veteres
Lacus Curtius
Vicus Tuscus
ROSTRA
AEDES CASTORUM
Lacus Iuturnae
ATRIUM VESTAE
REGIA
Fornix Fabianus ?
BASILICA AEMILIA (?)
VIA SACRA
Gradus Aurelii ? A'?
Sacellum Cloacinae
Aequimelium
Tabernae Novae
BASILICA FULVIA (?)
A C D A'
B?

Just in front of the tribunes, on the edge of the Comitium, was the traditional site of the tribunal of the *praetor urbanus*,[71] while the minor officials called *triumviri capitales* had an established seat for judging criminal offenses near the fourth-century Columna Maenia on the western edge of the Comitium.[72]

On the eastern side of the Comitium, looking onto the broader spaces of the Forum proper, stood the Rostra, a curved speakers' platform, adorned with statues—for instance, of Camillus or, more recently, of Sulla and Pompey. It was the normal place from which the people were addressed. As we will see, when violence became a regular feature of *contiones* and of meetings of the *comitia tributa,* physical control and occupation of the Rostra became a crucial objective.

Along both the north and the south sides of the Forum stood two major second-century basilicas. On the north side, fronted by the Tabernae Novae, lay one whose name is now disputed (between Basilica Aemilia and Basilica Fulvia), and on the south, with the Tabernae Veteres, lay the Basilica Sempronia. Both were equipped with first-floor galleries, called *maeniana,* from which spectators could watch the complex scene (or sets of different scenes) in the Forum. An anecdote retailed by Valerius Maximus shows a defendant in an extortion trial watching from a *maenianum* for the indication that the verdict would go against him and committing suicide before sentence was passed.[73]

The jury courts, or *quaestiones,* of the late Republic were presided over by a praetor or a *quaesitor* appointed ad hoc, seated on a low tribunal of perhaps about a meter in height; there was a jury of *iudices,* of between thirty and fifty persons; and there were a number of prosecutors and *patroni* speaking against or for the accused, as well as witnesses on either side. Around them, as was essential to both the public character of the occasion and the nature of the oratory that needed to be deployed, was a shifting crowd *(corona)* of spectators, whose reactions played a vital part in the course of the case.[74] The various *quaestiones,* more than one of which might be in session at the same time, thus demanded quite a considerable open space.

Toward the eastern end of the Forum, which seems to have been the

71. See J.-M. David, "Le tribunal du préteur: Contraintes symboliques et politiques sous la République et le début de l'Empire," *Klio* 77 (1995): 371.

72. See Cicero *Div. in Caec.* 16/50 and scholiast.

73. Val. Max. 9.12.7.

74. See David, *Patronat judiciaire,* esp. 463–64.

part in which *quaestiones* normally met, we encounter various fundamental problems of topography, as regards the stage reached in the late Republic. The entire monumental structure of the area was subsequently to be altered irrevocably by the erection of the temple of Divus Julius, voted in 42 and dedicated in 29, whose podium still dominates the area. The character of this zone *may* have been altered also in the 50s by the erection of a transverse basilica, running northeast from the temple of Castor and Pollux to the end of the Basilica Fulvia(?). This building may be the basilica referred to as under construction by Aemilius Paulus in a letter of Cicero's in 54.[75] But doubts have been raised about the archaeological basis of this hypothesis.[76]

What is certain about the monumental context of the southeast corner of the Forum is, first of all, the prominence of the fifth-century temple of Castor and Pollux itself, whose massive podium, the result of successive reconstructions during the Republic, stood between the Vicus Tuscus and the small shrine of Iuturna, the Lacus Iuturnae, also adorned with statues of these two deities.[77] Often referred to just as the Aedes Castoris, the temple was a major feature of Roman collective life, its projecting podium serving as an alternative speakers' platform, and it itself being used in the 50s as a sort of fortress, or springboard, for the physical domination of the Forum area (chap. 6). The antiquity of the temple, which tradition recorded to have been voted after the brothers Castor and Pollux had appeared at the battle of Lake Regillus in the early Republic, gave its two deities a special place in collective ideology.

Thus, near the end of his never delivered fifth oration against Verres, Cicero, notionally speaking in the open air at this end of the Forum, duly invokes Castor and Pollux: "You, the arbiters of all the business of the Forum, of the most important councils, of the laws and the law courts, situated in the place most frequented by the *populus Romanus,* Castor and Pollux . . ."[78] It was indeed somewhere in the area in front of this

---

75. Cicero *Att.* 4.16.8 (89). See E.M. Steinby, "Il lato orientale del Foro Romano: Proposte di lettura," *Arctos* 8 (1987): 139.

76. See, e.g., E. Carnabucci, *L'angolo sud-orientale del Foro Romano nel manoscritto inedito di Giacomo Boni* (Rome: Academia Nazionali dei Lincei, 1991).

77. See I. Nielsen and B. Poulsen, *The Temple of Castor and Pollux*, vol. 1 (Rome: De Luca, 1992); E.M. Steinby, ed., *Lacus Iuturnae*, vol. 1, *Analisi delle fonti* (Rome: De Luca, 1989).

78. Cicero *Verr.* 2.5.72/186. For the use of topographical allusion in Cicero's speeches in the Forum, see A. Vasaly, *Representations: Images of the World in Ciceronian Oratory* (Berkeley: University of California Press, 1993), esp. 34–35.

temple that the *quaestiones* sat. Thus Cicero, defending Scaurus in 54, could appeal to the fact that Scaurus' grandfather, Metellus, had carried out one of the successive repairs of the temple: "L. Metellus himself, this man's grandfather, seems to have established these most holy gods in that *templum* before your eyes, jurors, so that they might appeal to you to save his grandson."[79] In front of the temple, it seems that, perhaps in 81, at the moment of Sulla's reform of the *quaestiones*, a permanent structure for jury courts, consisting of a *tribunal Aurelium* and *gradus Aurelii* (Aurelian steps) had been established. Their physical appearance is not well understood, and no clearly identified archaeological traces of them have been found. But it is no surprise that Cicero, harking back in his *Pro Cluentio* to events in the year 74, speaks of the *gradus Aurelii* as having the role of a theater: "those *gradus Aurelii,* which were then new, seemed to have been built almost as a theater for that jury court."[80]

The two ancient shrines at the east end of the Forum, the Regia and the temple and atrium of Vesta, are very little mentioned in contemporary oratory, and their character and function remain remarkably obscure.[81] What plays a much larger part in contemporary discourse is the Sacra Via, which entered the Forum at its northeast corner and has generally been thought to have led down from the saddle on which the Arch of Titus was later to be placed; Coarelli, however, has argued that the Sacra Via ran further northeastward, across the area later occupied by the Basilica of Maxentius.[82] Whatever the precise topography, it is certain that there was a zone of substantial houses in the area of rising ground to the east of the Forum, in which it was common for prominent officeholders to live. From there they could "come down" *(descendere)* the short distance to the Forum, accompanied by large crowds of followers. At approximately the point where the Sacra Via entered the Forum, there stood what was so far the only triumphal arch in the heart of the political center, the Fornix Fabianus, erected by Q. Fabius Maximus after his victories in Gaul in 121. We see both the ritualized public display by the holders of power and the increasingly violent reactions of the crowd in an anecdote of 75, reported in a poorly preserved fragment of Sallust's *Historiae.* The two consuls were coming down the Sacra Via, escorting,

79. Quoted in Asconius 27–28C (repairs were carried out by L. Caecilius Metellus Dalmaticus, at the time of his triumph in 117).
80. Cicero *Clu.* 34/93. See further chap. 3.
81. See, e.g., *LTUR* 1, s.v. "Atrium Vestae."
82. Coarelli, *Foro,* 1:11–12.

or literally "bringing down" *(deducentes),* a candidate for the prae-torship, when the crowd, enraged by the high price of corn, assaulted them and forced them to retreat into the nearby *domus* of Octavius, which served as a fortress *(propugnaculum).*[83] The question of the extent to which these houses could be defended and could thus function as limitations on the power of the crowd will reappear several times later in this book.[84]

The Fornix Fabianus itself was one of the most prominent dynastic monuments so far erected in the political center of Rome, and it too was visible from where the *quaestiones* sat. It was repaired by the curule aedile of 57, Q. Fabius Maximus, and inscriptions show that it was adorned with statues of at least two of the famous second-century mem-bers of his family, Aemilius Paullus and Scipio Aemilianus. Thus it was easy for Cicero, delivering his *In Vatinium* in the following year, to find the appropriate way to praise him.

> Nothing that Maximus did was alien either to his own *virtus* or to those most famous men the Paulli, Maximi, and Africani, whose glory we not only can expect to be renewed by his *virtus* but can even now see.[85]

The Sacra Via served as the route for the processions that opened the *ludi Romani,* held in the Circus Maximus, and (in the opposite direction) for triumphal processions, which would come down the slope, across the Forum, and up the Clivus Capitolinus. That fact should remind us that the essential feature of the Forum is that the same space was used for many different sorts of public collective activity—not merely everyday trading and money changing, but gladiatorial *munera* offered by individu-als; theatrical performances *(ludi),* which were part of the established official calendar; the taking of oaths by officeholders; trials (both *iudicia populi* and *quaestiones*); funeral orations by members of the families of deceased persons; and, above all, *contiones,* informal meetings called by officeholders and devoted to speeches addressed to whoever was present. This alternation of function within the same space is perhaps best illus-trated by the fact that in 43 the Senate honored the memory of Servius Sulpicius Rufus not only by erecting a bronze statue of him on the Rostra

---

83. Sallust *Hist.* 2.45 M = 2.42 McGushin.
84. See pp. 131, 140–41, 157, and 182 below.
85. Cicero *Vat.* 11/28; see Degrassi, *ILLRP,* no. 392.

but by reserving for his descendants a space of five feet around the statue from which they would be able to watch *ludi* and gladiatorial shows.[86]

It is significant also that the Senate's vote in memory of Servius Sulpicius laid down that the reasons for the voting of the honors to him should be embodied in an inscription on the base of the statue. Given that the fundamental political function of the Forum was that the *populus Romanus,* as represented by whoever was present, should see the actions performed in its name and have those actions justified to it in words, it is important to stress that both permanent written texts (like the inscriptions on the Fornix Fabianus) and temporary ones played a part. We have already seen earlier in this chapter the way in which the names of jurors in the extortion court had to be written up in public. Thus not only the content of major novel steps, such as *leges,* had to be put up *(proposita)* in public for people to read—Cicero, for instance, describes how he sent *librarii* to copy the text of Rullus' agrarian law in December 62.[87] But also, for instance, the *praetor peregrinus* (and thus presumably anyone else giving jurisdiction) had to have the *stipulationes* relevant to his jurisdiction written up on an *album* (a whitewashed board) while he was sitting in judgment; the names of the *viatores* and other attendants who assisted the magistrates had to be posted on one wall of the temple of Saturn; and the sections of the *Tabula Heracleensis* relating to Rome reveal that the names of those who were (for reasons not made clear) listed as not entitled to free corn should be posted on an *album* in the Forum while the distributions were being carried out. The same text shows that the aedile had to put the details of any prospective contract for the upkeep of roads in front of his tribunal in the Forum for ten days before the contract was let out. He had also to see to it that the letting itself was conducted by the quaestor of the Aerarium "openly, in the Forum."[88] Writing, public action, and spoken words all played a part in guaranteeing publicity.

These small details are enough to reinforce our conceptions of that ideology of publicity that pervaded every aspect of Roman communal life. But did that ideology amount merely to the passive right of witnessing, of having the actions of the powerful conducted before the gaze

86. See Cicero *Phil.* 9.7/15–16.

87. Cicero *De leg. ag.* 2.5/13. See chap. 5.

88. *Lex Rubria* (CIL I², no. 592; Crawford, *Roman Statutes,* 1: no. 28, lines 23–25); *lex Cornelia de XX Quaestoribus* (CIL I², no. 587; Crawford, *Roman Statutes,* 1: no. 14 and 2: nos 38–41; *Tabula Heracleensis* (CIL I², no. 593; Crawford, *Roman Statutes,* 1: no. 24, lines 14–17, 32–37).

(conspectus) of the people? We will look further, in chapter 8, at the question of how far, if at all, this complex system, heavily marked by archaic elements, deserves the name of democracy. But at this point it need only be reiterated that the normal annual magistracies could only be gained by direct election and that those elected were obliged to take a public oath within five days of the commencement of their office, to declare that they would obey the laws. If they would not take such an oath, they had to resign.[89] They also, as we will see in more detail in chapter 5, had to take an oath relating to their conduct when they left office.

Was it only those who held office who could address the people? Was there a right, or at least some possibility, for the ordinary person to intervene in political debate? It is clear that a *contio* could be held only by someone holding office and that permission to speak was dependent on that officeholder. But it is quite certain that those who were allowed to speak included persons who were at that moment technically *privati* (persons not holding office). When the two prominent conservative ex-consuls Catulus and Hortensius spoke against the *lex Manilia* of 66, both were *privati.*[90] We need not really doubt that deference dictated that public persuasion was in fact confined to the office-holding class, however we define it. But it should be stressed that the evidence does suggest that, in a formal sense, *contiones* could begin with an invitation to whoever wished to address the people to come forward and do so. This evidence is not extensive, and in considering it, there is always the danger of overinterpreting the implications of passing items of narrative material. Nonetheless, Livy records that when a *tribunus plebis* of 167 was putting a *lex* to the vote, "there was an opportunity for *privati* to speak about the law," and Servius Sulpicius Galba, who held the modest rank of tribune of a legion, did so.[91] Similarly, Dionysius represents a herald as inviting "whoever wished" to do so to speak about a law.[92]

We can hardly take these passing allusions even as demonstrating the existence of a formal right for every citizen to speak, let alone as establishing that there was a social convention by which they actually did so. Nonetheless, it should be strongly stressed that any citizen who wished to

---

89. See Livy 31.50.6−7.
90. See chap. 4.
91. Livy 45.36.1−6.
92. Dionysius *Ant.* 10.41.1. See G.W. Botsford, *The Roman Assemblies* (New York: Macmillan, 1909), 145−46.

do so could hear opposing views on any topic, either at different *contiones* held by different officeholders or, sometimes, at the same *contio*. We shall also see many examples of how those holding *contiones* obliged other officeholders (by what means is not clear) to appear on the tribunal and to submit themselves to public questioning.[93] If we think in terms of freedom of speech, the Roman *res publica* had at any rate no means of checking on or repressing private speech. And if it did not provide a positive vehicle for free public speech on the part of all citizens as individuals, its conventions certainly provided ample opportunity for *hearing* open public debate in the Forum. So Cicero, for instance, speaks of the opportunities for hearing famous orators that had been open to him in his youth, specifically in the year 90.

> As for the others who were then regarded as political leaders [*principes*], they were then in office and could be heard by me al-most every day in *contiones*. For C. Curio was then *tribunus plebis,* although he indeed fell silent, after on one occasion he had been deserted [while speaking] by the entire meeting. . . . but Q. Varius, C. Carbo, and Cn. Pomponius [all of whom we know to have been *tribuni plebis*] were skilled speakers, and these indeed "lived" on the Rostra; similarly C. Iulius, as *aedilis curulis,* delivered carefully com-posed speeches almost every day.[94]

Such was the tradition of a permanent political theater (a metaphor consciously used, for example, by Cicero, who referred to events "on-stage, that is, at a *contio*."[95] This theater was available at a fixed tradi-tional location to those who were interested, and in it the crowd (which itself could be described as a *contio*) was not necessarily a passive audi-ence but could intervene with shouts or an explicit dialogue with the speaker or could show its opinion simply by drifting away. The same crowd could moreover be transformed into a sovereign assembly of vot-ers simply (in principle) by being instructed by the presiding magistrate to separate *(discedere)* into its voting *tribus*.[96] Moreover, in contrast with

---

93. E.g., see chaps. 3–5.

94. Cicero *Brut.* 89/305.

95. Cicero *De amicitia* 26/97: "in scaena, id est in contione."

96. So writes Asconius (71C): "cum id solum superest ut populus sententiam ferat, iubet eum is qui fert legem 'discedere': quod verbum non hoc significat quod in communi consuetudine *est,* eant de eo loco ubi lex feratur, sed in suam quisque tribum discedat in qua est suffragium laturus."

the *comitia centuriata*, the structure of which gave an explicit precedence to the upper classes throughout the Republic (see discussion earlier in this chapter and in chap. 8), no biasing in terms of social class marked the *comitia tributa*, except for the rule that *libertini* should be confined to one of the four *tribus urbanae*. What served to limit participation was thus not class but distance, a factor that should be interpreted as having given all the more power to the *plebs urbana*. If it is true, as suggested earlier in this chapter, that people who belonged to one of the thirty-one *tribus rusticae* tended in practice to remain in that *tribus* even after migrating to Rome or its vicinity, then the capacity of local residents to "represent" the whole *populus Romanus* was even greater. It is hardly surprising therefore that Sulla, backed by military force, was able briefly to invalidate the sovereign power of legislating enjoyed by the crowd in the Forum—or that Cicero, after that curb had once again been removed, came to express ever more fervently as time went on the vain hope that the tumults of the people might be, and ought to be, controllable by their betters.

III

Popular Politics in the 70s: The Demand for the Restoration of Sovereignty

The decade from 80 to 70 represents the only time in the history of the Republic since (at least) the early third century when the people did not possess the unrestricted right to legislate, by passing *leges* put before them by tribunes of the plebs. Why this right was lost is in general terms obvious, though in fact we have no direct evidence for either the ideology or the precise content of Sulla's reactionary reforms in the late 80s. Some evidence from the previous three decades will however suggest various reasons for the step Sulla took, in which he was going against a long tradition, deeply embedded in Roman history and Roman political practice. On some constructions of the character of Roman politics, namely, those that see the system as marked by the secure domination of an oligarchy, or aristocracy, it might seem surprising that such a reform was needed—or alternatively that it lasted only ten years. The view of the late Republic suggested here makes the Sullan reaction intelligible, and will also bring out the immense force exerted by the presence of the *populus* in the Forum. Though the evidence is relatively poor and scattered until we reach the year 70, we then see, in Cicero's *Verrines* (both in the one speech that was delivered and in the five that were not), a more vivid literary reflection of the force of popular opinion than in any other evidence. Since the main theme of this book is the power of the *populus* to legislate, it may seem paradoxical to argue that crowd politics in the Forum was at its most effective precisely in the only period when the unconditional power to legislate had been lost. But so, it may be suggested, it was.

Precisely what features of the evolution of the *res publica* and the character of its public life over the previous few decades led to Sulla's measure is a matter of speculation. It is, however, easy to point to a number of features that could easily have triggered a sense of the need for constitutional measures to reinforce the power of the Senate.¹ Obvious possible candidates are the repeated tribunician laws relating to the extortion court and the status of its *iudices;* other tribunician legislation affecting the constitution of the *res publica,* such as Gaius Gracchus' law that only the people could set up a court with the power to condemn someone to death; Domitius Ahenobarbus' legislation of 104 transferring the appointment of public priests to popular election; or Saturninus' legislation defining *maiestas.* Laws establishing corn distributions at limited prices or the repeated *leges* relative to the management of the *ager publicus,* the distribution of land to civilians or soldiers, and the foundation of *coloniae* were also clearly matters of major controversy.

But perhaps (it is a matter of pure speculation) it was the obtrusion of tribunician legislation into the areas of foreign and provincial policy and of military commands which did most to provoke a reaction. One relevant example would be the law proposed by C. Mamilius Limetanus in 109 to set up a court of equestrian jurors to try alleged collaborators with Jugurtha.² But far more significant is the comprehensive law on the administration and strategic control of Rome's empire in the eastern Mediterranean, apparently passed by a tribune of either 102/1 (recalling that *tribuni plebis* entered office on December 10) or 101/100, and at any rate anticipating the entry into office of the already elected consuls of 100. The text, of which large parts survive in Greek translation in inscriptions from Delphi and Cnidus, is at any rate full enough to illustrate how very detailed the control by the *comitia tributa* could be.³ Like the exactly or approximately contemporary legislation of Saturninus (tribune of 101/100) on the distribution of land, this tribunician law imposed on officeholders the obligation to take an oath that they would observe its provisions.

> The magistrates now in office, except for tribunes and governors, within the five days [next after] the people pass this statute, and

---

1. The evidence will not be rehearsed here. For a sketch, see F. Millar, "Politics, Persuasion, and the People before the Social War (150–90 B.C.)," *JRS* 76 (1986): 1. For a detailed up-to-date treatment, see A. Lintott, "Political History, 146–95 B.C.," in *CAH*² 9, *The Last Age of the Roman Republic, 146–43 B.C.,* ed. J.A. Crook, A. Lintott, and E. Rawson (Cambridge: Cambridge University Press, 1994), 40–103.

2. See Sallust *Bell. Jug.* 40.1–2; Cicero *Brut.* 33–34/127–28.

3. For the Greek inscriptions, see M. Hassall, M. Crawford, and J. Reynolds, "Rome and the Eastern Provinces at the End of the Second Century B.C.," *JRS* 64 (1974): 195, trans. also in R.K. Sherk, *Rome and the Greek East to the Death of Augustus* (Cambridge: Cambridge University Press, 1984), no. 55. See now Crawford, *Roman Statutes,* 1: no. 12. The section translated here is the Delphi copy, block C, lines 10–15, as in *Roman Statutes,* 1:255.

whoever shall hereafter hold a magistracy, except for governors, whoever of them [shall be] in Rome, within the five days next [after each of them] shall take up his magistracy; they are to swear by Jupiter and the ancestral gods to do all the things that have been laid down in this statute.

Complex provisions for enforcement and the prosecution and fining of offenders then follow.

Equally significant may have been tribunician intervention in the allocation of *provinciae*. A law of Gaius Gracchus had already laid down that the Senate should determine the two consular *provinciae* for the next year before the consular elections were held. The intention was presumably that the people should (up to a point) know what roles would be filled by those that they were electing. The previous procedure had been that the newly elected consuls themselves put a *relatio* to the Senate at the beginning of their term of office and that the Senate then exercised the very important strategic choice of deciding which *provinciae* would that year go to the two consuls and would thus have consular armies. This decision now had to be made earlier. But a crucial element of indeterminacy still prevailed (under both the old and the new system), for the lot *(sortitio)* was normally used to determine which consul went to which of the two *provinciae*. The consuls could alternatively be allowed to agree the allocation between them, but *sortitio* was normal. Its function seems not to have been to determine the will of the gods but simply to remove this crucial question from the area of competition and conflict.[4] Considerable scope for political and strategic decision making by the Senate still remained, for it also had to decide which existing proconsuls, already in command in a *provincia,* should have their imperium prolonged *(prorogatio)*. Precisely this issue is the context of Cicero's *De provinciis consularibus,* a speech delivered in the Senate in 56.

The fact that these decisions, which were both delicate in terms of mutual competition for honor and military glory, and extremely important strategically, lay within the sphere of the Senate must have made it all the more shocking and offensive when it came about that established custom was overridden by popular sovereignty, in the form of tribunician laws. Take, for example, the situation in the year 108 and the political debates over the command in the war against King Jugurtha of

---

4. See now N. Rosenstein, "Sorting Out the Lot in Republican Rome," *AJPh* 116 (1995): 43.

Numidia. The consul of 109, Q. Caecilius Metellus, was currently in command as proconsul. Under Gaius Gracchus' law, the Senate must have determined in advance of the elections which should be the consular *provinciae* for 107 (at what point prorogations were decided at the time is not clear). At any rate, this decision had already been made when the consular elections took place. These elections are described later in Sallust's somewhat overripe prose. Marius, then also serving in Numidia, was one of the candidates.

> Moreover, seditious officeholders were stirring up the vulgar mob, demanding the head of Metellus at every *contio* and exaggerating the *virtus* of Marius. Finally, the *plebs* was so excited that all the workmen and peasants, whose survival and credit depended on their labor, left their work and followed Marius, and they regarded their own needs as less important than his election to office. With the *nobilitas* thus thrown into consternation, after many stormy conflicts the consulate was entrusted to a *novus homo*. Moreover, after that, when the *populus* was formally asked by the *tribunus plebis* T. Manlius Mancinus whom it wished to conduct the war with Jugurtha, a large assembly voted that it should be Marius. But a little [earlier, the Senate(?)] had decreed. That vote was now invalid.[5]

Whatever decision was overridden by the sovereign *populus* in this case, it was evidently a vote by the Senate *(decreverat)*. A decision and strategic choice that had previously been subject to a complex constitutional procedure was now the subject of public debate and popular voting. With that, moreover, a first hint begins to appear of the connection between popular sovereignty, imperialism, and the concentration of power in the hands of an individual.

The same issue arose in 88, but at an even later stage in the normal procedure, and it affected Sulla himself. It must have been in 89 that news came, in the middle of the Social War, that the forces of Mithridates of Pontus had invaded the praetorian province of Asia.[6] It would then have been decreed by the Senate that one consul should have as his *provincia* the northern sector of the war in Italy and the other the command in Asia.

---

5. Sallust *Bell. Jug.* 73.

6. For the chronology, see A.N. Sherwin-White, *Roman Foreign Policy in the East, 168 B.C. to A.D. 1* (London: Duckworth, 1984), 121–22.

L. Cornelius Sulla and Q. Pompeius Rufus were elected and evidently drew lots *(sortitio)*. This sequence of events is presumed in the narratives by Velleius Paterculus and Appian, who both say that Asia fell by lot to Sulla.[7] Then, when Sulla was already in office, Sulpicius Rufus, one of the ten *tribuni plebis* of the year, proposed to the *comitia* that the command against Mithridates should be transferred to Marius, who was then a *privatus* and had not held public office since 100. As is well known, Sulla went to the forces encamped at Nola, gained their support, and returned to Rome to impose the reversal of Sulpicius' measures by force. There is also a hint that he at that time passed some laws affecting the constitution: if Appian's brief report is not misleading, the intention was that no law should be proposed without prior senatorial approval and that elections should (all?) be conducted in the *comitia centuriata* rather than the *comitia tributa*.[8] It is not worth speculating about the details, but the general import of the proposals is intelligible enough.

We need not pursue other details of the history of the 80s, in that period when Sulla, while in command of the East, operated in effective independence of the *res publica* in Rome. But it is absolutely essential to stress that we have good evidence that when his forces landed in southern Italy in 83 and advanced toward Rome, the future character of the Roman constitution was already quite explicitly at issue. Cicero records in his *Twelfth Philippic* the topics of negotiations between Sulla and the consul of 83, L. Cornelius Scipio, when they met in the area of Cales and Teanum: "the *auctoritas* of the Senate, the votes of the *populus,* and the constitution of the state."[9]

The three relevant provisions of Sulla's eventual legislation, after he had been elected dictator following his military victory, were the restoration of senators to the function of acting as the jurors in *quaestiones* (and the apparent multiplication of *quaestiones* for different crimes), the abolition of the right of *tribuni plebis* to propose legislation to the people, and a further law debarring the tribunes from further elective office. All three

7. Vell. Pat. 2.18.3: "sorte obvenit Sullae Asia provincia"; Appian *BC* 1.55/241: Σύλλας μὲν ὑπατεύων ἔλαχε στρατηγεῖν τῆς Ἀσίας καὶ τοῦδε τοῦ Μιθραδατείου πολέμου.

8. Appian *BC* 1.59/266. See Gabba's commentary ad loc. There are various possible interpretations, especially of the second provision.

9. Cicero *Phil.* 12.11/27: "de auctoritate senatus, de suffragiis populi, de iure civitatis." The latter phrase could reasonably be translated "the right of citizenship." But it does not seem that provisions on the boundaries of citizenship played an important part in Sulla's legislation.

provisions played a part in public debates in the 80s, and by the end of the decade all three had been reversed.

The direct evidence for these three measures of Sulla's is poor, and in particular it is impossible to be certain of the precise nature of his legislation on the powers of the tribunate. It seems certain at least that, as Caesar was to say to his troops in 49, Sulla left untouched the tribunes' right of *intercessio* on behalf of citizens, or what Cicero calls the "power of bringing help" *[potestatem . . . auxilii ferendi].*[10] On the negative side, the epitome of Livy states flatly that Sulla removed from the tribunes "all right of passing laws"[11]—which, if taken literally, means that they could not now pass legislation even with prior senatorial authority. It also seems from a passing allusion in Cicero's *First Verrine* that Sulla's legislation placed some limit on the contexts to which the tribunician veto could be applied. At any rate, Cicero records that Opimius was accused of having used his power of *intercessio* while tribune of 75 in a way that was against a *lex Cornelia.*[12] The nature of this restriction is quite unclear.

Again, the fragmentary nature of our evidence makes it futile to waste time on speculations. The general force of the legislation is clear enough: the tribunes were to retain at least some negative rights of extending protection to citizens but were not to have the power to put legislation to the people. Whether they could do so if they had secured the prior approval of the Senate is not clear. What mattered in any case was independent legislation, put directly to the people.

It might have been expected that the effect of these provisions would have been to destroy the role of the Forum as the stage for public debate. Cicero, indeed, in his *Pro Cluentio* of 66, implies just this, saying that it was only the tribunate of Quinctius in 74 that brought the Rostra back to life.

It was because he had seized the Rostra, which had long been vacant, and that place that since the advent of Sulla had been bereft of the tribunician voice, and because he had recalled the multitude, long unaccustomed to *contiones,* to something resembling their old customs, that for a short time he was popular with a certain sort of men.[13]

---

10. Caesar *BC* 1.5.1, 1.7.2; Cicero *De leg.* 3.9/22.
11. Livy *Per.* 89: "omne ius legum ferendarum ademit."
12. Cicero *Verr.* 1.60/155.
13. Cicero *Clu.* 40/110.

The record of the 70s, however, shows a more complex picture than this, though it certainly suggests very clearly that the force of popular politics, or of crowd politics in the Forum, increased rapidly toward the end of the decade, to culminate in the legislation of 70. The evidence, it must be admitted, is relatively poor, consisting primarily of fragments of Sallust's *Historiae* and of passing references to events of this decade in Cicero's speeches, above all in the *Verrines* of 70 and the *Pro Cluentio* of 66. Even in this period, it should be stressed, "the people" did pass legislation, and nothing in Sulla's laws served to make the Senate itself into a legislative body. But the people did so on the proposal of consuls (and perhaps, in principle, of praetors) and could perhaps do so (if we take the implications of Sulla's abortive legislation of 88) only after a senatus consultum. In that sense, therefore, the people had not lost its sovereign power to legislate, and we in fact know of a number of *leges* passed by them in the 70s.[14] But, as the story of these years, however fragmentary it is, will show, the long-established right to have legislation put to the people by their own representatives was fundamental to popular conceptions of the place of those representatives in the *res publica*.

In any case, it is important to recall that the essential principle of publicity remained. Nearly all the functions of the various elements of the *res publica*, with the significant exception of meetings of the Senate, had to be acted out in front of the people, involved persuasion addressed either directly or (in the case of speeches before *quaestiones* in the Forum) indirectly to them, or required them actually to vote, in elections, legislation, or trials. In that sense the stage was almost literally set for the demands for the restoration of tribunician legislation that were crowned with success in 70.

Even from this comparatively ill-attested decade, it will be necessary only to offer a few examples. Elections, for instance, involved the recommendation of candidates to the people by their supporters. So Cicero, for instance, in the *Pro Plancio*, looks back to an episode in 80 when the consul Q. Metellus Pius, at the praetorian elections for 79, appealed to the people on behalf of Q. Calidius, who as tribune in 98 had carried the law that restored Metellus' father from exile. Metellus' speech was notable for the

---

14. In brief summary, and omitting various problematic cases, *lex Aemilia frumentaria*, 78 B.C. (consular); *lex Aurelia de tribunicia potestate* and *lex Aurelia de iudiciis privatis*, 75 B.C. (consular); *lex de locatione censoria*, 75 B.C. (author unknown); *lex Aurelia de iudiciis privatis*, 74 B.C. (consular—abrogation of law of 75 B.C.); *lex Terentia Cassia frumentaria*, 73 B.C. (consular); *lex Cornelia de pecuniis exigendis*, 72 B.C. (consular); *lex Gellia Cornelia de civitate*, 72 B.C. (consular).

fact that he had described Calidius, of much less distinguished birth than himself, as the *patronus* of his family.[15] The word Cicero uses of Metellus' speech is *supplicare,* "to beseech." The anecdote is only one of many indications that election speeches were made, often focusing on the personal merits and services of the candidate, and recalling events in the past, both recent and distant.

Metellus almost certainly addressed the people in the Forum, where, as we have seen, different elected officeholders occupied their accustomed tribunals or benches, while a now increased number of established *quaestiones* functioned in the central and eastern area, with the new *gradus Aurelii* forming a sort of theater for trials.[16] The topography of the Forum was familiar to all, and indeed many of the extant allusions to it come from speeches delivered there, where the various features were immediately visible to the audience. Thus, in his immensely complex *Pro Cluentio* of 66, Cicero recalls to the jurors an episode from the earlier 70s when someone had been seized by his opponents and brought by force "before the feet of Q. Manlius, who was then triumvir." But Manlius, Cicero says, was no credit to the electoral system: "from being an insolent and disreputable hanger-on, he had during the civil war arrived by the *suffragia* of the *populus* at that column, to which, amid the abuse of the mob, he had often been dragged [as a defendant]."[17] The *triumviri capitales* occupied a modest rank in the long list of officeholders elected every year, and the "column" to which Cicero refers was the Columna Maenia at the southwest end of the Forum, beside which they sat in judgment.

The mutual visibility of the various elements of the Forum, and thus their potential interplay, was an essential feature of public life. It has to be remembered, for instance, when we read accounts of how the Greeks who had been despoiled by C. Antonius while serving under Sulla in the 80s prosecuted him before the *praetor peregrinus,* M. Lucullus, in 76. When Lucullus' verdict favored the Greeks, Antonius "appealed to the tribunes and swore that he could not get a fair trial." It was perhaps some one hundred meters from the tribunal of the *praetor peregrinus* to where the *tribuni* took their regular seats under the *Tabula Valeria,* on the side of the Curia.[18] "Appeal" in this sense is not a bureaucratic process but a

---

15. Cicero *Planc.* 29/69; see Val. Max. 5.2.7.
16. See chap. 2.
17. Cicero *Clu.* 13/38–39.
18. For the quoted account of Antonius' appeal, see Asconius 84C. For a hypothetical plan of the disposition of the Forum, see p. 40.

ritual conducted in the open air, consisting of a movement across a public space and an address to the *tribuni* on their bench.

The presence of concurrent functions or jurisdictions being exercised within sight of each other might function as a means of control of improprieties or (depending, of course, on the observer's point of view) as a means of exerting improper pressure on officeholders. The former conception is clearly illustrated in Cicero's pejorative description of Verres' exercise of his jurisdiction as urban praetor in 74. On Cicero's account, Verres repeatedly gave judgment in terms that contradicted his own *edictum,* causing his colleague as praetor, L. Calpurnius Piso (whose precise function is unknown), to fill up a series of codices with the record of his intercessions to correct Verres' judgments: "I think you have not forgotten what a crowd, and what class of persons, used to gather around Piso's judgment seat *[sella]* while he [Verres] was praetor. If he [Verres] had not had him [Piso] as a colleague, he would have been buried under a hail of stones in the Forum."[19]

An alternative picture of mutual pressures is provided by Cicero in the *Pro Cluentio,* in the same passage that we have seen before in connection with the recent construction of the *gradus Aurelii.* He is referring to the activity of Quinctius as *tribunus plebis* of 74, to which I will come back later in this chapter. In this instance, Cicero illustrates how the public meetings called by a tribune in one part of the Forum could be used to assemble popular support for an accusation that he then proceeded to make before a court sitting in another part.

> The accuser was a *tribunus plebis* and was the same man whether in *contiones* or at the *subsellia* [the seating for the court]. He used to approach the *iudicium* not only [directly] from a *contio* but with a *contio* [in the sense of the crowd itself]. Those *gradus Aurelii,* which were then newly constructed, seemed, as it were, to serve as a theater for that *iudicium.* When the accuser [Quinctius] had filled them up with the mob that he had gathered, those on the side of the accused were robbed of the power of speaking and even of getting up.[20]

It was in reality not just the new *gradus Aureli* but the whole Forum which functioned as a public political theater. This immediate physical

---

19. Cicero *Verr.* 2.1.46/119.
20. Cicero *Clu.* 34/93; see chap. 2.

context has to be borne in mind constantly if we are to understand what is really meant by the pressure for the reversal of Sulla's reforms (the closing of any further career to tribunes, the loss of independent tribunician legislation, and—less prominent in our sources until the very end of the decade—the transfer of the jury courts to senators). If we do not visualize concretely the relationship between an elected officeholder and the crowd in the Forum, it will never be clear how these constitutional changes came to be reversed.

The question of the historic rights of the tribunate was the focus of public debate from almost the beginning of the decade, being raised first in the consulship of Aemilius Lepidus in 78. At first, so our evidence suggests, the issue was brought forward by some or all of the tribunes of that year, who addressed to Lepidus a demand that their traditional powers should be restored. Our narrative source for this, Granius Licinianus, does not need to say explicitly that the demand was made in public, before a *contio*. This fact emerges when the narrative continues: Lepidus replied that such a restoration of powers would not be in the public interest, and he gained the assent of a large proportion of the people at the meeting *(contio)*. Granius adds that, in his time, the text of the *oratio* still survived ("et exstat oratio").[21]

Unfortunately, this text has not survived into the modern world. Its loss is all the more regrettable since precisely how Lepidus justified his position at this moment before the public would have been of real interest. What we have instead seems to be a representation of a later stage in Lepidus' position, namely, a speech that Sallust attributes to him and that contains a general denunciation of Sulla's tyranny, expressed as if Sulla were still alive. No concrete proposal is contained here, but the indications of a reaction against the Sullan constitution are unmistakable.

> So it is the victorious army which gives me the greatest confidence, which at the cost of so many wounds and toils has gained nothing except a tyrant. Unless of course they actually set out to overthrow the *tribunicia potestas* established by their ancestors by force of arms, and to rob themselves of their rights and courts.[22]

For any consistent representation of the *tribunicia potestas* as a public issue that was raised over the next few years, we again have to rely on a

---

21. Granius Licinianus 33.14 Flemisch; Malcovati, *ORF*, 332; 35.33 Criniti.
22. Sallust *Hist.* 1.55 M = 1.48 McGushin.

speech inserted in Sallust's *Historiae,* in this case that which he gives to Licinius Macer, the *tribunus plebis* of 73. In the words quoted, he is addressing the people.

> Do you think that there is a question of anyone standing in your way when you are united on an objective, when they who feared you [even] when you were apathetic and listless? Unless, by chance, C. Cotta, a consul from the very heart of the ruling faction [75], acted from anything other than fear in restoring certain rights to the *tribuni plebis.* And although L. Sicinius [tribune of 76], the first to dare to speak about the *tribunicia potestas,* was brought down while you merely murmured, nonetheless they began to fear your hostility even before you became tired of the injury done to you. . . .
>
> A disturbance arose in the consulship of Brutus and Mamercus [77], and then C. Curio [consul of 76] carried his domination to the point of destroying a guiltless tribune. You saw last year [74] with what spirit Lucullus [as consul] attacked L. Quinctius *[tribunus plebis];* how great finally are the storms now raised against me. . . . Thus other issues have flared up for a time, from license, hatred, or greed, but one thing alone has remained, as the concern of both sides [in the civil war], and has been torn from you for the future: the tribunician power *[vis tribunicia],* the weapon prepared by our ancestors for the defense of liberty.[23]

Even more than with the surviving texts of *orationes* actually delivered, we have almost no means of knowing how closely a "speech" written for insertion in a narrative history approximated anything actually said at the time. All that is clear is that the surviving written versions of speeches in the Forum are marked, first, as this example is, by the recall of previous events—recent in this case, often much more distant; Macer is in fact represented as going on later to talk of incidents from the "Struggle of the Orders" in archaic Rome. Second, it is a common characteristic for them to represent previous political issues in terms of public conflicts between rival elected officeholders. And third, they share a common concern with public opinion, both with the immediate reactions of the people present in the Forum and with longer-term undercurrents.

The speech that Sallust gives to Macer sufficiently catches the main

---

23. Sallust *Hist.* 3.48.8–12 M = 3.34 McGushin.

themes of these years, so it is not necessary to rehearse all the attested details. A few valuable sidelights are revealed by Cicero's references to this period and by the explanations offered by his commentator Asconius. Thus Cicero recalls that Sicinius in 76 had once "produced" the consuls Curio and Octavius (that is, had obliged them to come to the Rostra to address the people) and that Curio had made a long speech while Octavius sat listening.[24] The political content of the exchange is not made clear; but the implications of the word *producere,* used in Cicero's account, are almost always that the person "produced" was under pressure to justify himself. Cicero and Asconius between them also reveal that Cotta, as consul of 75, whether moved by fear of the people or not, had made many political enemies by proposing a law to allow former tribunes to hold further elective office, thus removing for good one of the elements of the Sullan reforms; as Asconius says, this took place "against the will of the *nobilitas* but with great enthusiasm on the part of the people."[25]

It would not in fact have been surprising if Cotta had indeed acted partly in order to head off popular anger, for these years were marked by repeated fears of food shortage and by demonstrations over the price of corn.[26] We have already seen how the two consuls of 75 were attacked on the Sacra Via by a crowd angered over the high price of corn (see chap. 2). In this same year, Hortensius, as aedile, not only gave notably lavish shows but made a distribution of grain to the people at a reduced price.[27] The claims of the *plebs urbana* both to public provision and to private *liberalitas* on the part of officeholders became even clearer during the last three decades of the Republic.

The same theme reappears immediately in the next year, 74, with the aedileship of M. Seius, who is recorded as having provided grain and oil for the people at reduced prices; as a result, statues of him were erected (during his life?) on the Capitol and Palatine, and when he died he was carried to his pyre on the shoulders of the people.[28] As is often the case with such reports, it is not clear whether the supplies he made available

---

24. Cicero *Brut.* 60/216–17.

25. Asconius 67C: "in consulatu *tulit invita* nobilitate magno populi studio"; 78C (quotation from Cicero's *Pro Cluentio*).

26. See C. Virlouvet, *Famines et émeutes à Rome des origines de la République à la mort de Néron* (Rome: École française de Rome, 1985), 15, 111; P. Garnsey, *Famine and Food Supply in the Graeco-Roman World* (Cambridge: Cambridge University Press, 1988), 200.

27. See Cicero *De off.* 2.16/57, *Verr.* 2.3.92/215.

28. See Cicero *De off.* 2.12/58; Pliny *NH* 15.1/2, 18.4/16.

derived from administrative measures, from personal *liberalitas,* or from a combination of the two. What is clear is, again, the highly visible connection between publicly demonstrated care for the interests of the urban population and subsequent popularity and potential political success (in this case, evidently cut short by death).

In political terms, however, this year, 74, was marked above all by the activity of the *tribunus plebis* L. Quinctius. As we saw, Sallust, in the oration given to Macer in the following year, records public conflicts between L. Lucullus as consul and Quinctius. It is attested that Quinctius campaigned for the restoration of the *tribunicia potestas,* though no details are recorded.[29] Much more vivid, if hardly clear in all their details and implications, are the reflections of Quinctius' role in relation to the *iudicia,* provided by Cicero's *Pro Cluentio* of eight years later. Earlier in this chapter, we have already seen one of Cicero's descriptions of how Quinctius brought a whole *contio* with him, right up to the *subsellia,* to bring pressure on a case at which he would act as accuser.[30] Quinctius had earlier defended one Oppianicus on a charge of poisoning, and after Oppianicus' condemnation, Quinctius prosecuted Iunius for improper conduct of the earlier trial.[31] Cicero describes the political context in vivid terms. Particularly noticeable is the close connection between the conduct of trials, the public role of senators, and popular reactions.

When Oppianicus had been condemned, immediately L. Quinctius, the most *popularis* of men, who had been accustomed to catch all the winds of rumors and *contiones,* thought that he had been offered the opportunity to advance himself by playing on the resentment against the Senate, since he thought that the courts, as manned by that *ordo,* were falling in public esteem. One *contio* and then another was delivered, vehement and serious. The *tribunus plebis* clamored that the *iudices* had accepted bribes to condemn an innocent man.[32]

Cicero referred to this series of events when he said that Quinctius came directly, followed by the *contio,* to act as prosecutor in the trial of Iunius,

---

29. Plutarch *Luc.* 5.4; *Schol.* p. 189 Stangl.

30. Cicero *Clu.* 34/93.

31. For the details, see Alexander, *Trials,* nos. 149 (Oppianicus), 153 (Iunius), 154 (Falcula).

32. Cicero *Clu.* 28/77.

who was duly condemned. A similar prosecution was brought by Quinctius against one of the jurors, Fidiculanius Falcula, who seems to have been acquitted. As Cicero represents it, Quinctius nonetheless "had by daily *contiones* of a seditious and turbulent character brought him [Falcula] to the height of unpopularity."[33]

We have of course to allow for Cicero's need, as regards the case for Cluentius, to portray the atmosphere of 74 in as sinister a light as possible. Nonetheless, 74 does indeed seem to have been the year when, as Cicero claimed, the tribunician *contio* reasserted its place in Roman public life.[34] We are, however, still in the period when the *tribuni plebis* had no independent right to propose legislation. That did not mean that popular feeling, aroused by tribunician *contiones,* could not lead to the formulation of a senatus consultum and thence to the proposal of a *lex* by the consuls. Exactly this type of occurrence (even though the law in question was in the end not passed) is perfectly described by Cicero in another section of the *Pro Cluentio.*[35] At some point subsequent to the condemnation of Oppianicus, Quinctius roused the people ("populo concitato"), bringing matters almost to open violence, and thereby pressured the Senate into voting a senatus consultum that would evidently, if passed into law, have set up a further *quaestio* to hear charges of corruption in *iudicia publica.* But neither L. Lucullus, as consul of 74, nor M. Lucullus and C. Cassius, consuls in 73, ever in fact put the consequential bill *(rogatio)* to the vote. Cicero makes quite clear that a measure initially undertaken to counter popular hostility was eventually dropped because popular indignation had died down: "it was brought about, first, by the fairness and wisdom of those consuls that what the Senate had decreed in order to counter the current storm of *invidia* they considered afterward did not need to be put to the *populus.*" At some point the prospective *rogatio,* which the *populus,* stimulated by Quinctius' denunciations, had demanded, does seem to have been debated at *contiones.* But the young son of Iunius was brought forward to excite pity (and prevent a further and more serious prosecution of his father?), and the people with loud shouts rejected the idea of a *quaestio.* As indicated, it *seems* that they were not voting but expressing their collective reaction

---

33. Cicero *Clu.* 37/103.

34. Cicero *Clu.* 40/110.

35. Cicero *Clu.* 49/136–38. For the significance of this episode as proving the absence in the 70s of a tribunician right to propose legislation, see J.-L. Ferrary, "La Lex Antonia de Termessibus," *Ath.* 63 (1985): 419, on pp. 441–42.

before the prospective vote, which in the end never took place. As Cicero comments, the *populus* was like a sea that would be calm unless stirred up by the *tempestates* of tribunician agitation.

Though Quinctius' tribunate does seem to have marked a turning point in the open expression of the popular will, the constitutional situation in fact remained unaltered. Thus the two consuls of 73, M. Terentius Varro Lucullus and C. Cassius Longinus, might have carried into law the senatus consultum on judicial corruption but did not; and when they came to pass a law authorizing extra purchases of grain in Sicily, they did so on the basis of another senatus consultum.[36] The needs or demands of the people were the same as in the previous years, but the procedures still remained under senatorial and consular control. The tribune of this year, Licinius Macer, as we have seen, continued the public campaign for restoration of tribunician rights—but our only evidence for this campaign is a speech that Sallust says Macer gave to the people, in which Macer duly implies that the corn law was just a sop to buy the people's acquiescence.[37]

The restoration that Macer seems to have demanded was not long in coming, and the decisive year was 71. In this year, we hear, for instance, of a tribune, M. Lollius Palicanus, producing before the gaze of the *populus Romanus* one of the victims of Verres' malpractices in Sicily,[38] and making a speech *(contio)* complaining of the way that he had been treated. Sthenius had in fact been condemned by Verres and therefore fell under an edict of the ten tribunes of this year, that no one condemned on a capital charge was allowed to remain in Rome. Cicero himself had had to appear before the ten tribunes to explain the circumstances of Sthenius' condemnation and obtain a decree that he should be exempt. It can be taken as certain that this case too was heard in the Forum, before the people.

Palicanus is listed among the *tribuni* who contributed to the restoration of tribunician powers, which was actually effected in the following year; but no details of his role are preserved.[39] It is beyond question that the two consuls elected in 71 for 70, Pompey and Crassus, committed themselves to this step. But were their intentions publicly known before the elections? If so, this would count as another case of an electoral campaign that focused not just on the personal merits and services of the

36. See Cicero *Verr.* 2.3.70/163, 2.3.75/173, 2.5.21/52.
37. Sallust *Hist.* 3.48.19–20 M = 3.34.17–20 McGushin.
38. Cicero *Verr.* 2.1.42/122, 2.2.41/100.
39. *Schol.* p. 189 Stangl.

candidates but on their political intentions.[40] Such a public commitment might in any case not have been necessary. Pompey had only recently returned, with his army, from completing the suppression of Sertorius' forces in Spain, and he had joined in with Crassus, who also now had an army outside Rome, in the final defeat of the major slave revolt under Spartacus.

Nonetheless, Greek narratives of these years, written under the Roman Empire, do clearly imply either, in general terms, that it was known or rumored, before the election, that Pompey would undertake measures, including the restoration of tribunician powers, to break up the Sullan constitution[41] or, more specifically, that Pompey and Crassus actually undertook, before the election, to do so.[42] But the one report that we have, from Plutarch, of Pompey making an election speech to the people does not specifically confirm this.[43]

In any case, either of our Greek sources on this matter, Plutarch or Appian, could easily have confused a preelection speech with the well-attested address to the people that Pompey made after election, as *consul designatus,* in which a public commitment to constitutional reform in the following year was absolutely unambiguous. We owe our knowledge of this scene to the highly rhetorical account of it that Cicero included in his *First Verrine* in 70. Whether he is being tendentious in implying that there was even greater popular concern over the senatorial jury courts (one of which he was addressing and urging not to disgrace itself again) than over tribunician rights, we cannot tell. But he is precise as to the circumstances, namely, that Pompey was already *designatus* but was speaking "near the city" [*ad urbem*], not in it (since he had still not laid down his military command). Cicero's words need to be quoted in full.

> When Cn. Pompeius himself for the first time as *consul designatus* delivered a *contio* near the city, in which, as seemed to be what was above all expected, he made clear that he would restore the *tribunicia potestas,* a noise and contented murmur on the part of the *contio* arose in response. But when he himself in the same *contio* had said that the provinces had been despoiled and ravaged, while the *iudicia* were becoming shameful and criminal—this was a mat-

---

40. See, e.g., Cicero *Planc.* 29/69, discussed above.
41. See Plutarch *Pomp.* 21.3–5.
42. See Appian *BC* 1.121/561.
43. Plutarch *Crass.* 12.

ter that it was his wish to see to and take steps about—*then*, indeed, not with a noise but with a great shout, the *populus Romanus* made clear its will.[44]

The sequence of events throughout 70 does not lend much support to Cicero's representation of the people's preferences. Both measures—the restoration of the *tribunicia potestas* and the ending of the senatorial monopoly of the *iudicia*—were indeed enacted. But the two consuls legislated on tribunician rights—and they had already done so before Cicero spoke in August—while the proposal of a compromise law on the *iudicia*, which had not yet been enacted when Cicero was speaking, was left to one of the praetors, L. Aurelius Cotta.

In the *Verrine Orations,* allusions to the monumental and historical context of the Forum and highly colored representations of popular reactions and feelings, against the senatorial jurors and against Verres in person, are fundamental aspects of Cicero's rhetorical procedures. It is therefore, paradoxically, to the words of Cicero, whose later works tend to devalue popular opinion in favor of the moderating force of the upper classes, that we owe our fullest set of literary evocations of political action and popular reactions in the Forum.

Our view of these processes, as they worked in 70, is not, however, wholly dependent on Cicero. The year was notable for the dinner given for the *plebs* by Crassus and for the three-month supply of grain he provided out of his own resources, details we owe to Plutarch.[45] It is, however, Cicero who alludes to notable additions to the calendar of *ludi*: the long-established *ludi Romani* of September were preceded by fifteen days of *ludi votivi* offered by Pompey and were followed by the *ludi Victoriae* recently established by Sulla.[46]

The special feature of Pompey's career and public position up to this point was that he had neither held any previous elective office nor been enrolled in the Senate. He was therefore still formally an *eques,* and he was thus able to parade with the other *equites* before the censors seated in the Forum and to answer before them that he had duly completed his military service—but under his own command. This story, and a description of the crowd's reaction, is again provided by Plutarch: "when they heard this, the people shouted out and were unable to restrain their

44. Cicero *Verr.* 1.15/45.
45. Plutarch *Crass.* 12.2–3.
46. Cicero *Verr.* 1.10/31.

shouts of delight, while the censors rose and escorted him home, thus giving pleasure to the citizens who followed along applauding."[47]

Plutarch follows this anecdote immediately with another, which also illustrates the interplay of official action and popular reaction. Pompey and Crassus were notoriously on poor personal terms. But toward the end of their year of office, when they were (as the story clearly implies) both seated on the Rostra in the Forum, an *eques,* who is recorded as never having played any public role before, ascended their tribunal and said to the crowd that he had had a dream in which Iuppiter had urged him to see that the consuls were reconciled before they left office. A symbolic reconciliation duly followed, with Crassus (at least) addressing the crowd.[48]

Long before this event, the consuls had put through a *lex* restoring the legislative powers of the *tribuni plebis.* They did so by the normal procedure, beginning with a *relatio* by Pompey to the Senate *de tribunicia potestate.* Cicero records that in response Catulus had said that if the senatorial order had conducted itself better in the *iudicia,* the people would not have so passionately demanded the restoration of tribunician rights.[49] As so often occurs, we see that debates in the Senate could be conducted in the full awareness of popular opinion. Perhaps surprisingly, however, neither Cicero nor any other surviving evidence provides any further reminiscences of the process by which the law was put through. It may be that the weight of popular demands had been such that the restoration was accepted as inevitable and hence that no incidents worth later recalling took place. As Cicero comments subsequently, in his *De legibus,* given how eagerly in the early Republic "our *populus*" had sought this right when it was still unknown, who would have tolerated its absence once it had been tried?[50] At any rate, we hear nothing either of opposition or of popular reactions at the moment when the law was passed. Instead, we have the ominous words of Cicero, notionally addressed to the senatorial *iudices* in the Forum, in the imaginary later stages of the trial of Verres.

> This *civitas* endured, as long as it could, and as long as it was necessary, that royal *dominatio* of yours [the senators], and it endured it in the *iudicia* and throughout the *res publica.* But on the

47. Plutarch *Pomp.* 22.
48. Plutarch *Pomp.* 23; cf. his *Crass.* 12.3–4.
49. Cicero *Verr.* 1.15/44.
50. Cicero *De leg.* 3.11/26.

day on which the *tribuni plebis* were restored to the *populus Romanus,* all that, in case by chance you do not yet understand it, was removed and torn from you.[51]

Over the next two decades, the truth of Cicero's words was to be proved over and over again, in ways that could hardly have been imagined in the summer of 70. Yet in 70 itself the constitutional and political effects of the restoration were not, so far as our evidence goes, felt so immediately. It is very probable, given the promises made in the previous year, that the restoration was accomplished early, and hence some months before Cicero might have spoken. But for some reason that is not clear, the reform of the *iudicia,* which had also been promised in 71, was still awaited when Cicero was speaking, or imagining himself speaking.

In the interval, we know of one item of what seems to have been tribunician legislation, the *lex Plautia,* the purpose of which was to restore the citizenship to the exiled followers of the consul of 78, Aemilius Lepidus. All we know of this *lex* is that the young Julius Caesar is reported by Suetonius as first having supported those promoting the restoration of the *tribunicia potestas* and then having delivered a speech *(contio)* in favor of what Suetonius calls the *rogatio Plotia.* It is worth noting that, although Caesar had gained an elective office by this time, as a military tribune, it was the most junior one, and he himself will have been only 30 and not yet a senator. In his *contio,* he seems to have spoken openly of the family interest that Suetonius notes, namely, the return from exile of his brother-in-law, L. Cinna. The single surviving quotation of the speech runs: "In my opinion, as regards our kinship *[necessitas],* I have lacked neither *labor,* nor *opera,* nor *industria.*"[52] As we will see, Caesar's unique talent for the public advertisement of himself and his family was not to go unused in the following years. It is probable that the same Plautius, as tribune in this year, also put through a *lex agraria* and a *lex de vi;* but the evidence for the date and political circumstances of both is too uncertain.[53]

What we do catch a glimpse of in the summer of 70 is the sequence of elections for the following year, and a highly adorned representation by Cicero of the influences brought to bear, unsuccessfully, to prevent his

---

51. Cicero *Verr.* 2.5.68/175.

52. Suetonius *Div. Iul.* 5.1; Aulus Gellius *NA* 13.3.5: "in oratione C. Caesaris, *Qua Plautiam Rogationem suasit.*" For the date, see Ferrary, "La Lex Antonia de Termessibus," 441 (n. 35 above).

53. See Broughton, *MRR,* 128.

own election as aedile (the position from which he was to imagine himself as next year bringing a prosecution against Verres before the thirty-five *tribus,* as discussed in chap. 2). As Cicero tells the story in his *First Verrine,* the election of the consuls and praetors for the next year took place first, and Hortensius, the famous orator and Verres' chief advocate, was elected consul. Cicero vividly portrays Hortensius being escorted back from the Campus Martius by a huge crowd. Their route evidently took them through the Forum, for as they reached the Fornix Fabianus in its northeast corner, another senator spotted Verres in the crowd and openly congratulated him on the fact that the result was as good as an acquittal in his case. Cicero put the anecdote to good use: "What? Will the *iudices* not follow the charges, the witnesses, the *existimatio* of the *populus Romanus?*"⁵⁴ Then lots were drawn for which *praetor* should have which function *(provincia),* and M. Metellus, another ally of Verres, gained the position of president *(quaesitor)* in the extortion court *(de pecuniis repetundis).* As Cicero represents the story, Verres was now safe, provided that the case could be dragged out until the next year, and provided also that Cicero was not elected aedile. The efforts of Verres' supporters were therefore concentrated on the elections for the aedile-ship. Money was collected, and for the first time in Roman politics, we hear of *divisores* meeting at the house of a candidate, with the aim of distributing bribes from him to their different tribes. That was not enough, however, and Hortensius, as one of the *consules designati* for the next year, appeared in public to campaign against Cicero.

> Meanwhile, the elections that involved myself began to be held, elections of which he [Hortensius] believed himself to be the master, as he did of the other elections of that year. That powerful man, with his amiable and popular son, rushed around the *tribus.* He met and greeted by name his "ancestral friends"—that is, the *divisores.* When all this was noticed and understood, the *populus Romanus* very gladly saw to it that the man whose wealth had not been able to distract me from my *fides* [as advocate for the Sicilians] would not succeed, by using his money, in getting me rejected from public office *[honor].*⁵⁵

---

54. Cicero *Verr.* 1.7/18–19.
55. Cicero *Verr.* 1.8–9/22–26; cf. 2.1.7/19: "cum iste infinita largitione contra me uteretur." For the established role of *divisores,* in distributing gifts made by richer persons to their fellow tribesmen, see Taylor, *Voting Districts,* 15.

We have of course no way of knowing what truth lies behind Cicero's report. What matters are the reminders this account provides: that the elections were both competitive and public, and that all rival forms of influence counted—from the prestige of a person's family, to his inherited connections, to his military role or his reputation as an advocate. So also did *largitio,* the distribution of cash. Later in the *Verrines,* Cicero says in passing that a group of officials in Sicily "did the same as people in our *res publica* who have gained a magistracy by *largitio* are accustomed to do; they made every effort to exploit their power so as to make up that shortfall in their wealth."[56]

Viewed in one light, the much greater prominence of electoral bribery in our sources for the last two decades of the Republic reflects the real power of the electorate, whose support had to be gained by all possible means. In a comparable way, the increasing violence aimed at physical domination of the Forum is a reflection of the central role of legislation and of the constitutional sovereignty of the *populus Romanus.* It did not take long, of course, for accentuated competition to break up the Republican system. But in the year 70, only twenty years before different forces were to take over, we have from Cicero the fullest and most vivid of all impressions of the *populus Romanus* in its historic role as audience, witness, and judge of what went on in its name in the Forum. The ideology of the Gracchan extortion law, that the court and the individual *iudices* were to perform in public a delegated function on behalf of the watching *populus Romanus,* finds its fullest expression here.[57]

These representations by Cicero are there, of course, because they suit his rhetorical purpose (or imagined rhetorical purpose, since some derive from the speeches that were never delivered). Throughout the speeches, radical reform of the *iudicia* is presented as imminently expected, and if the senatorial *iudices* have any chance of avoiding the loss of this central constitutional and political role, it is only by not disgracing themselves again, that is, by condemning Verres. The alternative seemed at the moment to be that the *iudicia* would once more be transferred wholesale to the equites.

What can we say against that praetor [Aurelius Cotta] who daily occupies the *templum* [the Rostra] and who says that the *res publica* cannot survive unless the *iudicia* are transferred to the *equester ordo?*[58]

56. Cicero *Verr.* 2.2.55/138.
57. See my discussion of the Gracchan law in chap. 2.
58. Cicero *Verr.* 2.3.96/223.

It is in fact surprising that we hear nothing of any of the tribunes of 70 except Plautius, and that the reform was to be put through not by one of the consuls or one or more of the tribunes but by a praetor from a prominent family. Cicero duly notes that too in speaking of the *equites,* "whom to be sure the *populus* now demands as *iudices,* [and] with regard to whom, in order that we may have them as *iudices,* we see a *lex* promulgated by a man who is not of our rank, not coming from equestrian stock, but from the most noble."[59] It is also puzzling, and not explained in any of our sources, that the precise reform that Cicero was anticipating, and which had clearly been promulgated as a *lex,* was not that which L. Aurelius Cotta eventually put through as praetor. Cotta's *lex* was, as is well known, a compromise, by which the *iudices* would be divided between three panels, made up of senators, *equites,* and *tribuni aerarii.*

We have no evidence to explain the altered content of the *lex* as eventually passed, and we have nothing to illustrate the process, or the political atmosphere, in which the revised law, which must have been seen as a compromise, will have been posted up for a *trinundinum,* subjected to *contiones,* and finally put to a vote, presumably by the *tribus* in the Forum. What we have instead is Cicero's evocation of an earlier stage, when a more radical reform, "another *ordo* to take on the task of judging," was evidently anticipated and demanded.[60] Once again, we have to think not just of an abstract "public opinion" but of the physical context of the Forum itself, with the magistrates in their accustomed seats, the courts in session, *contiones* going on, and the crowd witnessing what took place, listening, and showing its reactions. As so often occurred, the *iudicia* met before the ancient temple of Castor and Pollux, which was the easiest visual symbol to evoke.

> For what am I to say of the daily talk and complaints of the *populus Romanus,* of Verres' most insolent theft, or rather his novel and unique form of brigandage? That he dared to leave in the temple of Castor, the most frequented and most famous monument—that temple that is situated before the eyes and in the daily sight of the *populus Romanus,* in which quite frequently the Senate is summoned to meet, in which the most crowded gatherings, concerned with matters of the highest importance, take place daily—to leave

---

59. Cicero *Verr.* 2.2.71/174. For the promulgation of a *lex,* see also 2.5.69/177–78.
60. See, e.g., Cicero *Div. in Caec.* 3/8–9.

in that place, in popular talk, an eternal monument of his own brazenness.[61]

More specifically, however, Cicero evokes the precise political context in which he is undertaking the prosecution: "in the very crisis of your *ordo* and your *iudicia*, when men stand ready to attempt to inflame by *contiones* and *leges* hostility toward the Senate."[62] Later he makes the same point in a different way: "this is the *iudicium* in which you will judge the accused, and the *populus Romanus* will judge you; in the person of this man it will be decided whether, with senatorial *iudices*, an extremely guilty and extremely wealthy man can be condemned."[63] Throughout the speeches, Cicero's arguments are framed by the imputed reactions of the *populus Romanus:* the expectation (in fact fulfilled) that Verres would not dare to show himself for the second session; the hostile *clamor* of the *populus Romanus* that broke out when Verres had confessed that he had not executed some pirate chiefs, but had kept them under guard in his house.[64]

The communal and political significance of the Forum, of the institutions that functioned in it, and of the crowd there that witnessed and judged personal reputation *(existimatio),* is nowhere more fully evoked than toward the end of the *Fifth Verrine,* when Cicero rhetorically asks whether Verres, while committing his crimes in Sicily, had never thought of the context in which, back in Rome, judgment would be passed on him. The immediate context is the allegation that Verres had imprisoned some Roman citizens in the quarries of Syracuse.

> For you [the *iudices*] think that the rights of *libertas* ought to be retained, not only here, where the *tribuni plebis* are, where there are the other magistrates, where there is the Forum full of *iudicia,* where there is the *auctoritas* of the Senate, where there is the public opinion *[existimatio]* of the *populus Romanus* and its physical presence *[frequentia]*.... Did the *iudicium* never come into your [Verres'] mind, never the *contio,* never this great crowd *[frequentia],* which now looks on you in so prejudiced and hostile a spirit? Did the *dignitas* of the absent *populus Romanus* never pass

---

61. Cicero *Verr.* 2.1.49/129. On the temple's place in politics, see chap. 2.
62. Cicero *Verr.* 1.1/2.
63. Cicero *Verr.* 1.16/47.
64. See Cicero *Verr.* 2.1.1/1; 5/12.

before your eyes and mind, nor the actual image of this multitude? Did you think that you would never return to their sight *[conspectus]*, never come into the *Forum populi Romani,* never fall under the power of the laws and the courts?[65]

Cicero's evocation of the presence of different elements in the Forum is valid, as is his conception that the enforcement of the *leges* adopted by the *populus Romanus* was in part dependent on the operations of the *iudicia* in the open air, in the inherited and very long-standing context of the Forum, where the face-to-face conflicts of an ancient nuclear city-state were reproduced still, in an age when Roman governors, and individual Roman citizens, might be found in Syracuse, or Gades, or Smyrna.

Not very many years later, and in a different rhetorical context, Cicero would represent the force of public opinion as felt in the Forum, not as reinforcing the values of the *populus* and the rights of *libertas,* but as storms that the institutions of the *res publica* could barely hold in check.[66] But in 70 he already knew, and represents himself as saying in public to the *iudices,* that with the restoration of the *tribunicia potestas,* everything had changed, and the brief *dominatio* of the Senate was over.

---

65. Cicero *Verr.* 2.5.55/143–44.
66. See chap. 8.

IV

The Crowd, Oratory, and Imperialism, 69–65

Cicero's view that on the day that the full *tribunicia potestas* was restored the domination of the Senate was over was fully confirmed in the five years that led up to his own successful campaign for the consulate of 63. A similar view was expressed also, retrospectively, by Sallust, even if he provides no more than glib moralizing.

> For after the *tribunicia potestas* had been restored in the consulship of Cn. Pompeius and M. Crassus, young men, who gained the height of power, and whom youth and high spirits made impetuous, began, by accusing the Senate, to rouse the plebs, and then by largesse and promises to inflame them further, and thus to make themselves famous and powerful. Against them the majority of the *nobilitas* strove with all their might, apparently on behalf of the Senate, in reality to preserve their own importance.[1]

No one could doubt that the open political struggles of the last two decades of the Republic were fueled by personal ambition and exhibitionism, along with the distribution of concrete benefits (and the promising of future ones) to the plebs, all of these associated with attacks on the conduct of affairs by the Senate. The end result of intensified political strife, and of the search for personal prominence, was the dictatorship of Caesar, which was only two decades away when Cicero composed his *Verrines* and was already in the past when Sallust wrote his account of Catiline's conspiracy. Consequently, retrospective accounts of the period, including of course the biographies of Caesar and his contemporaries, pick out for us prime examples of the various paths to personal prominence that were open to ambitious men, even without their holding the tribunate.

---

1. Sallust *Cat.* 38.1–2.

However, if we interpret what we find in our evidence in personalized or moralizing terms, or simply as competition between officeholders, we may miss its true significance for the structure of politics. It does indeed show how the early stages of the public career of an ambitious youngish man were in the literal sense public, involving self-advertisement before the people, the delivery of *contiones* about new laws, the prosecution of prominent persons before *iudicia,* and the laying on of expensive shows for the *plebs urbana.* Cicero too had emphasized again and again in his *Verrines* both how his election as aedile for 69 was a sign of popular favor and how his conduct of the office was to be devoted to care for the city and the festivals *(ludi)* of its gods, the *procuratio* of their temples, and the delivery of benefits *(munera)* for the people.[2] He afterward admitted openly that the *ludi* that he gave as aedile in 69 had helped his candidacy for the consulship of 63.[3] When he later discussed the proper bounds of *largitio* during a man's aedileship, he claimed that his own expenditure had been modest.[4] But in fact, so Plutarch records, the grateful Sicilians, while Cicero was aedile, had sent free supplies of corn that enabled him to reduce market prices in Rome.[5]

At any rate, he could reasonably claim, as a first-generation senator from Arpinum, that his election as quaestor for 75, aedile for 69, and praetor for 66 had been the result of personal merit in the eyes of the *populus Romanus,* not of his birth or name.

> When the *populus Romanus* made me *quaestor* among the first [to be elected], *aedilis* as the first of two, and *praetor* first by the votes of all, it was granting that *honor* to my person, not my family; to my *mores,* not my *maiores* [ancestors]; to my attested *virtus,* not my reputed *nobilitas.*[6]

Roman public life was a constant dialogue, or a set of competing dialogues, between the individual actors who sought public office *(honor)* by the *beneficium* of the people and the mass of the people themselves, who at times were not merely an audience but became actors themselves in

---

2. For Cicero's representations of his prospective aedileship, see chap. 2 and esp. *Verr.* 2.5.14/36–37.

3. Cicero *Mur.* 19/40.

4. Cicero *De off.* 2.16–17/57–59.

5. Plutarch *Cic.* 8.1.

6. Cicero *Pis.* 1/3.

many different contexts, and were leading players in the drama when it came to elections and the voting of laws.

How an individual displayed himself to the people was of course a matter of personal circumstances and personal talent. Suetonius' brief but extremely pointed record of the rise of Julius Caesar in the early 60s— even though, by its nature, it benefits from hindsight—illustrates a different side of the political competition and self-promotion to the people that individuals practiced in those years. As we have seen in chapter 3, Suetonius records that Caesar's military tribunate was the first office he received by the votes of the *populus,* and he says that in 70 Caesar supported the movement for the restoration of the *tribunicia potestas* and delivered a *contio* in favor of the *lex Plotia* (or *lex Plautia*). Then, as quaestor in 69, Caesar was able to advertise himself to the people in precisely the way that Cicero could not, by delivering funeral orations from the Rostra for both his aunt Julia and his wife Cornelia. Suetonius quotes an extract from the legendary family histories that Caesar incorporated into the oration for his aunt.

> The maternal side of my aunt Julia's family took its origin from the kings, and the paternal one is linked with the immortal gods. For from Ancus Marcius there descend the Marcii Reges, which was the name of her mother's family; from Venus descended the Iulii, to which *gens* our *familia* belongs.[7]

Julia had been the wife of Marius, and Plutarch, in his *Life* of Caesar, notes that in her funeral procession Caesar displayed images of Marius, on public show for the first time since he and his followers had been declared public enemies by Sulla; some criticized this step, but the people reacted with loud shouts of applause.[8]

Caesar's quaestorship was spent in Spain, and his next public office, as aedile in 65, was marked by vast expenditures in which he wholly overshadowed his fellow aedile, Bibulus—on the Comitium and Forum and the surrounding basilicas, and on porticoes on the Capitol. There were also *venationes* (wild-beast hunts), *ludi,* and a gladiatorial show *(munus),* slightly reduced in scale by a measure limiting the number of gladiators that any one person could keep in Rome.[9] If we may believe Pliny the

---

7. Suetonius *Div. Iul.* 6.
8. Plutarch *Caesar* 5.1–2.
9. See Suetonius *Div. Iul.* 10.

Elder, the occasion was a *munus funebre* on the death of Caesar's father, and was the first time that silver had been used for the decoration of the arena and the weapons of the gladiators.[10]

Such stories of extravagant *munificentia* are built into the record of the public life of the late Republic and could be repeated endlessly.[11] Repetition with ever more extravagant variations was precisely their function, and any attempt to integrate a catalogue of examples into an analysis of political relations would prove merely burdensome. So this famous example must, except for occasional very special cases, serve as a reminder that exchanges between an officeholder and the people were not just matters of words but involved practical benefits, the laying on of entertainments, and visual symbols. It was thus also as aedile that Caesar replaced on the Capitol the trophies of Marius' victories over the Cimbri and Teutones, which Sulla had removed.[12]

By this time, however, much more urgent issues of military policy and of the management of the empire had come to dominate public debate. Rome had in the previous few years entered a quite new phase in its history as an imperialist power, and with that change had come, after the restoration of the *tribunicia potestas,* a new level of open public debate and conflict and of popular involvement, which is also much more fully attested then than in any previous phase. The issues were far too profound for it to be appropriate to analyze them simply in terms of personal ambition and competition.

The new phase of Roman imperialism had in fact originated in the period of senatorial *dominatio*—to be precise, in 74—when the weight of Roman strategic effort shifted to the East and, for the first time ever, both consuls (Lucullus and Aurelius Cotta) received commands in Asia Minor.[13] Cotta was in command in the newly acquired province of Bithynia, while Lucullus had as his *provincia* Asia and Cilicia. In the same year, one of the praetors, M. Antonius, was given what was called an *imperium infinitum* (without geographical limits) to confront piracy in the Mediterranean.

10. Pliny *NH* 33.16/53.

11. The stories are best surveyed by P. Veyne, *Le pain et le cirque* (Paris: Seuil, 1976), part 3, trans. as *Bread and Circuses* (London: A. Lane, Penguin, 1990).

12. See Suetonius *Div. Iul.* 11; Plutarch *Caes.* 6.1–4.

13. For the significance of this decisive step, see A.N. Sherwin-White, *Roman Foreign Policy in the East* (London: Duckworth, 1984), esp. 163; idem, "Lucullus, Pompey, and the East," in *CAH²* 9, *The Last Age of the Roman Republic, 146–43 B.C.,* ed. J.A. Crook, A. Lintott, and E. Rawson (Cambridge: Cambridge University Press, 1994), 229.

There is no need to follow the details of subsequent operations here, except to note that in the early 60s Lucullus, by successive prorogations, was still in Asia Minor and, in spite of major victories and of having advanced across Mithridates' kingdom into Armenia, had still not brought the war to a decisive end. The area of Roman military dominance and imperialist activity had, however, been extended from what the Romans called "Asia" (western Turkey) and Cilicia, to include not only Bithynia but the whole of Anatolia as far eastward as Armenia and the far side of the Euphrates. Moreover, since Tigranes of Armenia, Mithridates' ally, was currently in occupation of Syria, yet another area was becoming exposed to Roman diplomatic claims and potential military intervention. As was soon to be demonstrated both visually and in words, Roman domination in the eastern Mediterranean was in the process of fundamental transformation.

While this new pattern was developing, the restoration of the *tribunicia potestas* had occurred, with momentous consequences for the nature and content of Roman public debate and conflict. To be more precise, tribunician legislation came very soon to be concerned both with the allocation of commands and with the way that the profits of empire were handled and exploited. Precisely how soon this shift in legislative focus occurred is not quite certain, but it may have been immediately in 69. For Dio records that in this year "the citizens" were dissatisfied with Lucullus' conduct of the war, transferred the command of Asia to "the praetors," and then, "after this," gave it to "the consul."[14] It is not, however, worth dwelling on which element of the *res publica* made what decision at this time. Perhaps Dio is referring to a decision by the Senate that Asia should no longer be a consular province and should hence be available for *sortitio* by the praetors. But what was involved may equally have been a tribunician law.

In any case, we have almost certain evidence from 68 for the role of tribunician legislation in the management of the empire in the East. For 68 seems to be the only year to which we can allot the *lex Antonia de Termessibus*, partially known from a bronze tablet found in Rome.[15] The law had been moved by (it seems) all ten tribunes of the year, and was intended to affirm the *libertas* and rights of the town of Termessos in

---

14. Dio 36.2.2.

15. See J.-L. Ferrary, "La Lex Antonia de Termessibus," *Ath.* 63 (1985): 419; Crawford, *Roman Statutes,* 1: no. 19. The section subsequently translated in the text is col. 2, lines 5–6.

Pisidia. Comparable issues will have arisen in the case of many other towns. The significance of this instance is simply that it is documentary evidence, that the law is a tribunician law (though, it must be noted, put forward on the basis of a senatus consultum), and that, in a manner reminiscent of the law on the eastern provinces of the very end of the second century (see chap. 3), its text includes categorical instructions about what may be done by Roman commanders on the spot.

> Let no magistrate or promagistrate or *legatus* or anyone else intro-
> duce soldiers into the town or the territory of the Thermenses
> Maiores Pisidae for winter quarters or bring it about that anyone
> else introduces soldiers there for the winter, unless the Senate has
> decreed by name that soldiers are to be billeted for the winter
> among the Thermenses Maiores Pisidae. And do not let any magis-
> trate or promagistrate or *legatus* or anyone else act or give orders
> with the effect that they should give or provide or have taken from
> them any more than is or will be appropriate for them to give or
> provide under the *lex Porcia*.

The local, detailed, and, in the wider context of the empire, not very important content of this *lex* is precisely what lends significance to the fact that it was a *lex,* had been proposed by the tribunes to the people in the Forum, and had been voted on by the *tribus*. Now that the power of legislation had been restored, it was only to be expected that it would also once again be used to shape military commands and the management of the empire.

The first use of this power probably belongs also to 68. At any rate, Dio, in the passage previously mentioned, goes on to say that subsequently the Romans, still dissatisfied with Lucullus, sent "the consul" as his successor. Dio seems to be referring to the second stage of the progressive replace-ment of Lucullus, namely, that by which Cilicia was transferred to one of the consuls of 68, Q. Marcius Rex. By 67, at any rate, Marcius Rex was in Cilicia as proconsul, with three legions.[16] This must have come about either through senatorial dispositions made already in 69 or (more proba-bly) through a tribunician law passed in the course of 68.

With 67, finally, all ambiguity as to the effects of the new constitu-tional framework disappears, and the names of two of the ten tribunes of

---

16. See Sallust *Hist.* 5.14 M = 5.12 McGushin. See Dio 36.15.1 and 36.17.2.

the year, A. Gabinius and C. Cornelius, dominate our accounts of decisions, debates, and conflicts. First, a *lex Gabinia* dismissed some of Lucullus' legions and gave the command of Bithynia and Pontus to one of the two consuls of the year, M'. Acilius Glabrio.[17] As we will see, the ideology of Roman imperialism in the 60s, as represented to the people in the Forum, is transmitted to us above all through Cicero's *Pro lege Manilia* of 66. So the words in which he reminds the people of this *lex Gabinia* are of crucial importance.

> L. Lucullus . . . compelled by your [the people's] order, because you considered, in accordance with ancient precedent, that a limit should be placed on the length of his imperium, dismissed part of his army, which had already completed its term of service, and handed over part to M'. Glabrio.[18]

It was indeed in accordance with ancient precedent that limits should be placed on individual commands. But that the people made this decision and that their order *(iussum),* expressed in a *lex,* had brought it about were not. On the contrary, the precedent was only half a century old, and its constitutional basis had been reestablished only three years previously.

We hear less about the *contiones* in Rome debating this law than about those debating the other, more famous *lex Gabinia,* to be discussed shortly. But Plutarch indicates that one of the praetors of the year (perhaps the same Quinctius who had been tribune in 75) was chiefly responsible for persuading the people, by saying that Lucullus was treating Cilicia, Asia, Bithynia, Paphlagonia, Galatia, Pontus, and Armenia as his own property to despoil.[19] This list of places may have suffered some rhetorical exaggeration, but the story clearly reflects the reentry of strategic issues, mingled with personal suspicion and resentment, into public debate in the Forum.

Eleven years later, when Gabinius himself, now an ex-consul, was proconsul of Syria, Cicero, in the *Pro Sestio,* made similar accusations against him of profiteering. He also accused Gabinius of being in the course of constructing "before the eyes of all" so great a villa that *that*

---

17. See Sallust *Hist.* 5.13 M = 5.11 McGushin: "Legiones Valerianae comperto lege Gabinia Bithyniam et Pontum consuli datam, sese missos esse . . ."
18. Cicero *Man.* 9/26.
19. Plutarch *Luc.* 33.5.

villa now seems "a mere hut which he himself, as *tribunus plebis,* formerly displayed a picture of at *contiones,* so that, pretending to be a man of integrity and not greed, he might bring into *invidia* a courageous leading citizen."[20] The reference can only be to Lucullus, and to Gabinius having a picture of one of Lucullus' villas erected in the Forum and then lecturing to the people on the extravagance and profiteering it implied. We may recall the story of Hostilius Mancinus, who had used a picture of Carthage to expound his own role in the siege and thus secure the consulship of 145 (see chap. 2).

What we know of the passage of the *lex Gabinia* so far is, however, insignificant compared to our knowledge of the major *lex Gabinia,* which entrusted to Pompey enormous forces and a Mediterranean-wide command against the pirates. Various very important stages of this process are reflected in contemporary sources, above all in Cicero's *Pro lege Manilia* of the next year, 66, and also in the very detailed commentary that Asconius provides on Cicero's *Pro Cornelio* of 65. In this case, it is certain that the law was debated both in the Curia (which was not a constitutional necessity) and in the Forum, and we know that Hortensius, the consul of 69, spoke against it in both places. Cicero recalls this debate, notionally addressing Hortensius in person, in his *Pro lege Manilia.*

> For in the Senate, you yourself, Q. Hortensius, spoke at length (and in a way that befitted your high degree of fluency and exceptional skill in speaking) against a brave man, A. Gabinius—and you did so with weight and style—when he had promulgated a *lex* for the appointment of a single imperator against the pirates; and from this very place [the Rostra], you also spoke at great length against that law.[21]

It also seems to have been against this law of 67 (rather than the *lex Manilia* of the following year) that Catulus, another prominent exconsul, had spoken and had engaged in a dialogue with the crowd. Cicero recalls this too.

> When he asked of you [the people] if you were to confer all power on one man, Pompey, and if anything happened to him, in whom

---

20. Cicero *Sest.* 43/93.
21. Cicero *Man.* 17/52.

you would repose your hopes, he gained a great reward for his own *virtus* and *dignitas,* when you all with almost a single voice said that it would be in him himself.[22]

Both Plutarch and Dio retell this episode and attribute it to the debates on the *lex Gabinia*. Plutarch adds that Caesar, alone of the senators, supported the law, and he reports that one of the consuls said to Pompey (evidently in public, before a *contio*) that if he persisted and emulated Romulus, he would meet the fate of Romulus; the consul then came close to being torn to pieces by the crowd. He also records a story that Roscius (in fact, a tribune of 67) tried to speak against the law but could not make himself heard and was reduced to gestures.[23]

The stories are later retold more fully by Dio, in the course of a long narrative that relates an attempt to kill Gabinius in the Senate and violent popular reactions to that attempt; the Senate's efforts to persuade tribunes to veto the law, only to find that only Trebellius and Roscius were not afraid to; speeches by Pompey and Gabinius; Trebellius' abortive veto of the law (discussed below); Roscius' use of gestures; and finally Catulus' dialogue with the people.[24] As he does so often, Dio manages to use a remarkable range of contemporary detail, without our being able to be sure that all points in his narrative, or the overall sequence, are really authentic. But he may not have been wrong in recording that Roscius' gesture was specifically intended to demonstrate to the crowd the need for two *imperatores*. The long-established principle of collegiality was indeed at stake.

The year 67 also provided two remarkable examples of public divisions among the ten tribunes, in which one would set out to veto a law proposed by another. In the case of the *lex Gabinia,* the opponent was L. Trebellius, and the whole story is told in impressive detail by Asconius, in his explanation of some allusions in Cicero's *Pro Cornelio*. Asconius' account deserves to be set out in full, not least because it is a rather rare example of a description of actual voting by the thirty-five *tribus*.

L. Trebellius is the *tribunus plebis* whom he [Cicero] does not name. When he persisted in interceding [against the law]—for he had promised the Senate that he would die before that law was passed—

22. Cicero *Man.* 20/59.
23. Plutarch *Pomp.* 25.
24. Dio 36.23–36.

Gabinius began to call in the *tribus* to vote on depriving Trebellius of his magistracy . . . and for a time Trebellius, not frightened off by that, remained on the spot and persisted in his *intercessio*, for he thought that Gabinius was threatening, rather than that he would persevere with it. But after seventeen *tribus* had accepted the *rogatio*, so that only one remained, and [thus] one was lacking to confirm the order *[iussum]* of the *populus*, Trebellius abandoned his *intercessio*.[25]

If we are to believe Cicero, the bill was attended by enormous popular enthusiasm. The strong impression created by the words with which he evoked the scene a year later remains, even if we cannot tell precisely what stage he is describing.

> Do you think that there is any shore so deserted that the fame of that day has not reached it, [that day] when the whole *populus Romanus,* with the Forum packed and every temple crowded from which this place [the Rostra] can be seen, demanded Cn. Pompeius as the sole imperator for the common war on behalf of all peoples?[26]

The major issue of a sole imperator, which we can readily accept as having genuinely had the significance that conservative voices attributed to it—the fundamental threat to the Republican system implied by concentration of power—was not the only one that provoked major public conflicts in 67. Most of the issues debated are associated with another of the ten tribunes of the year, C. Cornelius. The issues and the sequence of events are of immense complexity, and all that is attempted here is to pick out a few salient events and scenes that illustrate the public, open-air drama of Roman politics.[27]

Cornelius seems to have begun by proposing to the Senate that it should pass a decree to prevent anyone from making loans to ambassadors from foreign states, which the Senate rejected on the grounds that the law already made provision against this. Cornelius seems then to have spoken about this in a *contio* and to have gone on to propose a law with a rather different content: that no exceptions from the *leges* should be

---

25. Asconius 72C.

26. Cicero *Man.* 15/44.

27. For a full account, see M. Griffin, "The Tribune C. Cornelius," *JRS* 63 (1973): 196. For a systematic treatment of the procedures and forms of communication to the voters involved in the proposal of laws, see C. Williamson, "The Roman Aristocracy and Positive Law," *Class. Philol.* 85 (1990): 266.

allowed except when voted by the *populus*. This was indeed the rule, but the right to grant such exceptions had gradually been usurped by the Senate. As Asconius comments, such a *lex* would diminish the *auctoritas* of the Senate and the influence of its most powerful members. So another tribune, Servilius Globulus, was "found" to veto it. Asconius' account of what followed is again worth quoting in full.

> When the day for passing the law arrived, and the herald *[praeco]*, with a *scriba* supplying the words of the lex, began to recite it to the people, he [Globulus] forbade the *scriba* to supply the text and the *praeco* to say it aloud. Then Cornelius recited [the text from] the codex himself. When the consul C. Piso vehemently complained that this action was improper and said that the *tribunicia intercessio* was being subverted, he was greeted with grievous abuse by the *populus*. And when he ordered those who had laid hands on him to be arrested by his lictor, the lictor's fasces were broken, and stones were also hurled at the consul from the back of the crowd. Disturbed by this tumult, Cornelius dismissed the meeting.[28]

Compared to the organized violence of the following years, this episode seems like a minor disorder, though it illustrates the fact that whatever had until now preserved order was not massive physical force at the disposal of the consuls. All order depended on deference and acceptance of the symbols of office. But far more important structural elements in Roman public life are revealed. The day for passing the *lex* of course will have followed a period of three *nundinae* during which it had been posted up. Nonetheless, the procedure required that a *scriba* should *subicere* the complete text (which must mean either holding it before the *praeco*'s eyes or dictating it in sections for him to repeat), and that the *praeco* should recite it aloud to the people. That step could be vetoed. But it seems to have been felt both that one tribune could not veto the actions of another in person and that using this device—the tribune acting in person—to frustrate a veto was improper, indeed criminal; Cornelius was accused of *maiestas* in 65 and acquitted (though largely for political reasons, Asconius implies).

The principle of publicity both in the posting up of a text of the law and in the recitation of its complete text on the day of voting was fundamental; in this particular case, a specific step in the public demonstration

---

28. Asconius 58C. For the fuller account, see 57–59C. For the subsequent trial in 65, see 60–62C.

of constitutional conflict was unprecedented, and there was no clear resolution of the disputed question of its validity.

With Cornelius' dismissal of the voting assembly, it seems clear that his *rogatio* lapsed. But he subsequently got through a compromise proposal by which a quorum of two hundred senators was required for a grant of exemption and by which no tribunician intercession was allowed when such a grant was subsequently put before the people. Some other measures of Cornelius' were also passed, while others were successfully vetoed by his colleagues.

One bill of his that did not pass concerned bribery at elections and penalties for *divisores.* Once again, what happened was the rousing of public opinion by the tribunes, met by a milder counterproposal, based on a senatus consultum and put forward by the consul Calpurnius Piso. This alternative proposal, though it met strong opposition, eventually passed, but not before a characteristic feature of the following years had appeared, namely, the need for physical control of the Forum for voting. A fragment of Cicero's *Pro Cornelio,* along with Asconius' note on it, reveals that Piso had first been physically driven out *(eiectus)* from the Forum, allegedly by a mob of *divisores,* and had then issued an *edictum* calling on those who wished for the safety of the *res publica* to rally to get the *lex* through: "and escorted by a larger band of followers, he had gone down [to the Forum] to carry the *lex.*"[29]

That the archaic character of the open-air process of legislation should lead to open trials of physical strength was of course ominous, and seemed so at the time to those concerned. Nonetheless, it should be stressed that all the issues over which conflicts had arisen in 67 were major questions affecting the constitution of the *res publica* and the government of the empire, and were the subject not only of physical conflict but of genuine debate on matters of principle. It also needs to be observed that the impropriety or otherwise of the use of force depended on the point of view of the observer.

For instance, in this particularly active period of tribunician legislation, it was evidently alleged that Cornelius had "given" (or passed on) the draft of a *lex* on the voting rights of *libertini* to a tribune of 66, Manilius (who will have taken office on December 10, 67). Cicero evidently mocked this idea in his *Pro Cornelio* of 65.[30] But later, in his *Pro*

---

29. Asconius 74–76C; see Dio 36.38.

30. Asconius 64C (also with comments on the alleged "giving" of the law by Cornelius to Manilius).

Milone, he referred obliquely, but in very positive terms, to the successful resistance that had been offered to Manilius' proposal. Addressing L. Domitius Ahenobarbus, who had been quaestor in 66, he said, "You had given the greatest proofs ever since your youth of how you despised the madnesses of the *populares.*"[31] What he was referring to is explained by Asconius.

> For at that time, when C. Manilius, the *tribunus plebis,* supported by a gang of *libertini* and slaves, was trying to put through a most disgraceful law to the effect that *libertini* would have the vote in all the *tribus,* and was doing this by violence, and was besieging the Clivus Capitolinus, Domitius had dispersed and broken up this gathering, so that many of the followers of Manilius were killed. By doing this he had offended the lowest class of the plebs and gained great *gratia* with the Senate.[32]

As we saw earlier, in chapter 2, the question of whether *libertini* should vote only in the four *tribus urbanae,* or might be registered in any of the other *tribus,* was and remained a contentious issue affecting the structure of the *res publica.* Fifteen years later, in a different and much more violent context, Cicero could look back on this episode of 66 as simply showing Domitius' creditable contempt for *popularis* frenzy. At the time, however, Cicero's position had been more open, and he himself had written and delivered before the people his famous oration in support of the most important law put forward by Manilius, the *lex Manilia* that gave the command against Mithridates to Pompey. In it he had put forward precisely those arguments that were to be most fatal to the survival of the Republic: that the necessities of empire were more important than the traditional limitations on individual power, and that the exceptional record and military services of Pompey made him worthy to be entrusted with a command on so exceptional a scale.

At the beginning of the *Pro lege Manilia,* Cicero claims it as the first political speech he had delivered from the Rostra, and it is certainly the earliest complete example of such a speech, by Cicero or anyone else, that has come down to us. Of course (to repeat), we have no way of knowing how far, in scale or in the arguments deployed, the written text represents

---

31. Cicero *Mil.* 8/22.
32. Asconius 45C. See Dio 36.42.1–3.

what Cicero actually said. We have no choice but to take it as it stands and see what it has to offer.

The central issue under debate remained the same as in the previous year, and the two aspects of the issue are directly linked by Cicero at several points in the speech: did the needs of the empire require a single imperator, and did this requirement outweigh the established practice of dividing, rather than concentrating, power? Thus, referring to 67, Cicero says:

> The *populus Romanus,* Q. Hortensius, reckoned that it was with good intent that you and the others who were of the same opinion said those things that you felt. But nonetheless, when the matter concerned their common safety, that same *populus Romanus* preferred to have consideration for its own distress rather than for your *auctoritas.*[33]

In 66 not all members of the Senate were in fact against the *lex.* Cicero lists at the end of his speech four prominent senators who supported it and who must surely have delivered *contiones:* P. Servilius, C. Curio, Cn. Lentulus, and C. Cassius.[34] A little earlier, Cicero had referred to the public opposition to the law by Catulus and Hortensius, and had said that their principles must give way to the necessities of war. An opinion that he attributes to Hortensius sums up in a sentence the central dilemma of the late Republic.

> What, therefore, does Hortensius say? That if all power is to be given to one man, Pompey is the most worthy. But that it is, nonetheless, not appropriate that all power should be handed to one man.[35]

Given the regular use of examples from earlier Roman history in public speeches, it would be interesting if Catulus really did, as Plutarch claims, say (paradoxically) that the Senate should retreat to a mountain refuge, as the plebs was alleged to have done centuries before in seceding to the Mons Sacer in the early stages of the "Struggle of the Orders." Plutarch does at any rate affirm that all thirty-five *tribus* voted for the law.[36] There had been ample opportunity to hear public arguments about its implications.

---

33. Cicero *Man.* 19/56.
34. Cicero *Man.* 23/68.
35. Cicero *Man.* 17/52.
36. Plutarch *Pomp.* 30.

It is not necessary to collect, for this year or any other, all the scattered evidence for how political conflicts were acted out in the Forum, via trials before *iudicia,* in the elections, or in the presentation of gladiatorial displays. But one episode from Plutarch's *Life* of Lucullus, evidently based on a Latin source, deserves to be examined.

With Lucullus' deposition from his imperium, public debate about his conduct of the war was not yet over. Returning to Rome, apparently still in the course of 66, he requested the right to hold a triumph. Since the triumph he eventually held did not take place until 63, the chronology of Plutarch's narrative is uncertain and is of no great importance. What matters is its vivid picture of the dependence of the returned commander on popular opinion. Lucullus' request was opposed by a tribune, Memmius, perhaps in 66, possibly later.

> Memmius . . . incited the people and persuaded them not to vote him [Lucullus] a triumph, on the grounds of widespread profiteering and having prolonged the war. When Lucullus began to vehemently contest this [charge], the leading and most powerful citizens mingled with the tribes and, by dint of much entreaty and urging, with difficulty persuaded the people to allow him a triumph.[37]

When the triumph was finally held in 63, it is noteworthy that Lucullus put on a display of enemy arms in the Circus Flaminius—and included in the procession boards on which were written the sums he had already paid to Pompey in 67, or to the treasury—and that he also gave (as we saw much earlier, in chap. 2) a dinner for the whole population in their *vici.*[38] The need to find all possible means of relating oneself to the people was overriding and was not affected by wealth, social status, or political attitude.

In 65, apart from the lavish building program and shows arranged by Julius Caesar as praetor (see the related discussion earlier in this chapter), only one episode stands out as adding in a significant way to our conception of politics as a public process enacted in the Forum. This event is the second trial of Cornelius, partially illuminated for us by the fragments of Cicero's speech in his defense and by Asconius' commentary on that speech. The issue was whether Cornelius' conduct as tribune in 67 (detailed earlier in this chapter) made him guilty of treason *(maiestas).* All

---

37. Plutarch *Luc.* 37.1–2.
38. Plutarch *Luc.* 37.2–4. On use of the Circus Flaminius, see chap. 5.

trials before *iudicia* were by their nature "political," because they took place in the same public space as did *contiones* and meetings of the *comitia tributa;* because they tended to involve persons engaged on political careers, careers that were profoundly affected by a person's conduct in such cases and by the good or bad reputation gained; and because they were exposed to and much affected by crowd reactions and, in this period, were often disturbed by outright violence. But this particular case is of greater significance than normal, first since it revolved around the rights of the tribunate, and second because, in speaking for the defense, Cicero appears, for perhaps the last time, to be taking up a public posture that he himself would certainly, in subsequent years, have labeled pejoratively as *popularis.* What he said on this occasion actually offers us some of our most striking evidence for the way in which *popularis* ideology in Roman public discourse was based on examples and precedents from earlier Roman history.

There had in fact been an initial, but abortive, attempt to prosecute Cornelius in 66. But on the first day the praetor due to preside at the case had failed to appear, either because of duties in relation to the public corn or as a favor to the defendant, and the accusers waiting in front of the tribunal had been attacked by "known leaders *[duces]* of gangs *[operae]*," to be saved only by the intervention of the consuls. On the next day, when the praetor did appear, the accusers had withdrawn the case.[39]

In 65, the year after Cicero's praetorship, he acted as advocate for Cornelius.[40] The case was a major political event, in which five leading citizens gave testimony against Cornelius. These citizens were Q. Hortensius, Q. Catulus, Q. Metellus Pius, M. Lucullus, and M. (or probably Mamercus) Lepidus. For any theory that sees Roman public life as dominated by the *principes civitatis,* it is interesting to observe that Cornelius was nonetheless acquitted by the *iudices.* Cicero had to argue that the fact that in 67 Cornelius had taken the unprecedented step of reading out the law from the codex himself did not constitute *maiestas.* For the prosecution case was—as might at first seem paradoxical—that the device used by Cornelius had amounted to the offense of diminishing the *maiestas* of the tribunate *(crimen imminutae maiestatis tribuniciae).* The tribunician

---

39. See Asconius 59–60C (the source for the quote in text); Alexander, *Trials,* 102.

40. For Cicero's *Pro Cornelio* and Asconius' invaluable explanations, see Asconius 57–81C; Crawford, *Fragmentary Speeches,* 67–68. For other references, see Alexander, *Trials,* no. 209.

right of veto, which was at stake, was, however, a weapon that could be used just as well in the interest of the status quo as in a *popularis* direction. In this case, therefore, the two primary aspects of tribunician rights, the positive (legislation) and the negative (intercession), came into direct conflict. It would hardly have been possible to devise an issue that so closely affected the Romans' perceptions of their own institutions and of their development through the earlier Republic.

It is therefore no surprise to find that the surviving fragments of Cicero's speech, as quoted by Asconius, are largely devoted to rehearsing and interpreting key episodes from Roman history: for instance, the *lex Licinia Mucia* of 95, which was agreed to have been "useless and damaging to the *res publica*"; the abrogation of some *leges* in 109 and again in 91; a controversy in 194 about the reservation of special seats at the *ludi* for senators; or the recent precedent set by Gabinius in having the *tribus* vote to depose Trebellius in 67 (discussed earlier in this chapter), a step that Cicero suggests was surely more serious than reading out a law oneself.[41]

Later on in his speech, Cicero evidently turned to the value to be placed on the tribunate itself and to the distant historical circumstances (in the "Struggle of the Orders") that had given rise to it. He evidently began by raising the possibility that the contemporary climate of opinion had once again turned against the *tribunicia potestas.*

> They say that your [the *iudices'*] minds, as a result of the rashness of that *tribunus plebis,* may be being changed to the point at which they are wholly alienated from the very name of that *potestas.* And that, of those who have restored that *potestas,* one can, as a single individual, do nothing against many, and the other is far away.[42]

Those who had restored the tribunician power were of course Crassus, who was present himself as one of the senatorial panel of *iudices,* and Pompey, who was in command in the East. In fact, according to Asconius, Cicero's suggestion about the jurors' attitude was wrong. For a variety of reasons, such as his not in general having given systematic offense to the *principes,* or his having been Pompey's quaestor, Cornelius was acquitted by the panels *(decuriae)* of *equites* and *tribuni aerarii,* and even gained the

---

41. Asconius 66–72C.
42. Asconius 76C.

votes of many members of the senatorial *decuria,* "except those who were friends of the *principes civitatis.*"43

Whether this was required for securing a favorable verdict or not, Cicero also felt it necessary to go back to episodes of early-fifth-century history, to the legendary struggle of the plebs against the powerful *(potentes).* Asconius comments that either Cicero or the copyists of the speech seem to have made some historical errors. For our purposes, however, this complication does not matter, for the purpose of retelling these episodes was their established place in legendary history. The true story was certainly irrecoverable in Rome in the first century B.C. or A.D. and was not important then, as it is not (in this context) important now. What matters is the representation of Roman history before the *iudices* and the *corona* of bystanders. Referring to the first secession of the plebs, Cicero wrote:

> So great therefore was their *virtus* that in the sixteenth year after the expulsion of the kings, on account of the excessive *dominatio* of the *potentes,* they seceded, established *leges sacratae* on their own behalf, elected two *tribuni,* and consecrated, as an eternal memorial, that mountain across the Anio, which today is called the Mons Sacer, on which they had encamped in arms. So, when the auspices had been taken, the following year *tribuni plebis* were elected by the *comitia curiata.*44

Later, Cicero came to much more recent episodes and to those *leges* that were regarded as constituting the foundations of popular liberty.

> I pass over also these more recent items: the *[lex] Porcia,* the fount of the most just *libertas;* the *lex Cassia* [137] by which the right and power of the vote gained its strength; or that other *lex Cassia* [104] that reinforced the *iudicia populi.*45

As Asconius explains, the first of the two *leges Cassiae* had provided for the use of a written ballot *(tabella)* in a *iudicium populi,* and the second had laid down that anyone condemned by such a *iudicium* could not be a member of the Senate. As we have seen earlier, in chapter 2, Cicero later,

---

43. Asconius 61C
44. Asconius 76C.
45. Asconius 78C.

in the *De legibus,* reflected the view that the *leges tabellariae* had been pernicious, precisely in liberating the people from the moderating influence of their betters.

In a second speech *Pro Cornelio,* Cicero approached the subject of the acceptability or otherwise of known examples of prominent tribunates, by reminding Catulus of the record of his uncle, Cn. Domitius Ahenobarbus, who had been tribune in 104.

> So then? Your uncle, a most distinguished man, with a distinguished father, grandfather, and ancestors, acted, I believe, amid silence—with the support of the *nobilitas* and with no one prepared to intercede—to give to the *populus Romanus,* and to take away from the colleges made up of the most powerful men, the power of co-opting priests *[sacerdotes].*[46]

Given the central role of the "colleges" of priests—the *pontifices, augures, septemviri epulonum,* and *quindecimviri sacris facundis*—in the working of the *res publica,* and given also the fact that these positions were lifelong, the question of whether they were to be filled still by co-optation from within or by election by the mass of citizens was of major importance. The issue had been raised unsuccessfully in 145 and then decided by Domitius' law of 104.[47] Cicero's words may already have been more controversial than they seem on the surface (since their explicit purpose is to represent Domitius' *lex* as an example of a noncontroversial item of tribunician legislation). For since 104, it seems that Sulla's legislation had included the reversal of Domitius' measure.[48] Two years after Cicero's speech, Labienus, as tribune of 63, reinstituted popular election as the means of appointing members to the colleges of priests.[49]

The various propositions incorporated by Cicero in his two speeches in defense of Cornelius have been worth exploring briefly because they remind us that speeches in the Forum, which were addressed in principle to the *iudices,* formed, or could form, almost as explicit a vehicle of political debate as speeches addressed directly to a *contio* of citizens assembled in the same space. They also remind us that the central subject

---

46. Asconius 79–80C.

47. See M. Beard, "Priesthood in the Roman Republic," in M. Beard and J. North, eds., *Pagan Priests: Religion and Power in the Ancient World* (London: Duckworth, 1990), 17.

48. Rotondi, *Leges Publicae,* 352. Only Dio (37.31.1) categorically states this.

49. See chap. 5.

of that debate was the ordering of the *res publica,* the steps by which in the past it had reached its present structure, and the question of further changes. Integral to all of this was the issue of the rights and powers of the mass of voters in relation to those of other elements in the *res publica.*

The powers which had been, or should be, granted to the tribunes inevitably represented one of the major areas of controversy in themselves: whether they should have the right to propose legislation, whether one tribune could properly call the *tribus* to vote on deposing another, or whether there was any legal and acceptable means by which one tribune could circumvent a veto by another.

Moreover, as Cicero had predicted, the restoration of the full *tribunicia potestas* in 70 had transformed the framework of political debate. For whether we look at issues relating to the internal structure of the *res publica* or (what was not in any case wholly a separate matter) at the passing of measures about provincial commands and the running of the empire, legislation, in particular tribunician legislation, now appears as the primary agent of change. Our evidence is scattered and allusive, and many possible items of legislation are of uncertain authorship, content, or date. But it must surely be significant that for the five years that followed the restoration of *tribunicia potestas,* 69–65, we know with reasonable certainty of no more than one *lex* passed, or at least proposed, by consuls; of none by praetors; and of about fifteen by tribunes.[50] A tribunician *lex* could be preceded by a debate in the Senate and might even be backed by a senatus consultum. But neither step was constitutionally necessary. By contrast, no form of legislation could be enacted without being put to the only body that normally legislated, the *comitia tributa* (the *comitia centuriata* could also legislate but is not recorded as doing so in this period). The *comitia tributa* assumed its constitutional function as the sovereign body in the *res publica* by being formed into its thirty-five constituent elements out of whatever crowd was present in the Forum or could be got there in time. We have unambiguous evidence that before that point was reached, the citizens did have ample opportunity to hear conflicting points of view at *contiones.* The system was indeed one in which persuasion of the voters, often by recourse to arguments from earlier Roman history, played a central role. But we also see, in this five-year period, clear indications of the growing need to muster and organize supporters to achieve physical dominance of the voting area. The next five years, 64–60, are much more

50. See Rotondi, *Leges Publicae,* 369–77; Broughton, *MRR,* 131–58.

fully illuminated by our sources, above all because it is to 63 that the bulk of the surviving speeches of Cicero to the people belong. This period was to see greatly intensified threats of physical violence, as well as complex debates and controversies over the constitution, over the exploitation of enormously increased overseas resources deriving from conquest, and over proposals about land distribution. Questions of internal regulation, of the limits of individual power and public status, and of the exploitation of the empire had become closely entangled.

V
***

Oratory, Disorder, and Social Problems,
64–60

The nature of Roman public life was in a state of constant change and development in the late Republic, so that even as regards its last thirty years a static analysis of how it worked could hardly be valid. First, the external circumstances of the Republic changed drastically. The few years considered in this chapter saw the ending of the wars against Mithridates, and then his death, and the sudden acquisition of Syria as a province. As we will see, the huge level of booty, the increased long-term tribute revenues, and the altered strategic shape of the empire in the East were clearly demonstrated to the *populus* in Rome. At the same time, there were threats to Rome's position in Gaul, as well as active local campaigning by Julius Caesar as propraetor in Lusitania in 61–60, both of which had momentous consequences.

Second, there were deep divisions about how to deploy the profits of empire, as well as continuing changes in the constitutional structure of the *res publica* and in the use made of already existing elements of it. One effect of the constant debate about the nature of the *res publica* and the exploitation of its resources is that in looking at the story, we ourselves are affected by changing perspectives. Roman political debates involved continuous reinterpretation of both the distant and the more recent past, so that (to take only one instance) debates in 63 revolved around precedents from the second century and earlier, while our evidence on those debates themselves is partly mediated through politically slanted reinterpretations of them dating from the 50s. More complex still, in its effects on our perceptions, is the fact that Sallust's *Bellum Catilinae* was written after the assassination of Julius Caesar as dictator in 44, while itself offering literary representations of arguments from earlier historical precedents, as put forward in 63.

In focusing heavily on the figures of Catiline himself and of Cicero, Julius Caesar, and Cato the Younger, the *Bellum Catilinae* also exemplifies a clear tendency in our evidence, one that has had a much more profound effect on our conceptions than is always realized. Narratives of the late Republic written in antiquity tended to see the struggles of these years primarily as representing competition or strife between a limited number of leading figures, and to leave aside even the now six hundred members of the Senate, let alone the mass of the people. This tendency is of course obviously true of the autobiographical works (even if written in the third person) of Julius Caesar, as it is of the later biographies, in Latin or Greek, of, for example, Pompey, Lucullus, Crassus, Cicero, Cato, Caesar, Brutus, or Cassius. But a similar tendency also marks the major historical narratives of Appian and Cassius Dio, written in Greek under the empire.

Such conceptions are not of course wholly misleading. Roman public life was indeed marked by individualistic competition for office, glory, and subsequent reputation and influence. A person's family background was very relevant to how that person was perceived, and equally a man's own style and personal conduct markedly affected his chances of electoral success. Trials in the Forum, as has been, if anything, too much stressed in modern literature, were, among other things, competitions in oratory and personal contests in which success or failure had drastic consequences. Above all, the rapidly accentuating competition for military glory had a fundamental effect on the evolution of Roman imperialism in the 60s and 50s.

Nonetheless, it has to be stressed that all these forms of individualistic competition were directed to an audience of the people, and that no one could gain any public office without direct popular election, whether through the *comitia centuriata* or the *comitia tributa*. More important still, changes in the *res publica*, new forms of exploitation of the empire, and new structures of military command required the voting of a *lex* by the people in the Forum. The people were the arbiters of success or failure, and they alone could validate structural change.

It is both an enormous advantage and, in some respects, a handicap that, in our attempts to perceive the structure of politics in terms of the role of the people, the later 60s are the first period from which we have a mass of contemporary testimony from Cicero. We have noted already the one surviving earlier example of a speech of his to the people, the *Pro lege Manilia* of 66. But from Cicero's consulate in 63, there are texts providing written versions of a whole series of speeches addressed by him to the people:

On the Agrarian Law 2
On the Agrarian Law 3 (both from early 63)
In Defence of Rabirius (addressed to the citizens in the *comitia*
    centuriata, defending someone accused of *perduellio*)
Against Catiline 2
Against Catiline 3 (both from November 63)

The importance of this group of texts can be underlined by pointing out that there are no surviving texts representing *contiones* to the people by anyone else (whole texts, that is; many fragments of course survive) and that, apart from these speeches of 63, there is one speech of Cicero's to the people in 57 *(Post reditum ad Quirites)* and two from the brief renaissance of the *res publica* in 44–43 (*Orationes Philippicae* 4 and 6)— a period that deserves political analysis in its own right.

These speeches to the people by Cicero as consul were not, however, the only ones he delivered during his year of office. In the course of discussing with Atticus in 60 how the historical record of his consulship should be presented, he sets out a list of his "consular" speeches.[1] The record is extremely revealing for the pattern of a consul's political activity in this period, when, by comparison with the pre-Sullan Republic, a consul stayed in Rome for all or most of his year of office.[2] The list reads:

In the Senate on the Kalends of January
To the *populus* on the *lex agraria*
On Otho
In Defense of Rabirius
When I renounced my *provincia* at a *contio*
When I drove out Catiline
Delivered to the *populus* on the day after Catiline fled
At a *contio* on the day that the Allobroges gave information
To the Senate on the Nones of November

He also lists his speeches as consul in the highly self-laudatory account of his own electoral career—through the quaestorship (75), aedileship (69), praetorship (66), and consulship (63)—and of his conduct of his consulship which is found in his speech against Piso in 55.[3] In this list, he leaves

---

1. Cicero *Att.* 2.1.3 (21).
2. See chap. 2.
3. Cicero *Pis.* 2–3/4–7.

out his *On Otho*, which related to the unpopularity of one of the praetors of the year 63, Roscius Otho, who as tribune in 67 had carried a law to establish that the *equites* should have reserved for them, as a sign of their social status, the first fourteen rows at theatrical performances; Cicero had delivered a speech to the people reproving them for their hostility.[4] He does give some details of the reasoning deployed in the speech in which he opposed restoring the right to stand for office to the sons of those men proscribed this right by Sulla, without making clear in what context the speech had been delivered. Dio tells us that the proposal was tribunician, but whether Cicero is referring to a speech of his in the Senate or at a *contio* remains unclear.[5] Cicero also gives in *In Pisonem* a reminiscence of the speech in which he renounced his *provincia* in favor of his fellow consul.

> Amid the protests of the *populus romanus*, I formally announced *in contione* my renunciation of the *provincia* of Gallia, which on the authority of the Senate had been voted and decked out with an army and funds, and which I exchanged with Antonius (the other consul of 63), since I considered that to be required by the circumstances of the *res publica*.[6]

This change involved no popular vote to override the Senate's previous arrangements; but it did still require to be enacted publicly before a *contio*. Cicero goes on also, in the same passage, to talk of the *contio* which he had been prevented from giving at the end of his year of office as consul; but we will return later in this chapter to this very important and revealing episode, which tells us so much about how relations between an elected officeholder and the public were conceived.

As the list of his public speeches clearly indicates, Cicero's consulship in 63 was marked by major constitutional issues affecting individual rights and statuses within the *res publica*; by an important agrarian bill, which Cicero opposed and which was not passed; by the capital prosecution of Rabirius before the *comitia centuriata*; and above all by the conspiracy of Catiline. The story of this episode, which cannot be told in any detail here, involves in its earlier stages valuable indications of the

---

4. See Plutarch *Cic.* 13; Pliny *NH* 6.30/117. See Crawford, *Fragmentary Speeches*, 209–10.

5. Dio 37.25.3; see Crawford, *Fragmentary Speeches*, 201–2.

6. Cicero *Pis.* 2/5.

patterns of popular politics in Rome and of the involvement in it of groups from elsewhere in Italy. But the conspiracy was ultimately brought to an end by military repression in Italy outside Rome. The execution of some of Catiline's associates at the end of 63 was, in the following years, to have fundamental implications for popular reactions and for the content of popular politics.

We will therefore look back at a few aspects of the consular elections for 63 and 62 before turning to an equally partial view of popular involvement in the major political and social issues of 63 and the following years. As we saw much earlier, in this last phase of Republican history, canvassing of potential voters could involve any part of the Italian Peninsula, including Gallia Cisalpina, which was still a *provincia,* and where only part of the inhabitants were Roman citizens (see chap. 2). In 65 Cicero was already thinking of spending some time there to canvass support for the consulship of 63.[7] In 64, when these elections took place, there were six competitors other than Cicero himself (four of whom were the rivals Cicero had been anticipating in 65); Cicero, the only competitor from a nonsenatorial background, was elected first, while a *nobilis,* C. Antonius, the son of the great orator M. Antonius, just defeated Catiline by a few *centuriae* and gained the other place. The speech Cicero delivered in the Senate in 64 against the supposed electoral coalition of Catiline and Antonius casts a flood of light on the traumatic aftermath of the Sullan regime, with its proscriptions and brutal public executions. Here, too, the importance of witnessing by the people is brought out. Referring to the murder of Marius Gratidianus by Catiline himself in the Sullan period, Cicero says, "How highly he valued the *populus* he showed when, with the people looking on *[inspectante populo],* he cut off the head of a man who was *maxime popularis.*"[8]

Cicero's speech does nothing, however, to illuminate popular voting patterns in 64, any more than does Sallust's novelistic evocation of the same process; he records only the same two facts as Cicero and Asconius, namely, the supposed (or hoped-for) coalition of Catiline and Antonius and the eventual election of Cicero and Antonius.[9] He records that Catiline nonetheless stood again in the consular elections of 63 for 62, was defeated, and only then turned seriously to planning the use of force both in Rome and in the Italian countryside, above all in Etruria, but also in

7. Cicero *Att.* 1.1.2 (10).
8. See Asconius 82–94C on Cicero's *In toga candida;* the passage cited is from 87C.
9. Sallust *Cat.* 21.3, 24.1.

Picenum and Apulia.[10] Utterly inadequate as Sallust's narrative is, it must of course be taken as raising one of the fundamental problems of the late Republic, namely, how far and in what way grievances that were felt among the population of Italy, all now Roman citizens, could in fact find expression through the constitutional machinery available in Rome.

If individuals or groups did wish to give expression by constitutional means to grievances and demands for change, they could only do so by coming to Rome and participating in person in the political process. As regards participation in the elections in 63, especially participation by groups from outside Rome, far more is revealed by Cicero's admittedly tendentious speeches of this year. The clearest representation of the context of the consular elections comes, however, not from his speeches of the second half of the year against Catiline but from his speech in defense of Murena, one of the two successful candidates for the consulship of 62.

Not listed among his "consular" speeches, as having been delivered before a *quaestio* on *ambitus* (electoral corruption), Cicero's *Pro Murena,* of which the original was delivered in November 63, belongs among our most important evidence for the workings of Roman politics. In it, Cicero defends his client against the accusations of a defeated rival, Servius Sulpicius Rufus (supported by Cato the Younger), by arguing that Murena's personality and career sufficiently explained his popularity, without the alleged recourse to improper influence having been necessary. The speech is a careful representation of the expected norms of electoral competition and of the public comportment of current or potential officeholders. Not all of Cicero's observations can be noted here. But in the particular context of 63, when Lucullus' army had returned for the triumph that he then held,[11] there is real significance in what Cicero says about the influence exercised by returned soldiers on behalf of a candidate who, like Murena, had been on campaign in the relevant area. Addressing Sulpicius, Cicero says:

Do these really seem to you to be insignificant sources of help and support for the consulship, namely, the goodwill of the soldiers? This is important, both in relation to their own numbers and in the influence that they have among their own people. But in particular the military vote has great weight among the entire *populus Romanus* in

---

10. Sallust *Cat.* 26–27.
11. See chap. 4.

electing a consul. For in the consular elections *imperatores* are being chosen, not interpreters of words.[12]

At an earlier moment in the speech, Cicero manages to make exactly the opposite point, more suitable to his own status as an *interpres verborum* (the description he applied to Sulpicius) who had never held military command (and had renounced his consular *provincia*).

> Weighty also and full of *dignitas* is that oratorical ability that has often been of influence in the election of consuls, that is, the capacity by advice and speech to move the minds of the Senate and the *populus* and those who judge cases. A consul is sought who can, on occasion, by speaking, repress the madness of the tribunes, who can bend the excited *populus* and can resist *largitio*.[13]

Reasonable regard had also to be paid to Murena's respectable senatorial ancestry, to his good military record, and to the sumptuous *ludi* he had laid on when praetor in 65.[14] As we saw earlier, he had also made good use of an opportunity to win favor when conducting the levy in Umbria.[15] It was therefore to be expected—and not to be attributed to bribery— that he would be attended by large crowds of followers in Rome.

Cicero argues, however, that the most urgent reason for not condemning Murena, and thus not destabilizing the *res publica* at a dangerous moment, was the continued threat posed by his defeated competitor Catiline. The elections earlier in the year had served to demonstrate this threat in very vivid form. Cicero recalls Catiline's posture as a consular candidate.

> They saw . . . Catiline meanwhile eager and confident, surrounded by a chorus of young men, protected by informers and assassins, buoyed up by hopes of the soldiers and, as he would imply himself, by promises from my colleague [Antonius], with an army of *coloni* from Arretium and Faesulae flooding around him; this mob was also marked out by a quite different group, men struck down by the calamities of the Sullan period.[16]

---

12. Cicero *Mur.* 18/38.
13. Cicero *Mur.* 11/24.
14. See Cicero *Mur.* 18/37–20/41.
15. See Cicero *Mur.* 20/42. See also chap. 2.
16. Cicero *Mur.* 24/49–26/53.

In the face of this threat, Cicero had had the Senate vote to put off the elections and hold a debate, in which he accused Catiline, and Catiline responded. But the Senate's decree had been less severe than the occasion demanded. Then, when the elections did take place, rumor had it that Catiline was coming down to the Campus Martius with followers armed with swords, so Cicero, as the presiding consul, had made sure that he had a substantial escort and had deliberately worn a breastplate as a sign of the immediate danger that threatened him. The opinion of those who wanted to see the *res publica* safe had moved then and there in favor of Murena.

Out of these various tendentious representations we can indeed gain some idea of the complex factors that influenced elections, from personal reputation, to an observed role as an orator in the Forum, to a good military record, the laying on of extravagant *ludi* or *munera* in the past, or perceptions of the present situation or of the intentions of the candidates. Connections with communities in different parts of Italy might turn out to be relevant, and groups from particular areas might make a visible appearance in Rome in support of one candidate or another.

The Roman political process was thus, or could be, to some extent an Italian process also, involving citizens from outside Rome. But the year 63, if anything, shows precisely how restricted the possibilities were for the expression of grievances felt in the Italian countryside. There is a striking contrast between the limited electoral or political influence that Catiline was able to exert in Rome and the forces—equivalent to two Roman legions—that he was able to assemble, in vain, in northern Italy.

What dominated politics instead was the interests of the *plebs urbana* in Rome. This domination is perhaps clearest of all in relation to the *lex agraria* put forward by Rullus, one of the tribunes of 63, and successfully resisted by Cicero. All we know of it, in effect, comes from Cicero's three speeches against it: one delivered in the Senate on the very first day of his consulship, January 1, 63; and two addressed to the people, arguing, in essence, that a law that appeared to be in the popular interest was in fact designed to give power to a small, self-interested group, in opposition to Pompey, who was just completing his major conquests in the East.

It is not necessary, for our purposes, to follow in detail the complex provisions of the bill, insofar as they are revealed by Cicero.[17] In broad

---

17. See the classic article by E.G. Hardy, "The Policy of the Rullan Proposal in 63 B.C.," *Journal of Philology* 32 (1913): 228, reprinted in *Some Problems in Roman History*

outline, the intention of the *rogatio* was to raise large sums by selling off both booty and newly acquired properties of the *populus Romanus* in the provinces, to use the money to settle *coloni* on *ager publicus* in Italy, and, beyond that, to buy land for citizens (apparently drawn in the main from the *plebs urbana*) who wanted it. A board of ten commissioners *(decemviri)* would be set up to carry this project out. It was, in other words, an attempt to use for the benefit of individual citizens the vastly increased capital resources that had come about through eastern conquests. Cicero is thus forced into the position of arguing repeatedly that a measure that seemed on the surface to be straightforwardly *popularis* was not so in reality. Conveniently for our purposes, he also happens to reveal, even if in tendentious terms, important aspects of the procedures involved in tribunician legislation.

The tribunes entered office on December 10 in 64, three weeks before the consuls and the other elected magistrates. On January 1, Cicero spoke in the Senate against the *lex agraria,* and then, on the same day, delivered his first speech to the *populus.* His opening words, of course designed to win popular favor, nonetheless reveal an essential aspect of the ideology of elected office at Rome: the conception that such an office was a *beneficium* conferred by the people.

> This is an established custom and institution of our ancestors, Citizens, that those who by your *beneficium* have [already] acquired *imagines* [of office-holding ancestors] for their *familia* should deliver an initial *contio* in which they combine thanks for your *beneficium* with praise of their own family.[18]

Cicero goes on to stress that, by contrast, he himself is a *novus homo* (in the fullest sense, namely, that none of his ancestors had held any elected office in Rome) and that his position is and will be truly *popularis.* He will thus act against the threat to *libertas* that hangs over the people. With a polite reference to the Gracchi, who had settled the plebs on *agri publici,* he then moves on to the current proposals.

What Cicero reports demonstrates, as clearly as anything could, the way in which the actions of officeholders were directed to the *populus,* and the degree to which the elected officeholders of any one year in no

---

(Oxford: Clarendon, 1924), 68. See also J.-L. Ferrary, "Rogatio Servilia Agraria," *Ath.* 56 (1988): 141; Crawford, *Roman Statutes,* 2: no. 52.

18. Cicero *De leg. ag.* 2.1/1.

way formed a "government" but acted independently without mutual consultation or exchange of information, and often in direct conflict with each other. As *consul designatus,* hence at some point from mid-64 onward, Cicero had heard that the *tribuni plebis designati* were composing a *lex agraria.* His attempts to gain their confidence were, he says, rebuffed, and he was forced to wait anxiously for the results of their secret meetings. At last the day on which the tribunes entered office (December 10) arrived; a *contio* on the part of the main mover, P. Rullus, was awaited.

> I was waiting for the man's *lex* and a *contio.* Initially, no *lex* is posted up, but he orders a *contio* to be assembled on the day before the ides [December 12]. People rush together with the highest expectations. He delivers an *oratio* that, to be sure, is long and expressed in very fine words. The only thing that seemed to me amiss was that out of such a large crowd *[frequentia]* not one person could be found who was able to understand what he said. . . . However, the more perceptive of those who had been standing in the *contio* suspected that he had intended to say something or other about a *lex agraria.* At some point, finally, while I am still *designatus,* the *lex* is posted up in public. On my instructions, various copyists *[librarii]* come together at the same moment, copy the law down, and bring it to me.[19]

Cicero does not say exactly where the law was posted up, though it *may* have been on the wall of the temple of Saturn, which functioned as the treasury of the *populus Romanus* and (which is not the same question as is at issue here) as the depository of *leges* once passed.[20] The place cannot at any rate have been far from the Forum. The implication is clearly that any citizen who could read, or could have someone take a copy for him, could have access to the complete text of the proposed *lex.* Cicero represents himself as reading through his copy of it sympathetically, but as finding nothing in it but the creation of ten "kings" *(reges),* to be elected not by all thirty-five *tribus* but by a selection of seventeen "in the same

---

19. See Cicero *De leg. ag.* 2.5–7/11–17; the passage quoted is 5–6/13–14.

20. See Cicero *De leg.* 3.4/11, "promulgata proposita in aerario cognita agunto," which certainly refers to the public posting up of texts of proposed laws at the Aerarium and not to deposition of archival copies, but which represents a *proposal* by Cicero and is still not proof of normal practice.

way as at the election for the Pontifex Maximus."[21] Here as elsewhere in the speech, his argument has the function of demonstrating that what seemed to be *popularis* was really a perversion, or inversion, of the known *popularis* measures of the past. A quite detailed knowledge of Roman history is presumed on the part of the assumed audience.

Later in the speech as published, Cicero does touch on the fundamental contradiction of the late-Republican system, the anomalous power and privilege enjoyed by the *plebs urbana*. But in this context he argues that the *plebs urbana* should not be ready to give up, in return for plots of land, the benefits that it enjoyed in the city.

> That, to be sure, is what was said by this tribune in the Senate, that the *plebs urbana* had excessive power in the *res publica;* it should be drained off. This was the expression he used, as if he were speaking of some dregs and not of a class of excellent citizens. But you, Citizens, if you are prepared to listen to me, keep hold of that which is yours: your *gratia, libertas,* votes *[suffragia], dignitas;* your city, Forum, *ludi,* festivals; and all your other advantages—unless of course you prefer to be dumped under the guidance of Rullus in the dust bowl of Sipontum or in the pestilential swamps in the territory of the Salpini.[22]

Though Cicero's choice of sites is of course simply rhetorical, his words do underline the contradiction that the profits of empire could indeed best be translated into plots of land for individual citizens, while only in the city could power be deployed and communal festivities enjoyed.

Toward the end of the published version of this speech, Cicero reminds the people that he owed his election to the consulship not to his ancestors but to his own merits. He argues that they could thus expect all the more vigilance from him.

> Am I the consul who would fear a *contio* or tremble at a *tribunus plebis,* who would rant frequently and without cause, who would fear that I would have to spend time in the *carcer* if a *tribunus plebis* ordered me to be led there? . . . If I had been afraid before, nonetheless with this *contio* and this *populus* I certainly would not fear. For

---

21. Cicero *De leg. ag.* 2.7/16–19. Passage quoted is 7/18.
22. Cicero *De leg. ag.* 2.26–27/70–71.

who has ever spoken with such a favorable reaction from the *contio* in urging a *lex agraria* as I have in speaking against one?[23]

Cicero seems to have been right. For reasons we do not know, no *lex agraria* was passed, and the consul did not have to go through the familiar ritual of being led to the *carcer* by a tribune. Cicero claims later that another tribune, L. Caecilius, had announced that he would veto the law.[24] Whether he did is not known. The debate over the *lex agraria* at any rate illustrates the complexity of the arguments that (as represented in published texts) could be put before the people, as well as the need to generate such arguments on both sides; Cicero's third speech *de lege agraria* is a response delivered at a *contio* to allegations by the tribune at an earlier *contio* that Cicero was acting in the interests of those who had acquired land in the Sullan period. We can never know which of these arguments were actually effective or indeed whether the content of public speeches, rather than (as often presumed) other forms of influence, determined the issue. It is certain that the question of land distribution surfaced repeatedly in subsequent years and continued to be the subject of public argument.

Among the arguments Cicero did present against the *lex agraria,* it is not impossible that the imputation that its purpose was to give power to Pompey's rivals carried particular weight. At any rate, we find that in the course of 63, two other tribunes, T. Labienus and T. Ampius, were able to carry a law permitting Pompey, on his return to Rome, to wear a gold crown and triumphal dress at the *ludi circenses* and a *toga praetexta* and a gold crown at the *ludi scaenici.*[25] In the context of the public arena of Roman politics and of the repeated measures aimed at limiting competition and preventing the excessive prominence of any individual, these measures were not trivial novelties, but mirrored the popular readiness, already expressed in 67 and 66, to elevate individual commanders, in real powers and in symbolic standing, above their senatorial competitors; these honors foreshadow ones given later to Julius Caesar as dictator.

They were thus of real significance in the context of the life of the *res publica,* just as was, in a much more immediate sense, Labienus' renewal,

---

23. Cicero *De leg. ag.* 2.37/101.
24. Cicero *Sull.* 23/65.
25. See Vell. Pat. 2.40.4 (for the reading followed in the text, see the 1997 edition by M. Elefante; Dio 37.21.4; cf. Dio 43.43.

apparently reversing a measure by Sulla, of the law of Domitius Ahenobarbus as *tribunus plebis* in 104, which had entrusted the selection of
priests to popular election. This tribunician measure (along with Sulla's
law) is specifically recorded only by Dio.[26] We can take it as historical,
however, for, as Dio goes on to record, there followed in the same year
the election as Pontifex Maximus of Julius Caesar, whose competitors
had been two senior and prestigious *consulares*. At this moment Caesar
was merely an ex-aedile, but he was popular as a result of his lavish
shows in 65 and was a successful candidate also for the praetorship of 62.

According to the only extended narrative of it we have, which also
comes from Cassius Dio, the prosecution of Rabirius for *perduellio*, instituted by Labienus as tribune, was also in reality a cooperative venture
between Labienus and Julius Caesar.[27] Once again the process involved
profound issues of constitutional law and was played out before the
comitia—though this time, uniquely for this period, before the *comitia
centuriata* meeting in the Campus Martius. Once again Cicero, speaking
for the defense in his *Pro Rabirio perduellionis reo,* was in the position of
arguing that a step that seemed to be based on a *popularis* principle—the
defense of the right of the ordinary citizen not to be exposed to violence
instituted by the consuls without the sanction of a vote by the people—
was in reality a move of a repressive, archaic, and anti-*popularis* character. The prosecution had indeed certainly been chosen as a constitutional test case. The charge was that Rabirius had followed the call of the
consuls thirty-seven years before, in 100, to defend the *res publica* against
the followers of the tribune Saturninus. The claim was that this summons
did not represent an adequate justification and, consequently, that
Rabirius, in having participated in the killing of Saturninus, was guilty of
murder and, by extension, of a form of treason *(perduellio)*. As is a
notorious problem, questions of what the sequence of procedures was
and of how Cicero's *Pro Rabirio* falls into the sequence of events recorded in the brief and allusive narrative of Dio has proved impossible to
resolve conclusively. It is clear at least that, according to Dio, Caesar
himself and L. Iulius Caesar were the two presiding judges at a trial at
which Rabirius was condemned, and that Rabirius appealed, was tried
before the *comitia centuriata,* and would have been condemned again but

26. Dio 37.37.1. See p. 91 above.
27. Dio 37.26–27. See E.G. Hardy, *Some Problems in Roman History,* chap. 4; Alexander, *Trials,* nos. 220 and 221.

for the operation of the procedural device of lowering the flag that was flown by archaic custom on the Janiculum. This step had the effect of causing the assembly to be dissolved.[28]

Cicero's *Pro Rabirio,* whether or not there is any way of relating it to Dio's story, belongs, as he listed it, to his "consular" orations, because in it he is addressing himself to the citizens *(Quirites),* as well as to Labienus in person as prosecutor. It is noteworthy that Cicero claims that people had come to support Rabirius from as far away as Apulia and Campania.[29] It was thus a *iudicium populi,* though nothing in the text of the speech itself formally confirms that it was delivered before the *comitia centuriata* in the Campus Martius, rather than the *comitia tributa* in the Forum (Dio's narrative would of course suggest the former). Cicero's speech in fact refers to both of these locations, but in such a way as to leave the question open.

So which of us in the end, Labienus, is *popularis?* You, who think it appropriate that executioners and chains should be inflicted on Roman citizens *in contione,* who give orders that on a spot rendered sacred by the auspices, in the Campus Martius, at the *comitia centuriata,* a cross for the punishment of citizens should be driven in and set up? Or I, who forbid a *contio* to be befouled by the contagion of an executioner, who say that the Forum of the *populus Romanus* should be purified of those traces of execrable crime, and who defend the duty to protect the purity of the *contio,* the sanctity of the Campus, the inviolability of the bodies of all Roman citizens, the unsullied right of *libertas?*[30]

Cicero claims that it had been proved that Rabirius himself had not killed Saturninus, and that even if he had, it would have been justified by the senatus consultum of 100, which had called on the officeholders of the year to take all measures to preserve the imperium and *maiestas* of the *populus Romanus.*[31] There is no need to enter here into the insoluble question of whether *we* should see such a senatus consultum (wrongly labeled by moderns as the *senatus consultum ultimum*) as having a valid

---

28. See chaps. 2 and 8.
29. Cicero *Rab. perd.* 3/8.
30. Cicero *Rab. perd.* 4/11.
31. Cicero *Rab. perd.* 7/20.

constitutional basis or not.[32] It is perfectly clear, not least from this very prosecution, that the point was fundamentally disputed in the late Republic itself. Cicero argues that the consensus of all the respectable elements in society, in rallying behind the consuls, justified the violence of 100 and would have justified Rabirius even if he had killed Saturninus. Now that there was no threat of force but only a pernicious accusation, dredged up by a tribune as an attack on the *res publica*, it was time to call the citizens not to arms but to use their votes against an attack on their *maiestas*.[33] Dio's story may suggest that, at one stage at least, these arguments did not in fact prevail, and a procedural device had been needed to prevent condemnation.

Once again all we have is a less-than-clear later narrative, and in this case we have the incomplete text of an oration addressed to the citizens. We can note that a major issue of internal sovereignty was at stake, and while we can observe the complex arguments from historic precedents that are employed, we are unable to be sure of the precise context or of whether any of these arguments were convincing to the people.

All that is certain is that later in the same year, the same constitutional issue—namely, which organs of the state had the right to execute citizens and in what circumstances—acquired an immediate contemporary relevance, of just the sort that Cicero denies in his *Pro Rabirio*. Only the barest outline of the familiar story of the conspiracy of Catiline needs to be told here, no more than the minimum necessary to bring out specifically the evidence for popular reactions and involvement.

When news of widespread preparations for revolt in various districts of Italy in the second half of 63 had been received, Cicero called a meeting, or possibly two meetings, of the Senate in the second half of October, at which the Senate passed essentially the same decree as it had in 100: "that the consuls should see to it that the *res publica* suffered no damage."[34] Military preparations were then put in hand. Meanwhile, Catiline was still in Rome, and it was only after an attempt to assassinate Cicero that, on November 8, the Senate was called to meet in the temple of Iuppiter Stator, where Cicero delivered his *First Catilinarian,* accusing Catiline and attempting to drive him from the city. Catiline replied in

---

32. See, e.g., A.W. Lintott, *Violence in Republican Rome* (Oxford: Clarendon, 1968), 149–50; J. Ungern-Sternberg, *Untersuchungen zum spätrepublikanischen Notstandsrecht: Senatusconsultum ultimum und Hostis-Erklärung* (Munich: Beck, 1970).

33. See Cicero *Rab. perd.* 12/35.

34. Sallust *Cat.* 29.

contemptuous terms, referring to Cicero's modest origins in Arpinum, but he then left Rome all the same, to join his forces in Etruria.

Nothing in the *First Catilinarian* makes any concrete claims about the attitude or involvement of the *populus* at large. Nonetheless, measures taken in the Senate were not sufficient, and on the next day, November 9, Cicero delivered his *Second Catilinarian* to a *contio* in the Forum. As in all such cases, we can tell neither how accurately the text as preserved reflects what was said at the time nor how the propositions in it were received. In the speech as we have it, Cicero analyzes the weakness of Catiline's support, describes the measures taken against him, and reassures the people that the *res publica* will be safe and that the city will be protected by the gods.

As is the case throughout the story of the conspiracy, what is striking is the absence of a strong popular movement in Rome itself. Sallust's narrative suggests, in very general and highly colored terms, that there was, or would have been, such a movement at about this point,[35] and he later claims that there had been a plan by which, as a prelude to violent action—including setting fire to parts of the city and attacking the houses of key figures, Cicero among them—the tribune-designate L. Calpurnius Bestia would call a *contio,* complain of Cicero's actions, and lay on him the blame for a most serious war.[36] But, before this took place, information about the conspiracy was obtained from emissaries of the Gallic Allobroges who were in Rome, and the news of the alleged plan to set fire to Rome converted the plebs to support for Cicero.[37]

After the arrest of those believed to be the leaders of the conspiracy, their examination by the Senate meeting in the temple of Concordia, and their being placed in custody, Cicero delivered his last consular *contio* to the people on December 3. Cicero's *Third Catilinarian* is the subsequent written version of what he then said. The text contains a detailed narrative of the exposure of the conspiracy, with (as might be expected) emphasis on the danger that had threatened the city and on Cicero's personal role in preventing it. It is, however, also unique among Cicero's public speeches as they are preserved, in putting so much emphasis on the role of the gods in the protection of the *res publica*. In particular, it makes very detailed rhetorical use of the major statue of Iuppiter, which on the very day of the arrest of the conspirators had been reerected on the Capitol after being

---

35. Sallust *Cat.* 37–39.
36. Sallust *Cat.* 43.
37. See Sallust *Cat.* 48.

struck by lightning two years earlier. According to Cicero, *haruspices* summoned to Rome in 65 had "ordered that a larger image of Iuppiter should be made and placed on an elevated spot and, contrary to how it had been before, should face east." Cicero continues: "They said that they hoped that if that statue, which you see, looked toward the rising sun, the Forum, and the Curia, it would be the case that conspiracies entered into secretly against the safety of the city and the imperium would be exposed to the light, so that they could be perceived by the Senate and *populus Romanus.*" It was surely, Cicero says, by the will of Iuppiter Optimus Maximus that it came about that, on the morning of that same day, when the conspirators and informers were being led through the Forum to the temple of Concordia, the statue was being erected.[38]

It could not in general be claimed that religious considerations play a dominant part in the reflections of public discourse in Rome that have come down to us. But what does in a very specific sense play an important part in the public oratory of the Forum is allusion to the ancient buildings and temples that surrounded it and were visible from it. The notion of *conspectus,* of having the march of events pass before one's eyes, could be attributed to the gods whose temples were grouped around the Forum area, as well as to the *populus* itself.

As is well known, the Senate then met in the temple of Iuppiter Stator on December 5 and condemned to death those conspirators who were under arrest. There is no need to discuss the notoriously complex details of who spoke and in what order at this meeting. Suffice it to say that the controversial legality of the decision was to affect the rest of Cicero's public career, as it did, in a different way, that of Julius Caesar, who (as all sources agree) spoke in the Senate against the decision. It is more relevant in this context to stress the way in which the whole process of execution was conducted in public, as a sort of ritual related to the topography of the Forum area.

The written version of Cicero's speech at this meeting of the Senate, the *Fourth Catilinarian,* evokes, for the reassurance of senators who feared that the physical force needed to carry through the executions was lacking, the sense of the whole area being full of carefully prepared supporters: "Full is the Forum, full the temples around the Forum, full all the approaches to this temple and place" (the precise location of the temple of Iuppiter Stator is unfortunately disputed, but it was certainly

38. Cicero *Cat.* 3.8/20–9/21.

somewhere between the Sacra Via and the lower edges of the Palatine Hill).[39] Cicero goes on to list the groups, in descending order of social status, who were present in the area in support of the Senate: the *equites Romani;* the *tribuni aerarii;* the *scribae;* a mass of freeborn citizens, even the poorest; and *libertini.*[40]

The picture is of course idealized. A number of sources indicate that at least the *equites* who surrounded the temple at which the Senate met were armed with swords. Nonetheless, Cicero's picture must be valid, at least negatively. For whatever reason, which we cannot hope to know, the mass of the people responded on this occasion as passive spectators, even as enthusiastic supporters of the action taken.

Our most vivid evocation of the interaction between the main participants and the watching crowd comes from Plutarch. The conspirators had by custom been detained in the houses of leading senators, which in this way, as in others, performed semipublic functions. Thus Plutarch describes how Cicero took the leading conspirator, Lentulus Sura, from the house of one of the praetors, which was situated on the Palatine, and led him down the Sacra Via, across the Forum (with the people watching in horror), and to the *carcer,* where he was strangled. The same ritual followed with each of the other conspirators. To make quite clear that all was now over, Cicero himself shouted out to the crowd, "Vixerunt!" (meaning "they have lived"—and are now dead). In the evening, so Plutarch says, the mood changed, and the people escorted Cicero back to his house (which lay near the Sacra Via) with applause, as the savior of the city.[41]

We cannot hope, given the nature of our evidence, to understand the true nature of the "conspiracy" or the extent and nature of popular support for it. All that seems clear is that there is a marked contrast between the quite substantial forces collected by its leaders from various parts of Italy, on the one hand, and the almost entirely passive reactions of the crowd in Rome on the other. We cannot know whether there was a change in public opinion, as Sallust claims, or whether, as in 100, the presence of significant numbers of armed supporters of the consuls was enough to repress dissent. It is clear that popular opinion, as manifested in the Forum, nearly always depended on the readiness of a leader, usually a tribune, to evoke it and that manifestations or countermanifestations of popular opinion in the Forum necessarily involved relatively

39. For the literary evidence, see *LTVR,* s.v. "Iuppiter stator."
40. Cicero *Cat.* 4.7–8/14–16.
41. Plutarch *Cic.* 22.

small groups in relation to the wider mass of voters. In what sense demonstration of hostility or support, directed toward actions or speeches by officeholders in the Forum, "really" represented much wider undercurrents of opinion is precisely what we cannot know.

In the slightly longer term, it evidently soon became obvious to all participants that physical control of the Forum area was an important political weapon. In the very immediate term, and even before the execution of the conspirators, it is clear that leaders taking a position hostile to Cicero were already presenting themselves. Cicero himself was aware of this, and in his *Pro Murena,* delivered in the second half of November, he addresses Cato, one of the accusers and one of the ten tribunes-designate for the next year.

> Do you not see the storm that is in prospect for your year of office? For already at yesterday's *contio* there thundered the pernicious voice of a *tribunus designatus,* your colleague, against whom your foresight has taken good precautions, as have all the *boni,* in urging you to stand for the tribunate.[42]

It is likely, but not certain, that the troublesome tribune-designate referred to was (Q. Caecilius) Metellus Nepos, and the allusion is enough to show that, whoever it was, he was taking up a public position even before the tribunes entered office on December 10. What that position was is unclear, except that Cicero felt it as a threat. The threat that did immediately transpire was symbolic but, in the context of the public rituals of Roman politics, of considerable significance. Custom, and perhaps even a law, required that a consul, on laying down office, should take a public oath (as he will have done also on taking up office); and it also allowed him to make a speech to accompany it. Metellus Nepos, however, in the interval between his assumption of office and the end of December, declared in a public speech that it was not appropriate for anyone who had condemned others to death to have the right of speaking in public *(potestas dicendi);* so, on December 31, the last day of Cicero's consulship, he used his veto to deny Cicero the right to give a speech *(contio)* to the people. Cicero responded by converting the words of the oath itself into (in effect) a brief *contio,* affirming his own role in the salvation of the *res publica.* He records this sequence of events in a letter of 62 to

---

42. Cicero *Mur.* 38/81.

Metellus' brother and also in more grandiloquent terms in his speech against Piso in 55.

> When, as I was giving up office at a *contio* and was forbidden by a *tribunus plebis* to say those things that I had intended, and when he permitted me only to take an oath, without any hesitation I swore that the *res publica* and this city had been saved by my sole efforts. And the whole *populus Romanus* at that *contio* granted me not just the congratulations of that day but eternity and immortality, when it approved my oath by swearing in similar terms, with a single voice and will. At that time my return from the Forum back to my house was such that there seemed to be no one out of the whole mass of citizens who was not with me.[43]

The preceding passage is typical of our evidence in that it reveals the existence of an established custom only in relation to one prominent episode. But the established ritual itself, in requiring an oath (that the speaker had obeyed the law, as he had sworn to do on entry?) and in allowing an accompanying speech, is very significant for the ideology of elective office. On this occasion, paradoxically, the veto imposed by the tribune is represented as having functioned to convert a monologue into a dialogue, in which the people made a formal response; and Cicero's later evocation of the scene characteristically converts the crowd that was present, and which then escorted him the few hundred meters back to his house, into the whole *populus Romanus*.

The year 62 provides classic instances of how conflicts between the various elected officeholders of the year could be played out in public in the Forum. Contemporary sources tend to allude to these dramatic events, rather than to record them, and detailed narratives are, unfortunately, offered only by writers of the imperial period. The central issue seems to have been the proposal by Metellus Nepos by which Pompey would be called back from the East with his army, to take military measures against the Catilinarian forces. Plutarch records that a debate was held in the Senate, at which Cato attempted in vain to dissuade Metellus. The scene then moved to the Forum. Cato and another tribune, Q. Minucius Thermus, made their way there, and on arrival "Cato . . . saw the temple of Castor and Pollux surrounded by armed men and its

---

43. Cicero *Pis.* 2–3/4–7 (quoted here); see also his *Fam.* 5.2.6–8 (2).

steps guarded by gladiators, and Metellus himself sitting up on the podium with Caesar." Cato nonetheless advanced and took his seat with Metellus and Caesar, after which there ensued a crude version of the ritualized confrontation of Cornelius and Servilius Globulus in 67 (discussed in chap. 4). The *scriba* produced the *lex*, Cato vetoed it, Metellus (like Cornelius) began to read it himself, Cato took it physically from him, Metellus began to recite it by heart, and Thermus silenced him by placing his hand over his mouth. Metellus' armed followers then briefly occupied the Forum, and he began the voting process, until a larger crowd appeared in support of Cato. Metellus was still able to make a speech of protest before immediately leaving the city to join Pompey.[44] As Cicero recalls in the *Pro Sestio*, Cato's personal courage had won the day against those occupying the *templum*.[45] This episode was nonetheless a step toward a situation where force determined which legislative acts could or could not be put through. A similar picture emerges from the anecdotes that Suetonius attaches to Caesar's praetorship in 62: a *rogatio* to transfer the rebuilding of the Capitol from Catulus, promulgated and then dropped in the face of optimate opposition; and Caesar's support for Metellus and persistence in the face of a *senatus consultum* calling for the removal of both men from office, followed by a retreat to Caesar's house and by his dissuasion of the crowd that offered to support him in asserting his *dignitas*.[46]

We need not dwell on other, inadequately recorded episodes of this year, except to note that Cato, as a concession to popular feeling, is said to have passed some little-known measure to resume corn distributions.[47] It also seems to have been Cato and another tribune of this year who passed a *lex* to impose controls on claims to the right to hold a triumph. An existing *lex* laid down that responsibility for a minimum of five thousand enemy dead was required before this right could be claimed. The new law laid a penalty on *imperatores* who incorporated inflated claims in their letters to the Senate, and it also obliged them, as soon as they entered the city, to take an oath before the *quaestores urbani* to affirm that the figures reported were correct. The reference must be to the quaestors who had charge of the Aerarium Saturni in the temple of

44. Plutarch *Cato Min.* 27–29, Loeb trans. with adjustments. Cf. the similar narrative in Dio 37.43.1–4.
45. Cicero *Sest.* 29/62.
46. Suetonius *Div. Iul.* 15–16.
47. See Plutarch *Cato Min.* 26.2; *Caes.* 15.

Saturn, and it can be taken as certain that the oath was administered publicly, before the crowd.[48] In a period of frequent and contentious triumphs, this measure was not bureaucratic but an assertion of the principle of public accountability, in the most literal sense.

The year 62 is also notable for the clear evidence that three different types of elected officeholders could propose *leges* to the people: tribunes, praetors, and consuls. Any such proposals might be preceded by discussions in the Senate; but this was not a formal necessity, and even where the Senate had voted against a proposal (as with Metellus' proposal in relation to Pompey), the officeholder in question could still go on to recommend his proposal in *contiones* and to call the *comitia* to vote on it. The separation, or conflict, of fundamental functions is thus clearly displayed.

The law which was proposed by the two consuls of 62, L. Licinius Murena, whom Cicero had defended, and D. Iunius Silanus, the Lex Licinia Iunia, also related to the ordering of public life and the need for publicity. It concerned the rules for the passing of *leges* and is frequently referred to in sources relating to the 50s. But the only clearly attested provision relates not, as is often claimed, to deposition at the Aerarium of copies of *proposed* laws but to the need for a formal public procedure for the registration at the Aerarium of copies of *leges* after they had been passed. The law states "that it should not be lawful to lodge a *lex* in the Aerarium *secretly*."[49]

It cannot be emphasized too strongly that all functions of the *res publica* had to be carried out publicly, and were frequently accompanied by verbal or written explanations or information addressed to the people. This appears nowhere more clearly than in the steps that followed the eventual return of Pompey to Rome in the winter of 62/1. It was very soon required of him that he should deliver a *contio* to the people, all the more so because his opinion was sought on the constitution of a court to try Clodius over the desecration of the rites of Bona Dea; I will leave until later in this chapter the bare details of this issue, whose further stages provide some of the clearest reports of the conflict-ridden working of

48. See Val. Max. 2.7.1. For the *quaestores*, see briefly F. Millar, "The Aerarium and Its Officials under the Emperor," *JRS* 54 (1964): 33. Compare the provision in the *lex Latina Tabulae Bantinae* (line 4): "[i]ouranto apud quaestorem ad aerarium palam luci per Iovem deosque Penat[eis]" (Crawford, *Roman Statutes,* 1: no. 7, line 24).

49. *Schol.* p. 140 Stangl: "Licinia vero et Iunia, consulibus auctoribus Licinio Murena et Iunio Silano perlata, illud cavebat, ne clam aerario legem *in*ferri liceret." For other sources, see Rotondi, *Leges Publicae,* 383–84. See Suetonius *Div. Iul.* 28: "mox lege iam in aes incisa et in aerarium condita corrigeret errorem." Cf. n. 20 in this chapter.

popular politics in the Forum. Soon after Pompey's return, and in the early stages of the Bona Dea affair, Cicero reported as follows to Atticus in February of 61.

> As for what Pompey's first *contio* was like, I wrote to you earlier—no pleasure for the poor, empty for the disreputable, no satisfaction for the well-off, not serious in the eyes of the respectable. It met such a frosty reception. Then, at the suggestion of the consul Piso, that most frivolous tribune Fufius brings forward *[producit]* Pompey before the *contio*. The affair took place in the Circus Flaminius, and there was in that very spot on the same day a crowd attending a market. He [Fufius] inquired of him whether he approved of the idea that the *iudices* should be selected by the praetor to function as the jury over which that same praetor would preside—for that had been laid down by the Senate for the Clodian sacrilege case. Then Pompeius spoke in the most aristocratic style and replied that in all matters the *auctoritas* of the Senate seemed to him supreme and always had—and he went on at great length.[50]

This scene displays yet another example of the "production" of a major figure before a *contio* by a tribune and of such a figure's apparent obligation to answer questions put publicly to him. It goes without saying that this dialogue was not private but rather, by its nature, was intended to be audible to the crowd.

The significance of holding the *contio* in the Circus Flaminius is quite unclear. Occupying a fairly restricted site in the southern part of the Campus Martius, the Circus certainly bore no resemblance in scale to the Circus Maximus.[51] Nonetheless, *ludi,* including the *ludi plebei,* took place there, and a few scattered indications suggest that it could have been an accepted alternative to the Forum for meetings of the people; we shall see later a further example of this use of the Circus Flaminius from the tribunate of Clodius in 58 (see chap. 6). If the example involving Pompey is valid—and Cicero's report of a market going on there at the same time suggests a proletarian context all the more unsuitable for Pompey's grand style of speech—it is of some note. Given the size of the city, the absence of any mention of proletarian quarters, serving as a source of strength and a location for protest, is in many ways remark-

---

50. Cicero *Att.* 1.14.1–2 (14).
51. For all details, see *LTUR* 2, s.v. "Circus Flaminius."

able. Verbal persuasion and legislative activity—and in consequence violence—were quite remarkably focused on, and limited to, the traditional location of the Forum itself.

It must have been at a different *contio* that Pompey addressed the people and directed their attention to the strategic significance of his victories in the East, in particular of the acquisition of Syria: "he had received Asia as the most distant of provinces and had restored it to his *patria* as a central one [in the empire]." It may have been in the same speech that he claimed to have fought twenty-two kings and to have invariably both taken up and laid down his commands earlier than expected.[52] What matters here is not the boasts about military glory, which we would expect, but the act of reporting at a *contio* the significance of having acquired a province (Syria) that lay well to the east of the existing province of "Asia."

There were other long-term consequences of Pompey's conquests, and these too were demonstrated, this time in visual form, in the course of Pompey's triumph in October 61. Plutarch's *Life* gives the most detailed account.

> Inscriptions borne in advance of the procession indicated the nations over which he triumphed. . . . In addition to all this the inscriptions set forth that whereas the public revenues from taxes had been fifty million drachmas, they were receiving from the additions which Pompey had made to the city's power eighty-five million, and that he was bringing into the public treasury in coined money and vessels of gold and silver twenty thousand talents, apart from the money which had been given to his soldiers, of whom the one whose share was the smallest had received fifteen hundred drachmas.[53]

As to whether these complex figures really were laid out in such a way that they could be read and understood, we can only speculate. And, of course, this event does not constitute any proof that the bulk of the crowd could read at all. The function of the figures was to add to the general display precise information both about short-term booty and about long-term tribute revenues. In that sense the figures were, and were intended to be, both a reflection of the sovereignty of the *populus Romanus* and a demonstration of the services rendered to it by the imperator. It would

---

52. Pliny *NH* 7.27/99 (quoted here); cf. Orosius 6.6.4; Plutarch *Pomp.* 54.1.
53. Plutarch *Pomp.* 45, Loeb trans.

not be a gross oversimplification to see this event as a very precise fore-shadowing of the official ideology of the early imperial period.[54]

As I noted earlier in this chapter, the winter of 62/1 was marked also by the Bona Dea affair, which in itself was of modest significance, but which happened to bring out very revealing strains in the *res publica,* and also to give rise, in Cicero's letters, to descriptions of crowd politics that are perhaps fuller and more circumstantial than any others we possess. The public issue arose, as is well known, from the accusation that, during the rites of the Bona Dea in early December 62, which had to be conducted by women only, in the house of the Pontifex Maximus (now Julius Caesar), Clodius had been present, dressed in women's clothing. Over this issue, which the pontifices declared to constitute a case of sacrilege of public rites, Pompey was publicly questioned by the tribune Fufius and answered pompously that he supported the opinion of the Senate (as quoted above).

The Senate's proposal was that a bill *(rogatio)* should be put to the people, under which a praetor would be appointed to preside over a specially constituted *iudicium,* and would have the power to select the *iudices* himself. What happened next is recorded by Cicero in the same letter in which he had described Pompey's unimpressive appearance in the Circus Flaminius.[55]

When the day came for the *rogatio* based on the senatus consultum to be voted on (that is, after the usual *trinundinum*), young followers of Clodius were prominent in pressuring the people to reject it. The consul Piso, who had the task of speaking in favor of the *rogatio,* expressed (at best) so little enthusiasm that Cicero says he was really its opponent *(dissuasor).* The wooden gangways *(pontes)* erected in the Forum, along which each voter proceeded in order, with the purpose that he would be protected from undue influence, were occupied by hired groups of followers *(operae)* of Clodius, and the *tabellae* handed out to each voter did not include any that indicated support for the *rogatio* (U(ti) R(ogas), "as you ask"). What then follows is puzzling, for the voting procedure seems to have come to a halt while *contiones* were delivered; but the normal principle, as we saw earlier, was that *contiones* could occupy the time up

---

54. See F. Millar, "Imperial Ideology in the Tabula Siarensis," in J. González and J. Arce, eds., *Estudios sobre la Tabula Siarensis* (Madrid: Consejo Superior de Investigaciones Científicas, Centro Estudios Históricos, 1988), 11.

55. Cicero *Att.* 1.14.2–5 (14).

to the moment when the presiding magistrate instructed the people to divide into *tribus,* but that after that no further debate took place.[56]

In Cicero's account, Cato "flew" to the Rostra and delivered a speech of reproof directed at Piso (it hardly seems from this that Piso can have invited him). Cato was followed by Hortensius and "many of the *boni.*" At that point, Cicero says, the *comitia* were dismissed. (It appears that the legislative meeting had indeed started and had then been interrupted by *contiones.*)

The Senate then met and passed a further decree, by some four hundred votes to fifteen, instructing the consuls to urge the people to pass the *rogatio.* But the tribune Fufius vetoed this decree. It would be hard to find a better example of the ultimate constitutional weakness of the Senate, even when it displayed a high degree of unity. Whatever the Senate wished, it could only be translated into law by the voters outside in the Forum. They meanwhile were being addressed in *contiones* by Clodius, who was one of the *quaestores* of the year. His speeches were filled with attacks on major senatorial figures—Lucullus, Hortensius, C. Piso (the consul of 67)—and on one of the current consuls, M. Valerius Messalla.

Cicero returns to the story in a letter of summer 61,[57] in which he goes back to events in the spring and describes how Clodius had continued to deliver *contiones* designed to bring Cicero's name into disrepute. Cicero had replied in kind, and from what he says about the *clamor* and *concursus* that greeted his speeches in defense of the Senate, it is clear that these *contiones* too were public. But his campaign of resistance was thwarted by Hortensius' compromise proposal that the tribune Fufius should propose a *rogatio* that was the same as the consular one (which he had vetoed), except for the manner of appointing *iudices* (now apparently to be selected by lot). This *rogatio* evidently went through; a jury mostly made up (in Cicero's eyes) of unreliable and disreputable senators, *equites,* and *tribuni aerarii* took their seats, and the trial proceeded amid the shouting *(acclamatio)* of Clodius' supporters. On the first day, nonetheless, Cicero, when called as a witness, had some popular success: "there came to me on the next day as large a crowd *[frequentia]* as that by which I was escorted home when laying down my consulate."

The *iudices* asked for a guard *(praesidium)*—Cicero does not explain how or by whom such a guard would be constituted. But in the mean-

---

56. See chap. 2.
57. Cicero *Att.* 1.16 (16); see Alexander, *Trials,* no. 236.

time, so Cicero claims, the *iudices* had been bribed. Twenty-five voted to condemn Clodius, thirty-one to acquit him.

We are not in a position either to accept Cicero's interpretation of these events or to reject it. But we can reasonably see the structure of this sequence of events as a classic instance of the functioning of the *res publica* in the context of the open-air theater of the Forum: a legislative proposal approved by the Senate, which a tribune then vetoes; and a trial in the Forum, before a large public, where the jurors are exposed to rival forms of oratorical persuasion on the one side, and to crowd reactions on the other.

Cicero's letter continues by describing debates in the Senate and then returns to an appreciation of the political situation in terms of popular reactions, in a style that all too clearly reveals the tension between the need for popular support, on the one hand, and privately expressed contempt for the mob, on the other. He himself, he says, despite his testimony against Clodius, has retained the favor of "the filth and dregs of the city"; he also describes the mob, almost untranslatably, as the *contionalis hirudo aerarii* [the meeting-going bloodsucker of the treasury], whose view of himself was helped by the notion that he was high in the favor of Pompey: "in consequence, at the *ludi* and at gladiatorial shows, I have been receiving wonderful tributes without any [hostile] shepherds' whistles." Cicero's correspondence from the following years will show just how much importance was attached to these signs of popular favor or hostility, as well as what rhetorical use could be made of allusions to them in political contexts.

Cicero finally turns to the prospects for the consular elections for the year 60, showing, as always, that all expectations were a matter of rumor and speculation and that there was no reliable means of predicting the results. Pompey was believed to be supporting L. Afranius (who was indeed elected), as was the consul Piso, who was maintaining *divisores* in his house. Two senatus consulta on measures to combat bribery had been passed, but more significantly another tribune had promulgated a *lex* on bribery *(de ambitu),* and the *comitia* had been postponed. There is nothing to show whether this law was passed or not. But again what matters for our conception of the political system was the publicly visible rivalry and opposed policies of leading officeholders and ex-officeholders, on the one hand, and the unavoidable necessity of votes by the people, whether electoral or legislative, on the other.

The other essential feature of this period was the continued presence of the consuls in Rome through all or most of their year of office (see chap. 2), which only served to afford more opportunities for direct public confrontations over legislation. The year 61 had also seen Pompey's great triumph, following on that of Lucullus in 63, as well as unresolved problems over the ratification of his settlement of the eastern provinces and over land distributions for his troops. As the abortive proposal by Rullus in 63 had already shown, the new conquests in the East raised the stakes in Roman politics, both as regards what would now count as real military glory and as regards the assets available for the benefit of the *plebs urbana.*

While all these factors showed themselves much more fully in 59, when Julius Caesar was consul, there were already significant effects on the public politics of 60, when Q. Caecilius Metellus Celer and L. Afranius were consuls. Afranius, according to Cicero, played little role, but Metellus found himself in public opposition to measures proposed by two of the ten tribunes, L. Flavius and C. Herennius; neither came from a prominent family, and neither is attested in our evidence for earlier years.

Once again, the most coherent narrative of the conflicts of this year is presented by Cassius Dio.[58] On Dio's account, ratification of Pompey's arrangements was opposed by leading personalities in the Senate, both for personal motives and because the complex settlements that Pompey had reached properly deserved detailed examination. The tribune Flavius proposed a law that would have given land both to Pompey's discharged veterans and to civilians. A complex demonstration of ritualized conflict then ensued: Metellus opposed the law (which must mean that he delivered *contiones* against it); Flavius used his tribunician powers to have Metellus placed in the *carcer;* the Senate then tried to meet there; Flavius placed his bench across the entrance, and, given tribunician *sacrosanctitas,* that meant that no one could go through; Metellus then had a breach made in the wall, so that the senators could enter; at this, Pompey, fearing popular anger, told Flavius to desist.

The precise rationale of the story is not entirely clear, unless in fact Metellus' speeches against the law had been likely to carry a majority. He was at any rate certainly not the only senator who addressed the people on this issue. For Cicero records that he himself spoke at a *contio* in partial support of the law, while trying to limit its effects. His report deserves to be quoted, for it is an exceptionally clear reflection of the way

---

58. Dio 37.49–50.

in which, as in the case of the *rogatio* of Rullus in 63, quite complex issues of personal rights and financial policy not only could be but had to be rehearsed before the people.

> An agrarian law was vigorously promoted by the tribune Flavius, at the instance of Pompey, but one that had nothing *popularis* about it except its supporter. From this proposal, I, with a favorable reaction from the *contio,* proposed to remove all those provisions that involved disadvantages for private persons. I proposed to exempt that land that had been in public ownership in the consulship of P. Mucius and L. Calpurnius [133]; to confirm Sulla's settlers in their holdings; to keep in occupation the people of Volaterrae and Arretium, whose land Sulla had made public but had not divided out; one provision I was not for rejecting, namely, that land could be bought with these adventitious sums that can be raised over the next quinquennium from new indirect revenues.

Cicero goes on to explain that preservation of private property was his overriding aim but that he had intended to satisfy both the *populus* and Pompey with the provision for the purchase of land: "if that were arranged with care, I thought both that the dregs of the city could be cleared out and that empty areas of Italy could be populated."[59]

Speaking to the people three years earlier, Cicero had adopted a quite different posture, warning them of how much they would lose if they allowed themselves to be taken out of the city and given lots in the countryside, and accusing Rullus of using in the Senate expressions very similar to his own in this letter (see the discussion of the *rogatio* of Rullus earlier in this chapter). We can be certain that in this year also such expression formed no part of the speech that he addressed to the people. Precisely because so much ultimately depended on persuasion (or other forms of pressure) directed to the people in the Forum, there was a marked tension between what might be said in a private letter or a private conversation, in political dealings between leading personalities, or in speeches in the Senate, on the one hand, and what might be said in the oratory of the *contio,* on the other.

The letters of this year do indeed show Cicero as deeply concerned about opinion within the Senate, over the question of a newly arisen

---

59. Cicero *Att.* 1.19.4 (19).

military crisis in Gaul, over satisfaction of Pompey's demands, and over the request by the tax contractors *(publicani)* for a reduction of the payment due from them for the revenues of Asia. He alludes to the elections, including the candidature of Julius Caesar, who had returned prematurely from Hispania Ulterior to stand for the consulship. One of his letters of December 60 also illustrates with perfect clarity the undeniable influence of lateral political connections among senators. For he records how he was visited by Balbus, an associate of Caesar, who was shortly to enter on his consulate, who said that Caesar would follow the advice of Cicero and Pompey in everything, and would also try to reconcile Pompey and Crassus. Such was the beginning of the coalition sometimes known, quite misleadingly, as the First Triumvirate. It was a product of circumstances, an attempt by one of the two incoming consuls, Caesar, to win over some of the leading ex-consuls. Cicero in fact declined the proposal that he should collaborate. But he already knew, as he records in the same letter to Atticus, what the major issue at stake would be: a *lex agraria*, which he would have to resist firmly, accept passively, or—as people said that Caesar expected—actually support.[60] It follows that it was already public knowledge before the end of the year 60 that a *lex agraria* would be proposed in the new year and that this time the proposer would be not a tribune, like Rullus, but one of the two consuls. Suetonius later recorded that the Senate, following the normal procedure, had already made the allocation of *provinciae* for the prospective consuls—who turned out to be Caesar and Bibulus—and that they had deliberately selected *provinciae* to which no prestige was attached.[61] If that report is correct, it might also have been expected that the legislative rights of the tribunes of 59 would be deployed once again to overrule the allocation and to create an appropriate field for the winning of military glory. But, whatever was already foreseen, Roman popular politics was about to enter a new phase and, with that, to embark on the last decade in the history of Rome in which major decisions would depend on the votes of the people assembled in the Forum.

---

60. Cicero *Att.* 2.3.3–4 (23).

61. Suetonius *Div. Iul.* 19.2: "opera ab optimatibus data est, ut provinciae futuris consulibus minimi negotii[, id est silvae callesque,] decernerentur." It is debated whether the words in brackets are original or were added (with or without good reason) by a commentator.

VI

Empire, Legislation, and Political Violence, 59–56

It has never been doubted that the consulship of Julius Caesar and M. Calpurnius Bibulus in 59 marked a decisive phase in the history of the late Republic. But it may nonetheless be worth stressing how clearly it brought out various features emphasized in this study. First, there is the late-Republican "politicization" of the consulship, in the literal sense that the consuls now stayed in Rome throughout all or nearly all of their year of office, rather than acting during most of it as military commanders. Second, there are the overt conflicts between the two consuls, as there also are between members of the "college" of ten tribunes, a feature that clearly emphasizes the way in which elected officeholders functioned in public as individuals, not as members of a "government." Third, there is an essentially novel feature, the presentation of controversial social legislation by a consul. It is very significant that, as we saw in chapter 5, the fact that there would be conflict over a *lex agraria* was generally known before the consuls entered office on January 1, 59. That is not to say that this prospective legislation had played any part in any "election campaign" by Caesar—his claims are more likely to have rested on his lavish displays as aedile in 65, his *popularis* stance in winning the position of Pontifex Maximus against more senior competitors in 63, his role as praetor in 62, and his recent campaigns as propraetor in Lusitania, for which he claimed a triumph that he abandoned to enter the city and stand for the consulship. It should, however, be stressed that the same letter of Cicero that shows that a *lex agraria,* proposed by Caesar, was anticipated shows that the political coalition sometimes misleadingly labeled the First Triumvirate was being put together by Caesar *after* his election and very shortly before he entered office (see chap. 5).

Above all, however, the year 59 illustrates, first, how major issues relating to the empire were debated in public and were decided by popular voting in the Forum. These issues concerned the disposition of the empire, the use of the massive revenues accruing from it, and the prospects for future military glory. Second, almost everything that happened in 59 did so, as it seems to us (given that we rely almost entirely on Cicero's testimony), not only against the will of the leading senators *(principes)* but via constitutional procedures that effectively brushed the Senate aside. It was in the open air, in the Forum, that the decisive political confrontations, and the decisive votes, took place, and there (paradoxically) that the novel steps were taken which within a decade sealed the fate of the classical Republic. As was to be the case throughout the 50s, physical domination of the Forum became a crucial weapon in politics. There is every reason for us to see this as an indication of the degradation of a Republican structure with very marked democratic features. It should, however, be stressed how precisely political violence was indeed focused on the Forum, and how closely it related to the ancient right of the citizen to vote on legislation in person.

From the point of view of the modern observer, the first half of the 50s is exceptionally rich in material that explicitly debates the values inherent in the Republican constitution, the rules that regulated (or should have regulated) conflicts between officeholders, and the proper vehicles for the expression of the popular will. Here, above all else, we find the now acceptable *popularis* legislation of the past being set against its disreputable and destructive contemporary equivalents. The evidence concerning Cicero's exile in 58 and his return in 57 also offers a whole range of points of view adopted by Cicero or attributed by him to others, just as do his public criticisms of P. Vatinius, the most influential tribune of 59, and above all the speech in defense of P. Sestius, tribune in 58, which Cicero delivered in 56. By now Cicero's views had shifted decisively to defense of what he conceived of as the established order, deserving support from all respectable elements in society. His testimony is priceless— but only if we read it as public persuasion functioning as one element in a complex public debate.

As is the case with the previous decade, a step-by-step narrative of events in the 50s is not always available and, insofar as it is, is offered primarily by Greek narratives written in the imperial period. No attempt to follow all the political events of the year in sequence will be made here, and the treatment in this chapter will emphasize those episodes that particularly illuminate the rapidly changing nature of the political scene, as well as the conflicting values that informed it.[1] As we have seen already, all contemporary material, even when embodying a narrative of events, simultaneously expresses a point of view or an interpretation.

Caesar's consulship began with the proposal of an agrarian law, which he first attempted, unsuccessfully, to have discussed and approved in the Senate. It seems to have been in this context that he threatened to have Cato, who spoke against the law, led out of the Curia by a lictor and taken to the prison *(carcer)*.[2] Here, as always, we have to remember the topography, and the public, open-air context, of any such symbolic step. The Curia stood on the edge of the Forum, and the process of publicly conducting someone from there to the *carcer* involved a walk of some forty meters (see the plan on p. 40). Such an act of imprisonment was a ritual that involved a purely symbolic use of force. Its purpose was to demonstrate the nature of political disagreement before the people.

It was now that Caesar turned to the people, proposing his legislation directly to them without a previous senatus consultum. What is striking about the political procedures deployed at this point, and at a series of other moments in the year, is the particular use made of the *contio:* the setting up of public dialogues, conducted before the people, whose function was to bring out the attitudes and positions of the main actors. As with so many aspects of the use of oral pronouncements in the Forum, it is easy to suppose that only very small numbers can really have heard or appreciated what was said. But in fact these public statements of position are regularly commented on by Cicero, even in cases when he had not been present in person, and they also enter the biographical and narrative record. Unlikely as it may seem, these oral statements of position—often offered unwillingly—did play a real part in contemporary perceptions.

Dio, indeed, on whose narrative of the early part of 59 we have to depend, states clearly that Caesar's first public step was to question his fellow consul Bibulus before a meeting, as to whether he approved of the agrarian law. When Bibulus replied in the negative, Caesar tried to persuade him (that is, he will have made a speech addressed formally to him but audible to the *contio,* beseeching him to agree—and also urging the people to join in this supplication). Bibulus' response, so Dio records, was

1. For an excellent recent treatment of Roman politics in the 50s, see T.P. Wiseman, "Caesar, Pompey, and Rome," in *CAH*[2] 9, *The Last Age of the Roman Republic, 146–43 B.C.*, ed. J.A. Crook, A. Lintott, and E. Rawson (Cambridge: Cambridge University Press, 1994), 368–423.

2. See Suetonius *Div. Iul.* 20.4; Dio 38.3.

to shout out to the people, "You will not have this law this year, not even if you all want it!"[3]

In form, this three-way exchange closely resembles a pattern we have seen on a number of occasions already, by which *tribuni plebis* "produced" (the verb used is *producere*) persons before a *contio* and invited or compelled them to explain their position before the people.[4] Whether the element of compulsion rested on tribunician rights (thus being parallel to the symbolic right to lead officeholders, even consuls, to the *carcer*) or was merely a matter of moral pressure exercised in public is not quite clear. At any rate this form of public exchange can be found on many occasions in the 50s. This instance, however, must belong in a rather different category, for the two parties are the consuls of the year, who are evidently sharing the tribunal.

Public role-playing and the importance of the public explication of legislative proposals through the medium of speeches addressed to the people are very marked features of Dio's excellent account of political exchanges in the early part of 59, on which we have to depend until contemporary observations restart in April or May, in the form of Cicero's letters. According to Dio, Caesar chose not to address public questions to any of the other elected officeholders of the year, for fear of provoking a similarly negative answer. Instead, he turned to the two prominent ex-consuls of 70, Pompey and Crassus, whose support, as we have seen, he had made efforts to attract just before entering office (see chap. 5). Dio notes that, formally speaking, both ex-consuls were *privati;* but the invitation to them to speak was designed both as a public honorific gesture and as a means of impressing public opinion. Pompey duly made a speech in favor of the agrarian law, going over every feature of it in detail, as Dio says. (We may recall similarly detailed expositions in relation to Rullus' agrarian bill of 63.)[5] Caesar asked him, clearly in public, for his support against the opposition "and urged the people to join in asking for his help." Pompey spoke again and was followed by Crassus.[6] If we are to understand the nature of Roman public life, it is not possible to exaggerate the significance of these exchanges. There is, first, the public, persuasive rehearsal of the content of legislation; second, the

3. Dio 38.4.2–3.
4. See chaps. 3–5.
5. See chap. 5.
6. See Dio 38.4.4–5.5 (the source for the quotation in text). For Pompey's *contio,* see also Plutarch *Pomp.* 47.

encouragement of the crowd not just to listen but to become a party to such exchanges; and third, the fact that such exchanges, even if literally audible only to a few hundred people at most, did affect public opinion more widely and did subsequently enter the historical record.

At this point, according to Dio's narrative, Bibulus took the extreme step of proclaiming a *iustitium* for the rest of the year, with the effect that no public business could properly be transacted. Caesar nonetheless gave the normal notice of the proposal of his agrarian law. When the day arrived for voting on it, the crowd that supported it occupied the Forum the night before, and Caesar began the proceedings by making a speech from the podium of the temple of Castor. Bibulus, with a body of supporters, forced his way through the crowd and up onto the podium, where he attempted to speak against the bill. As he was thrown off the podium, his fasces were broken, and he, the tribunes who supported him, and his other followers suffered injuries. The ominous pattern of the following years, in which so much would depend on physical domination of the Forum, was already manifest.[7]

It was at this point, after a last attempt to persuade the Senate to take action, that Bibulus retired to his house for the rest of the year, and responded to all subsequent legislative proposals by issuing *edicta,* whose contents were also delivered to Caesar by Bibulus' *apparitores,* stating that the unfavorable omens for which he would be watching rendered public proceedings invalid.[8]

Dio's account of the 50s is in fact a remarkable achievement, a clear and forceful narrative that manages to incorporate a considerable proportion of the significant details that we can glean from the extensive contemporary evidence, which itself amounts to no coherent account of the sequence of events. He could not, however, given the economy of his massive history of Rome, catch everything. From Dio, for instance, it would appear only that Vatinius, one of the pro-Caesarian tribunes of the year, intended, at this stage, to have Bibulus placed in the *carcer,* but was prevented by some of his colleagues.[9] It should be noted that, according to Cicero, of the ten tribunes of this year, two had taken a strongly *popularis* position, three had taken a not at all ("minime") *popularis* one, and the others, by implication, had been hostile.[10] Cicero's words repre-

---

7. See Dio 38.6.1–3.
8. See Dio 38.6.4–6.
9. Dio 38.6.6.
10. Cicero *Sest.* 53/113.

sent a convenient demonstration of the disparate positions that could be taken up by a college of ten persons, elected at the same time by the same procedure. The attitude that would be adopted by each might on occasion be known, or rumored, in advance; but it could only be put to the test by being publicly demonstrated in the course of his year of office.

In the case of Vatinius, we happen to know from Cicero's speech interrogating him during the trial of Sestius in 56, that while Bibulus was still functioning in the Senate, Vatinius had used the archaic rules that governed the conduct of public life on the Forum to carry through an attempt to take the consul to the *carcer* and to prevent his own tribunician colleagues from interposing a veto. The scene that Cicero describes relies on the positioning of the tribunes' bench, which was placed outside the Curia, and under the third-century painting known as the *Tabula Valeria,* which hung on its outside wall; past it the ritual procession would have to go, on its very short journey to the *carcer:*

> When you were leading him, the consul, into imprisonment, and when from the *Tabula Valeria* your colleagues were ordering his release, did you not, by joining up the *tribunalia,* construct a "bridge" in front of the Rostra, through which a most moderate and constant consul of the *populus Romanus,* with *auxilium* cut off, his *amici* shut out, with the violence of depraved men aroused, was led, as a most shameful and wretched spectacle, not merely to the *carcer* but to punishment and death?[11]

Pons (bridge), as used here, can hardly mean a complex structure raised above ground level, over the top of which Bibulus was led; the implication is rather that wooden benches were joined up ("continuatis") so that the non-*popularis* tribunes on their bench could not physically intervene to have Bibulus released. As Coarelli observes, nothing could more clearly demonstrate the archaic nature of the rules governing public life.[12] If the tribunes could not physically lay hands on the person whom they wished to release, their attempts to bring *auxilium*—which evidently were made, but only vocally—would be ineffectual.

This act of imprisonment, which clearly did take place, equally clearly did not lead to the drastic effects implied by Cicero. Bibulus was soon

---

11. Cicero *Vat.* 9/21. See the plan of the Forum on p. 40.
12. See Coarelli, *Foro,* 2.53–54.

released, and at some later stage he withdrew formally to his house, intervening subsequently only by issuing written material.

This episode is unique in Republican history but nonetheless does cast some light on the workings of politics. It would cast even more if only our evidence supplied a little more topographical detail. There is nothing to indicate even the approximate location of Bibulus' house. Nor is it clear whether the *edicta* and the texts of his (presumably earlier?) *contiones* which Bibulus posted up publicly were displayed, like other written material, in the Forum (see chap. 2), or outside his house, or somewhere else. All that is clear, from two letters of Cicero's to Atticus, written in the summer of 59, is that these texts attracted a high level of popular attention. We know from the use made of them later by Suetonius that they included observations on Caesar's career and abusive allusions to his earlier homosexual relations with the king of Bithynia and to his present aspirations to kingship for himself, all of which no doubt increased their popular appeal.[13] At any rate, Cicero claims in his first letter that Bibulus enjoys huge popularity and that people "copy down and record his *edicta* and *contiones.*"[14] In his second letter, also of course concerned to make the most of signs of popular hostility toward Pompey, Cicero reveals that the effect of the *edicta* had been such that in late July, Pompey had held a *contio* about them.

> I could not hold back my tears when on July 25 I saw him address-
> ing a public meeting *[contionantem]* about Bibulus' *edicta*. He who
> previously had been accustomed to preen himself so magnificently
> in that very place, with the most profound affection of the people,
> with all in support of him—how humble, how dejected he was;
> how he displeased not only those present but himself also![15]

Cicero goes on to say that one could not get past the place where the *edicta* were put up, for the crowd of persons taking pleasure in reading them. The location must, by implication, have been a prominent spot, somewhere in the political center of the city. Like other evidence, it shows that there was a substantial literate public for political material that was made available in written form, without of course providing any proof of what proportion of the voters could read a continuous text. Cicero also

---

13. Suetonius *Div. Iul.* 9, 10, 49.
14. Cicero *Att.* 2.20.4 (40).
15. Cicero *Att.* 2.21.3–5 (41).

refers to Caesar, in what seems to have been a different *contio,* trying to persuade his hearers to attack Bibulus' house. It is implied that they knew where it was, as was true of the houses of most leading figures (even if we do not). But although Caesar's words were highly seditious (and therefore calculated to be popular), he had not been able to evoke any sound in response. However tendentious Cicero's words may be, they still reflect the volatility and unpredictability of popular reactions and the possibility of an absence of reaction, accentuated of course by the fact that, unless a *contio* was organized in advance, the speaker could not know who would be present.

For the sequence of events during this momentous year, which profoundly altered the political map of Rome, we can, but to a surprisingly limited extent, follow the main lines through the contemporary evidence of Cicero's letters, primarily those to Atticus. The actual passage of the *lex agraria* is illustrated only by the later account in Plutarch's *Life* of Cato the Younger (32), in which he records how Cato spoke from the Rostra against the law and was ordered off to the *carcer* by Caesar. The Senate followed him in a public display of shame, and public reaction was such that Caesar had to persuade another tribune to perform the necessary formal act of bringing "help" and having him released. By May, it is clear that this first *lex agraria* had been followed by a second, which took the revolutionary step of including the Ager Campanus, the vast stretch of land in Campania that had been Roman public property since the Second Punic War and whose rents Cicero regarded as one of the ultimate safeguards of the financial stability of the *res publica*. This view appears in a letter of late April or early May. Cicero has evidently just heard of this new proposal and is profoundly shocked.[16] We need not follow the details, except to note that a letter of Cicero's to Atticus, written in June, makes clear both that there had been by now more than one *lex Iulia* relating to *ager publicus,* that one of them was labeled for convenience the *lex Campana,* and that a public oath, reminiscent of the historic conflicts of the year 100, was required of all current candidates for office. Once again, it is necessary to stress the significance that the *contio* could have, namely, that of a passive act of witnessing the performance of a legal duty. Cicero says that in the current atmosphere, there was general despair.

For the *lex Campana* includes a clause requiring a curse *[exsecratio]* to be pronounced on themselves before a *contio* by candidates [for

---

16. Cicero *Att.* 2.16.1 (36).

office in 58], if they were to make any proposal to the effect that land might be held under any conditions other than those under the *leges Iuliae.* The others do not hesitate to swear, but Laterensis is regarded as having taken an admirable step in giving up his candidature for the tribunate rather than take the oath.[17]

Once again, it should be noted that indications of what political posture candidates might take up and what concrete proposals they might make formed a normal aspect of their self-presentation during the elections. It was precisely for that reason that the device of imposing the condition of a publicly accepted and binding reticence was so effective.

What reports we have of wider public reactions in this period are to some extent mutually contradictory. In his following letter to Atticus, Cicero claims that Bibulus was highly popular and Pompey in disgrace; at the *ludi Apollinares,* lines spoken in the theater could be understood as referring to Pompey—e.g., "to our misfortune, you are Magnus"—and were greeted with loud applause, while Caesar's entry was met with silence and that of Curio (the son of the Curio who was consul in 76) with great enthusiasm.[18] The significance of this last point is explained by Cicero's claim in his previous letter that, in the general state of fear and oppression, the *adulescens* Curio was the only one to speak ("loquitur") and offer open opposition: "For him there is great applause and extremely favorable greetings in the Forum *[consalutatio forensis perhonorifica].*"[19] The way that Cicero expresses this popular favor seems to imply the making of public speeches in the Forum. If the occasions for Curio's opposition were really political speeches at *contiones,* it should be noted that Curio was young, in his early twenties, and would not hold the quaestorship until the later 50s, and the tribunate until 50 (see chap. 7). But Cicero's words are also compatible with the possibility that Curio's "opposition" was expressed in the form of comments on the current political scene that were made in the course of advocacy in the Forum. In either case, the acute sensibility of contemporaries to the overtones of speech and reaction in the Forum hardly needs to be stressed.

The major step taken in 59, which in effect determined the course of events for the rest of the 50s and, in the longer term, the end of the Republic itself, was the law passed by Vatinius, Caesar's chief supporter

17. Cicero *Att.* 2.18.2 (38).
18. See Cicero *Att.* 2.19.3–4 (39).
19. Cicero *Att.* 2.18.1 (38).

among the ten tribunes of the year, by which the *provincia* of Gallia Cisalpina and Illyricum was given to Caesar, thus overriding the senatorial dispositions made in the previous year (see chap. 5). Its constitutional significance is brought out clearly by Cicero in his interrogation of Vatinius in 56, which refers to what Cicero takes to be an even more scandalous innovation, namely, the authorization by the *populus Romanus* of the selection of the *legati* by Caesar.

> You had [already] snatched from the Senate the power to allocate a *provincia*, the choice in selecting an imperator, the disposition of the *aerarium*, which the *populus Romanus* never sought for itself, since it never attempted to transfer to itself the direction of the highest policy. Well, some of these things have been done in other cases. It is rare, but it has happened, that the *populus* might choose an imperator. But who ever heard of *legati* [nominated] without a senatus consultum?[20]

Cicero thus refers to an aspect of central decision-making functions that the Senate did regularly carry out, namely, the allocation of forces and funds to provincial commands and the approval of the list of *legati* selected by the governor. These functions had now been taken by the people. But even here, he passes over the further constitutional innovation embodied in the *lex Vatinia*, namely, that the double *provincia*, with three legions, was voted to Caesar for five years. It is not necessary in this context to go into the process (which itself hardly fits with any previous procedure) by which the Senate later added Gallia Transalpina, with one further legion, with momentous and unforeseen consequences.

Though Plutarch's *Life* (33) claims that Cato spoke against the law and warned the people—with entire justification, if indeed the report is true—that they were establishing a tyrant in their own citadel, there is a complete absence of contemporary evidence on the passage of this *lex*. A much more detailed picture is, paradoxically, available of events in the Forum in relation to a quite minor and insignificant event, the claim that someone called Vettius, perhaps inspired by Bibulus (and Cicero and Cato?), was going to attempt the assassination of Pompey (and perhaps also of Caesar). The truth of the matter is undiscoverable and of no importance. But the procedures adopted are revealing. According to a

---

20. Cicero *Vat.* 15/36.

letter from Cicero to Atticus, an examination of the alleged facts was first conducted in the Senate. Then the resultant senatus consultum was read out *in contione.* On the next day, Caesar "produced" *[produxit]* Vettius on the Rostra, and Vettius held forth at length, giving a somewhat different version from before. Cicero's account breaks off at the point where Vettius is due to stand trial on charges of violence ("de vi").[21]

What is relevant here is the evident need for any complex political affair to be explored in public before the people. This appearance by Vettius seems in fact not to have been his only one, for Cicero comes back to this episode also in his interrogation of Vatinius. As tribune, Vatinius had evidently proposed a *rogatio* relating to this affair.

> Were you not a man of such cruelty that you tried to remove and destroy, by your *rogatio,* distinguished men and *principes civitatis,* when you produced before a *contio* L. Vettius, who had confessed in the Senate that he had been equipped with a weapon and had intended to kill with his own hands Cn. Pompeius, a most eminent and famous citizen? You thus placed [Vettius] on the Rostra, on that inaugurated *templum* and place, I may say, on which, as a function of the exercise of their authority, the other *tribuni plebis* have been accustomed to produce *principes civitatis*—there you wished that that informer Vettius should offer his tongue and voice in the service of your criminal purpose. And did not L. Vettius, in that *contio* of yours, when interrogated by you, declare that he had had as his promoters, backers, and associates in that crime just those men after whose removal from the state—which was what you at that moment were seeking—the state could not stand?[22]

By implication, Cicero's characterization of Vatinius' conduct reflects an established norm, whereby the "production" on the Rostra of leading citizens was accepted as being an aspect of the public function of the tribunes. Whether their appearance was in each case willing or unwilling, the underlying notion was that the health of the political system required that they should explain themselves and their views on current issues of policy.

In the meantime, Clodius had had his transfer from the status of *patricius* to that of *plebeius* put through by Caesar as consul and had then been elected tribune for 58, while Gabinius (the former tribune of 67) and

---

21. See Cicero *Att.* 2.24.3 (44).
22. Cicero *Vat.* 10/24.

L. Calpurnius Piso had been elected to the consulship. Whereas the year 59, despite its crucial importance, happens to offer us less evidence for exchanges in the Forum than we might expect, 58, the year of Clodius' tribunate and of Cicero's exile, as well as of the consulship of the two men whose record Cicero was to attack in both *In Pisonem* and *De provinciis consularibus,* provides far more material. Toward the end of 59, however, two episodes do vividly illustrate the public conduct of communal affairs and the shift of power that had happened over the last few years.

In November or December, and hence long after the consular elections, Cicero describes how the young C. Porcius Cato had attempted to prosecute Gabinius for electoral bribery *(ambitus);* the situation thus precisely reflects that of the prosecution of Murena in late 63 (see chap. 5). What Cicero reports comes in a single paragraph of a letter to his brother, Quintus.

> We have completely lost the *res publica,* to the extent that Cato, a young man of no judgment, but still a Roman citizen and a Cato, has scarcely escaped with his life. The reason is that, when he wanted to prosecute Gabinius *de ambitu* and, over a period of several days, the *praetores* could not be approached and would not make themselves available, he mounted [the Rostra] for a *contio* and called Pompeius a *privatus dictator.* He could not have come closer to being killed—and from that you can judge the state of the *res publica.*[23]

It was apparently from this attempted prosecution *de ambitu* that, according to Cicero, Gabinius later boasted that he had been rescued by hired gangs *(operae).*[24] These very brief reports should not be taken as clear evidence that, against all known precedent, Cato had simply mounted the Rostra and begun to speak, without being "given" a *contio* by a current officeholder. But they are obviously evidence for the fact that physical force could now be deployed to prevent the delivery of *contiones* whose content was unwelcome.

Another episode of late 63 was also, and much more closely, replicated at the end of 59. According to Dio, Bibulus now emerged from seclusion in his house and entered the Forum with the intention of adding to his

23. Cicero *Q.f.* 1.2.15 (2); see also his *Sest.* 8/18.
24. Cicero *Sest.* 8/18.

end-of-office oath a speech about the present state of affairs. But Clodius (already in office for some three weeks) vetoed the speech.[25] Once again, it would seem from Dio's words that the taking of the oath itself could not be vetoed. Bibulus does not seem to have followed Cicero's device of expanding the text of the oath itself to form a brief self-justificatory oration (see chap. 5).

Only a few salient points from the wealth of material for the year 58 need to be stressed here. It is in effect from 58 that we first have extensive and consistent evidence for the organized use of violence to put through legislation or to disrupt courts of law. The events of the year inevitably form the main focus of the speeches that Cicero delivered after his return in 57, as they do of his *Pro Sestio,* delivered in 56. In this speech, Cicero produces his most systematic account of the recruitment of supporters throughout the city and of organized efforts to dominate the Forum. As was noted earlier (see chap. 2), we can dimly perceive here a relationship between events in the Forum and the vast mass of population in the different quarters *(vici)* of the city. But we gain no impression of which quarters or of their social structure. As is true throughout, the existence of a huge urban population that *might* be mobilized has always to be remembered. But its political action is visible only when it shows itself, or is persuaded to show itself, on the public stage of the Forum. With one rather slight exception, to which I will return in a moment, most of the city of Rome is politically invisible. All political organization and activity was directed to the Forum.

This new phase in Roman political life is evoked twice by Cicero, in slightly different rhetorical forms. The first comes in the form of an address to Clodius contained in Cicero's *De domo sua,* a speech delivered in 57.

> When on the *tribunal Aurelium* you were openly enrolling not only free men but even slaves called up from all the *vici,* to be sure you were then not preparing violence! When by your *edicta* you were ordering the *tabernae* to be closed, you were aiming not for the violence of the ignorant mob but for the modesty and prudence of respectable men! When you were having weapons carried into the temple of Castor, you had of course no end in mind other than that of preventing anything being done by force! When you tore down

---

25. Dio 38.12.3.

and removed the steps of (the temple of) Castor, you then aimed to bar rash men from access and ascent to the temple, in order that you might be able to conduct business peacefully! When you instructed to present themselves those who, at a meeting of decent men, had spoken about my restoration, and [when you] broke up the presentation of their case with blows, weapons, and stones, then, to be sure, you demonstrated your intense dislike of violence![26]

The same physical context, namely, the eastern end of the Forum, where the *quaestiones* now sat (see chap. 2), is reflected also in Cicero's words in the *Pro Sestio* of the following year, 56.

> With those same consuls looking on, the recruitment of slaves was carried out in front of the *tribunal Aurelium* in the name of the *collegia,* while *vicus* by *vicus* men were being conscripted and enrolled into units *[decuriarentur]* and were being incited to violence, to blows, to murder, to looting. Under the same consuls, weapons were being openly carried into the temple of Castor, the steps of the same temple were being torn up, armed men were controlling the Forum and the *contiones* . . . [27]

While the setting and the events that Cicero is alluding to in each oration are clearly the same, it is noticeable how he picks out different features in each of the two speeches (the presence of the consuls or the role of the *collegia*). It is of course an immense gain to have testimony that is charged with the meaning that events had for participants. But, at the same time, no such utterance can be taken merely as a *description*. In the speeches, above all, such representations are persuasive evocations, exploiting the associations and expectations that can be presumed on the part of their hearers.

That said, it remains significant that the quite extensive evidence for the political life of the Forum over the previous two decades contains no earlier allegations of a comparable level of organization in the deployment of force. We can never assess the significance of voting in the Forum for the vast mass of the urban population or (in reality) know which social groups were represented there or by what channels the involvement of some was organized. But it would be hypercritical not to accept that

26. Cicero *Dom.* 21/54.
27. Cicero *Sest.* 15/34.

with 58 we do reach a new phase in the organization of efforts to control voting. Yet that focus of organizational effort also demands emphasis. The organization of force was narrowly focused, in a topographical sense, precisely because it was about voting on legislation.

New legislative acts were indeed a fundamental feature of the politics of 58. Without examining all the details, which are not the central concern of this study, we can note, for instance, Dio's typically efficient summary of the legislation put forward by Clodius as tribune: the establishment of a free corn distribution; the restoration of the legal status of *collegia;* a restriction on the rights of the censors; and another restriction on the power to prevent the conduct of public business by observing, or claiming to have observed, unfavorable omens.[28] Given the relatively limited scope of government and politics in the ancient world, these were far-reaching (and, in the case of the free corn distributions, very long-lasting) measures, which represented a coherent set of ideological positions and touched on the nature of the *res publica* and of the exercise of power within it.

So, equally, did the next measure of which Dio speaks, namely, the legislative steps that led to the exile of Cicero. Initially, these steps took the form of the enforcement of a constitutional principle, the denial of civil rights (or "interdiction from fire and water") of anyone who had put to death a Roman citizen who had not been formally condemned. Between, on the one hand, the later Greek narratives of Appian, Plutarch, and Dio that tell the whole story of the events leading up to Cicero's departure from Rome but inevitably do so from a distance and, on the other, the tendentious allusions to episodes from this context provided by Cicero himself, the only contemporary source, it is not worth trying to reconstruct a precise sequence of the events or to determine the positions taken up by contemporaries. What is relevant is the clear evidence that the issue of Cicero's responsibility for the execution of the Catilinarian conspirators in December 63 was the subject of open debate at *contiones.* For instance, Cicero recalls how Clodius, addressing the crowd at a *contio,* had said that either Cicero must perish or he would have to be defeated all over again. The anecdote belongs in a passage where Cicero declares that he could have resisted only by evoking physical violence.[29]

---

28. Dio 38.13. For a more detailed, contemporary survey, bringing in other legislative acts of Clodius, see, e.g., Cicero *Sest.* 25/55–26/56.

29. Cicero *Sest.* 19/43: "cum quidem in contione dixisset aut mihi semel pereundum aut bis esse vincendum." See more generally 19/43–44 for the context.

On other occasions, Clodius had claimed to the people in *contiones* that his campaign against Cicero had the support of Pompey, Crassus, and Caesar.[30] On another, Gabinius as consul had been "produced" by Clodius at a *contio* held in the Circus Flaminius. As we saw earlier, in chapter 5, this location is perhaps the only one in Rome of which our (very slight) evidence might serve to suggest that it functioned as an alternative focus for popular gatherings, distinct from the Forum. Cicero's recall of this occasion in the speech that he delivered in the Senate after his return in 57 does not lack the rhetorical color that one would expect.

> But when he [Gabinius] first stepped forward before a *contio* in the Circus Flaminius, not like a consul *productus* by a *tribunus* but a pirate chief summed by a brigand, what a man of *auctoritas* he seemed! Reeking of wine, slumber, debauchery, his hair perfumed and his locks carefully arranged, his eyes heavy and his cheeks limp, in a voice that was constricted and trembling, this weighty authority declared that, to him, the fact that the execution of citizens who had not been condemned had been carried out was gravely displeasing.[31]

Behind the personal abuse lies the real importance held for the public life of the Forum by the image and style (both in appearance and in manner of speech) of the major actors; the significance attached to their attitudes, or alleged attitudes; and the fact that a major constitutional issue really was at stake. The same issue had after all been raised in 63 (see chap. 5): did a vote by the Senate calling on officeholders to take all necessary steps to prevent damage to the *res publica* serve to override the standing rule that only a legally constituted court could condemn a citizen to death?

Gabinius evidently addressed the same issue on at least one other occasion, on which (it seems) he had not been *productus* by anyone else. On this occasion, Gabinius had said that he would seek to punish the *equites Romani* who had assembled to protect the Senate when it met in December 63 to vote on the execution of the conspirators. Even "his man" Catiline, Cicero comments, if he had come back to life, would not have dared to say that.[32]

After Cicero had left Rome, a *rogatio* specifically naming him and declaring him an exile (that is, as forbidden to come within four hundred

---

30. See Cicero *Sest.* 17/39–40.
31. Cicero *Post red. in Sen.* 6/13.
32. Cicero *Post red. in Sen.* 5/12; see also 13/32 and *Sest.* 12/28.

Roman miles of the city) was put to the people and passed, while his house on the slopes of the Palatine was destroyed and a shrine to Libertas was erected on its site. The assertion of popular sovereignty is perfectly exemplified in the fact that one clause in the *rogatio* formally forbade any discussion of the matter in the Senate; Clodius put the text on the doorpost of the Curia itself.[33]

I will come later to complex steps taken in the last months of 58 to try to repeal the *lex* passed against Cicero. For the moment, it will be more significant to observe how the public arena was the scene, perhaps more explicitly than ever before, for the expression of competing ideologies. The forced departure of Cicero and the erection of a shrine of Libertas on the site of his house represented one view of the situation. Cicero, of course, looking back after his return, saw these actions as a sign of mass violence and as the exercise of tribunician tyranny. For a start, public power had invaded the realm of private property. Then there was the question of the deified personification of Liberty, on which Cicero expatiates in the speech about his house that he delivered before the pontifices. As elsewhere, in this passage he is notionally addressing Clodius.

> But what goddess is this? She ought to be the Bona Dea, since she was dedicated by you. "Libertas," he says. So you have placed on the site of my house her whom you have removed from the whole city? You, when you deny that your colleagues, invested with the highest power, were free men; when access to the temple of Castor was open to no one; when this most distinguished man . . . you order in the hearing of the *populus Romanus* to be trodden on by your footmen; when you exile me, uncondemned, by the imposition of tyrannical *privilegia;* when you keep the leading man of the whole world [Pompey] shut up in his house; when you occupy the Forum with armed bands of desperadoes; when you are establishing a statue of Libertas in that very house that itself was the symbol of your most cruel domination and of the most wretched servitude of the Roman people?[34]

On the one hand, in this representation of the dominance of force in Rome as it was in 58, we can see the recurrence of traditional sites, the Forum and the temple of Castor; on the other, as we already have seen,

---

33. See Cicero *Att.* 3.12.1 (57), 3.15.6 (60).
34. Cicero *Dom.* 42/110.

we can accept that the organization of force to control communal spaces reached a new level in these years and, furthermore, that political violence now extended to effect the houses of prominent politicians, whether Cicero's, somewhere on the north side of the Palatine, or Pompey's, a little further north still, in the district called the Carinae.

In the case of Cicero's house, its destruction followed a formal public act. In that of Pompey's, we see how the incitement of the crowd in the Forum did lead to consequences that there had never been any effective means to prevent, but that, by an unspoken social convention, had not in earlier periods come into effect. The houses of the leading citizens had always tended to occupy areas not far from the Forum, so that these individuals had high visibility and could easily proceed from their homes, normally with a large band of followers, to perform their functions in public (see chap. 2). But we do not find, in earlier periods, that public discourse in the Forum led to threats to, or even real physical effects on, the prominent houses in its neighborhood. So it turns out to be, however, in the earlier 50s. Cicero later recalls Clodius saying at a *contio* that he would like to build another portico in the Carinae, to match that on the Palatine, in the area of Cicero's house. Pompey took this as a threat and remained in his house in a state of siege. This siege at some point became quite literal; armed guards under the command of Damio, a freedman of Clodius, are recorded as having besieged the house and cut Pompey off from public life.[35]

In this period, conservative elements began to organize a rival deployment of force, notably on the part of T. Annius Milo, whom Cicero would later defend (unsuccessfully) in 52, on a charge of murdering Clodius (see chap. 7). This organization of force too could of course be denounced publicly as an affront to tradition and communal order. Cicero records how Vatinius had been *productus* before the people by Clodius and had complained that Milo was using gladiators and wild-beast handlers *(bestiarii)* to besiege the *res publica*.[36]

The conduct of the different elements of Roman public life in fact depended absolutely on the observance of limits and on an unspoken acceptance of norms of conduct. Just as there never had been any systematic means by which the crowd in the Forum could have been prevented from attacking houses in the neighborhood, so the parallel exercise of different functions within the Forum itself also depended on the

---

35. See Asconius 46–47C.
36. Cicero *Vat.* 17/40.

acceptance of limits and conventions. Thus, Cicero, in his interrogation of Vatinius, speaks with particular force of the fact that Vatinius, accused before one of the praetors of 58, not only had appealed to the tribunes but had thereby evoked the physical breaking up of the court over which the praetor had been presiding. For this sequence of events to be intelligible, it has to be recalled that the bench of the tribunes will have been easily within sight of the area at the east end of the Forum where the *quaestiones* sat (see chap. 2). Cicero emphasizes that it was unheard of that Vatinius, when summoned to court by the praetor Memmius, should have appealed to the tribunes to prevent the trial taking place.

> I ask you, Vatinius, whether any defendant in this *civitas* since the foundation of the city has appealed to the *tribuni plebis,* so as to avoid standing trial, whether anyone has mounted the *tribunal* of his judge and thrust him off by force, has scattered the benches, thrown down the urns [for voting tablets]—in short, committed in the course of breaking up the court precisely all those offenses that are the reason why courts have been set up. Are you aware that Memmius then fled, that your accusers had to be rescued from the hands of yourself and your followers, while the *iudices* of the *quaestiones* were driven away from the neighboring *tribunalia?* In short, that in the Forum, in daylight, with the *populus Romanus* looking on, a *quaestio,* the magistrates, ancestral custom, the laws, the *iudices,* the accused, the penalty—all were subverted?[37]

Within the context of an undeniably increased level of violence, however, the business of the *res publica* continued, even if, in content, as well as in the methods used, the legislation that was passed represented a sharp break with the established order. So, for instance, as regards the allocation of *provinciae,* the pattern established in 59 was repeated. The Senate must have decreed *provinciae* in advance for the two consuls, but whatever these dispositions had been, they were again set aside by tribunician legislation put forward by Clodius, which gave Macedonia to Piso and gave Cilicia, for which Syria was then substituted, to Gabinius. It is easy to overlook the significance of this latter step. Syria had been acquired as a province only a decade earlier. This was the first time that this command became consular, and the proposal voted on by the people

---

37. Cicero *Vat.* 14/33–34.

in the Forum reflected a decisive change in the strategic shape of the empire. The dispatch of Crassus to Syria three years later (also by popular legislation; see the discussion later in this chapter) inaugurated centuries of Roman military concentration on the eastern frontier.

If we may judge from Cicero, contemporaries were more conscious of the political and constitutional aspects of the votes. In the *Pro Sestio*, Cicero represents the two consuls Piso and Gabinius as having made a pact with Clodius as tribune, by which, in return for handing over the *res publica* to him, they would get whatever *provinciae* they wanted, along with the relevant funds and armies: "there were promulgated at one and the same time, by the same *tribunus, rogationes* concerning my destruction and about the *provinciae* of the consuls by name."[38] It was of course precisely that, the allocation by name of a *provincia* to a particular magistrate, that the use of *sortitio* had been designed to prevent (see chap. 2).

Cicero's is, however, not quite the only point of view available to us for the legislation passed in 58. The damaged text of a bilingual inscription from Delos records how the two consuls, speaking from the podium of the temple of Castor, proposed to the people a law on the privileges of the island. The text of the law contains grandiloquent references to the suppression of piracy under the *lex Gabinia* of 67, to the *dignitas* and *maiestas* of the *populus Romanus,* and to the extension of the empire and the achievement of peace throughout the world, all of which reflects a conception of present circumstances and a form of current rhetoric infinitely removed from those found in Cicero's speeches.[39]

The empire of the *populus Romanus* was indeed in the process of amplification in this year, not only through the initial campaigns of Julius Caesar in Gaul, but in the concrete form of the acquisition of the minor Ptolemaic kingdom of Cyprus. Caesar of course owed his command to tribunician legislation that not only overrode both the previous senatorial determination of the consular *provinciae* and the subsequent allocation of them by lot but granted him the command for five years (as mentioned earlier in this chapter). His was thus very precisely an *extraordinaria potestas*. It is therefore very striking both that tribunician legislation in 58 was deliberately used to bring the acquisition of Cyprus into a comparable category and that Caesar allegedly wrote from Gaul to congratulate Clodius on the success of this constitutional device. For the person to

---

38. Cicero *Sest.* 10/24–25; cf., e.g., his *Post red. in Sen.* 7/18.
39. See C. Nicolet et al., *La loi gabinia-calpurnia de Délos (58 av. J.-C.)* (Rome: École française de Rome, 1980); Crawford, *Roman Statues*, 1: no. 22.

whom Clodius' *lex* entrusted the mission to Cyprus was Cato the Younger, one of the most prominent opponents of personal grants of exceptional powers. More than that, the connection between the demands of successful imperialism and expansion and the need to override the normal rules for the exercise of individual power was made quite explicit in speeches delivered to the people. For Clodius read out at a *contio* what was alleged to be a letter from Caesar congratulating him on the success of this constitutional device. Cicero's words on this event, recorded in his *De domo sua,* are notionally addressed to Clodius.

> By your *rogatio* you conferred on this man office and command irregularly *[extra ordinem]* and by name *[nominatim].* Moreover, you were so unrestrained that you could not conceal the rationale of this criminal act of yours. For you read out at a *contio* a letter that you said had been sent to you by Gaius Caesar . . . [and in which] he congratulated you on removing Marcus Cato from your tribunate and on depriving him for the future of the freedom to speak about *extraordinariae potestates.* As for this letter, either he never sent it to you, or, if he did, he did not wish it to be read out *in contione.*[40]

According to Cicero elsewhere, Clodius himself openly declared, in this or another *contio,* that he had "torn out the tongue" from Cato.[41] Whether the letter from Caesar was genuine or not, the connection between imperialism and constitutional change was made absolutely explicit.

However great were the changes brought about by the organized use of violence, the functioning of the inherited constitution remained a serious issue, and the open public discussion of its rules and procedures remained a prominent feature of communal political life. We can see these aspects very clearly, for instance, in two episodes reported from the closing months of 58.

According to Cicero, as Clodius' tribunate was drawing to a close, he suddenly took up the issue of the observance of unfavorable omens and the standing rule that if such omens were observed, public business could not continue; under this rule, any legislation passed under these circum-

---

40. Cicero *Dom.* 9/21–22. For a detailed treatment of this episode and of the appointment of Cato as *pro quaestore* to this mission, see E. Badian, "M. Porcius Cato and the Annexation and Early Administration of Cyprus," *JRS* 55 (1965): 110.

41. Cicero *Sest.* 28/60: "in contione palam dixerit linguam se evellisse M. Catoni."

stances was invalid. As Cicero can hardly fail to observe, Clodius' posture in favor of this rule was paradoxical, because it would imply the invalidation of his own transfer to plebeian status in 59 and hence of his election to the tribunate. What concerns us in this context, however, is not the complexity of Roman religious law but the form in which these issues were brought out before what appear to have been at least two separate *contiones* of the people, one held by Clodius, and one held by his brother Appius Claudius Pulcher, who happened to be praetor. Cicero describes the procedure as follows.

> You, when your tribunate was declining and enfeebled, suddenly emerged as the *patronus* of the *auspicia;* you "produced" M. Bibulus, as you did the *augures,* before a *contio;* in response to your interrogation, the *augures* replied that when the sky was being watched [for omens] business could not be conducted with the *populus.* In response to your question, M. Bibulus replied that he had watched the sky. He himself also said *in contione,* when *productus* by Appius, your brother, that, because you had been adopted despite the *auspicia,* you had not become *tribunus* at all.[42]

This drastic conclusion was not in practice drawn, any more than anyone seriously set out to act on the assumption that the entire legislation of Julius Caesar as consul in 59 was invalid. It is still very significant for present purposes that the device of public question and answer, before a *contio,* was used to expose the rules that were supposed in principle to govern Roman public life. Once more, it is important to stress that such exchanges, which cannot have been literally audible to more than a few hundred people at most, nonetheless did become generally known and did form part of the material of political and constitutional argument in subsequent years.

An equally complex constitutional issue arose when toward the end of October 58, eight of the ten tribunes of the year began a series of measures designed to lift the sentence of exile passed on Cicero. They faced a particular problem in that Clodius' legislation had incorporated a clause making it illegal to reopen the question. But could any such clause in fact bind the sovereign people? Or did a subsequent law abrogating a previously passed one thereby serve to abrogate any such clause, if the earlier

---

42. Cicero *Dom.* 15/40; cf. his *Har. resp.* 23/48.

law contained one?[43] Once again, we may concentrate on the successive public steps taken in late 58, rather than on constitutional niceties. Cicero was, naturally enough, following the issues closely from the other side of the Adriatic, and he reported on them in a letter to Atticus of November 29. On October 29, the eight tribunes had promulgated a *lex* made up of three clauses, which must mean that they posted up copies in public (see chap. 5). Whether they held *contiones* on the subject is not stated, though Cicero records (as he also does later in a speech after his return) that they had spoken about it in the Senate. Clodius at any rate commented on the constitutional aspect at a *contio* on November 3, specifically in regard to the position of the tribunes-designate (due to enter office on December 10). Rival drafts of another law had already been prepared for use by two of these incoming tribunes, Fabricius (or Fadius?) and P. Sestius. Once again, very technical constitutional matters were being exposed, in writing and in speech, before the people, and only they, if anyone, could vote Cicero a restoration of his citizen status and validate his return. Not surprisingly, Cicero urges Atticus to do whatever he can, even to the extent of deploying a "bought crowd" *[comparata multitudo]*.[44] Not until the following year, however, did Cicero's supporters find a means of arranging a popular vote for his return.

The year 57, as it is represented in our sources for the conduct of political life in the open air, could be divided into three phases: continued debate and combat over proposals that Cicero should be restored from exile; the celebrated vote of the *comitia centuriata* which we have encountered already (see chap. 2), and which marked Cicero's triumphal return; and very vividly described episodes from the last quarter of the year in which the question of the general corn supply (and not only the now established free monthly distributions) gained an unprecedented prominence and also served to underline the weakness of the Senate in the face of popular demands. To characterize the year, as far as it offers distinctive evidence for popular politics, in these very personalized terms is of course to emphasize that what is offered here is not a "history" of Rome or of the *plebs Romana* but a selection of some of the images and reports that our very full but very one-sided evidence happens to make available. What is available is heavily biased by Cicero's inevitable concern with his own fortunes and by the fact that in the following year, he defended

---

43. On this issue, see Ph. Moreau, "La rogatio des huit tribuns de 58 av. J.-C. et la clause de sanctio réglementant l'abrogation des lois," *Ath.* 67 (1989): 151.

44. Cicero *Att.* 3.23.1–4 (68); see also his *Post red. in Sen.* 2/4.

Sestius, who as tribune in 57 had been his most prominent supporter. Cicero's *Pro Sestio* has to be regarded as the most important and consistent expression of the "optimate" or conservative interpretation of Roman politics. Though the use of any terms that have a connotation in modern politics inevitably tends to distortion, it is in fact not a distortion to characterize the ideology of the *Pro Sestio* in this way. For its fundamental propositions are, first, that the health of the *res publica* depended on respect for established institutions, the Senate above all; and, second, that the "good" or "respectable" people *(boni)* were those persons, of any social class, who did value and support these institutions.

The expression of this position, especially when it takes place in the context of a defense of the role of one of the ten tribunes in a particular year, necessarily leads Cicero to offer detailed propositions on popular opinion, of a highly partial kind, as well as to present very detailed representations of scenes from public life. We may begin with Cicero's evocation of the enthusiasm generated by the appearance of Sestius at a gladiatorial show given by Metellus Scipio to mark the death of his adoptive father, Q. Metellus Pius. As was stressed earlier, it was a crucially important characteristic of Roman public life that a wide variety of events took place, on no clearly regulated timetable, in the same physical space, the Forum. It was in this space that the *populus Romanus* played a variety of roles, from idle spectating to the exercise of their sovereign rights as voters. To convert the Forum for a gladiatorial *munus,* all that was needed was to line it with barriers, *cancelli* (for theatrical *ludi,* in contrast, an actual temporary wooden theater might be constructed). This was the context which Cicero chooses to represent as a better indicator of popular opinion than the *contiones* which might occupy the same space.

> But the most decisive judgment of the whole *populus Romanus* was manifested by the crowd at a gladiatorial show; for there was a *munus* given by Scipio, worthy both of himself and of that man, Q. Metellus, for whom it was being offered. It was indeed the form of *spectaculum* that is attended by a whole crowd and every rank of men, and in which the multitude takes the greatest delight. At this meeting, there appeared P. Sestius, *tribunus plebis,* who while occupying that magistracy concerned himself with nothing except my cause. He arrived and showed himself to the people, not out of desire for applause, but in order that our enemies themselves should witness

the will of the whole *populus*. He made his entry, as you know, from the Columna Maenia. So great a burst of applause was stirred up from every vantage point, right down from the Capitol, so great a burst from the *cancelli* of the Forum, that it was commented that there had never been any greater or more open expression of the consensus of the entire *populus Romanus* regarding any cause.[45]

We need not doubt that Sestius was indeed applauded when he appeared on this occasion. But what his motives were and what part thoughts of the exiled Cicero played in the minds of the people were (and are) a matter of speculation. All that is certain is that no actual propositions were being put to the people to vote. Moreover, as is always the case, "the people" remains for us an anonymous crowd, whose social and political composition is unknown.

Cicero of course felt the need to defend his claim that the true public opinion was that which could be expressed through applause for an individual officeholder, rather than that manifested at properly political assemblies, whether *contiones* or *comitia* for voting. The first claim to make was therefore that in fact more people came for a gladiatorial *munus* than for such political gatherings; hence expressions of the popular will there were more significant. The next step was to argue both that *contiones* were now conducted in an improper manner and that those who turned up at them had been hired to do so. This characterization applied to the *contiones* held by Clodius' brother, Appius Claudius Pulcher, as praetor in 57.

But indeed that praetor, who, in the manner not of his father, grandfather, great-grandfather, in short, of all of his ancestors, but following the custom of mere Greeks, used to interrogate the *contio* concerning me, as to whether they wished me to return, and when he received a shout in response, from the half-dead voices of hired men, used to declare, "The *populus Romanus* says no!"—that man, when he went each day to see the gladiators, was never spotted at the moment of his entry. He used to emerge suddenly, after creeping under the planks.[46]

45. Cicero *Sest.* 58/124. For the physical context, see, e.g., G. Ville, *La gladiature en Occident des origines à la mort de Domitien* (Rome: Ecole française de Rome, 1981), 380–81.

46. Cicero *Sest.* 59/125–26.

It is clear enough from this passage that the question of Cicero's possible restoration was a very visible public issue, that the positions taken up in relation to it by current officeholders were well known, and that *contiones*—sometimes involving explicit questions designed to evoke a response from the crowd—were delivered before the people.

Discussions of this issue had indeed begun (or continued from the previous year) immediately at the beginning of January. A long stretch of narrative in the *Pro Sestio* vividly portrays the sequence of events, both in the Senate and out in the Forum.[47] On the first of January, Cicero says, there was a crowded meeting of the Senate, high expectations among the *populus,* and a gathering of ambassadors from all of Italy; as I noted earlier (chap. 2), the citizenship of Italy could now be expressed not only in individual voting but via the dispatch of *legati* by local communities. A debate was held in the Senate, evidently followed by others. Finally, on February 25, the day came for the proposal of a bill *(rogatio),* put forward by one of the tribunes, Q. Fabricius. The new conditions in which the passing of legislation functioned are perfectly illustrated by the fact that he took the precaution "to occupy the *templum* [the Rostra]" some time before dawn. But Cicero's opponents, so he says, had forestalled him, in the middle of the night filling the Forum, Comitium, and Curia with armed men, most of them slaves. These men then made an attack on Fabricius and his entourage, killing some and wounding others. When another *tribunus,* M. Cispius, was entering the Forum, they drove him off. In the middle of general violence, Cicero's brother, Quintus, evidently reached the Rostra, in order to beg the people for Cicero's return; but he was thrust off the Rostra and lay injured in the Comitium, covered by the bodies of freedmen and slaves, and eventually escaping under cover of night.

Cicero goes on later to contrast this victory of brute force with the formal methods that might have been used to thwart Fabricius' proposal: an announcement of the observation of unfavorable omens, *intercessio* by a colleague, or actual votes *(suffragia).*[48] But the issue had never been allowed to come to a vote. The contrast is important, because Roman political life had always functioned via the independent, and often opposed, actions of different elected officeholders, exercising their functions in public. But it thereby depended on the presumption that the mass of citizenry would not be incited, or organized, into physical intervention.

47. See Cicero *Sest.* 33/72–35/77.
48. Cicero *Sest.* 36/78.

Even after this attack on Fabricius, Cicero claims, Sestius, whom he was defending on a charge of public violence *(vis),* had not resorted to organizing armed followers. On the contrary, on an occasion that was evidently that of the proposal of a *lex* by one of the consuls in the Forum, he had approached the temple of Castor to announce the observation of unfavorable omens. At that point a *Clodiana multitudo* had assaulted him, using swords, rods, and bits of the *saepta*—the barriers put up to channel the voters of the thirty-five *tribus.* Sestius was left for dead. Only then, Cicero implies, had Sestius, like Milo, turned to the organization of gangs of followers to meet force with force.[49]

It is against this context, of public violence and of the alleged hiring of men to attend *contiones,* that Cicero presents his admittedly partial analyses of how popular opinion could be expressed and explicitly defends the steps taken by both Sestius and Milo to meet force with force. Nonetheless, the device that was finally used to bring about a vote that would restore Cicero was to shift the context of popular voting, both in a constitutional and in a topographical sense; that is to say to revive the rarely used power of the *comitia centuriata* to pass legislation (see chap. 2) and, with that, to transfer the place of voting to the Campus Martius. Thereby there will have come about also, of course, a substantial change in the composition of the voting groups. For, whereas there was no social hierarchy within the thirty-five *tribus*—and, as we have seen (chap. 2), it is also quite likely that the "rustic" tribes were in practice largely "represented" in voting by individuals who had migrated to Rome and its neighborhood—the *centuriae* of the *comitia centuriata* voted in an order determined by census ratings. This principle of priority is explicitly defended by Cicero in his *De re publica* (see chaps. 2 and 8), and it certainly will have played a major part in the decision by his allies in Rome to use this procedure. But what is stressed by Cicero in his numerous allusions to the moment of his triumphal return is not this social change but the participation of voters from all over Italy. The two factors are of course connected, since it can be accepted without specific testimony that the better a man's social position, the fewer were the barriers to his making the journey to Rome to vote.

This highly unusual concurrence of voters from outside Rome was brought about by a senatus consultum, moved by one of the consuls, P. Cornelius Lentulus Spinther, which laid down, in Cicero's words, "that

---

49. Cicero *Sest.* 37/79–39/84.

all those from all over Italy who wished for the salvation of the *res publica* should assemble for the restoration and defense of myself."[50] It is notable that it was only when that *incredibilis multitudo* had arrived that Spinther called another meeting of the Senate, which this time assembled on the Capitol. The other consul, so Cicero says, laid aside personal hostility to support the motion also; and the Senate voted for Cicero's return by 417 votes in favor to 1 against. For any modern scholar who is tempted to believe in the secure domination of the Senate over the workings of Roman politics, the next step is of very clear significance.

> And on that day on which you [the Senate] had delivered your judgment, in most serious terms and at great length, to the effect that it had been my measures [in 63] that had saved the *res publica,* that same consul saw to it that on the next day those same things should be said *in contione* by the *principes civitatis*. On this occasion indeed, he himself argued my case most eloquently and brought it about, with all of Italy standing there and listening, that no one heard the harsh voice of any hired or disreputable person, or of one hostile to the *boni*.[51]

In short, on this occasion, the leading figures in the Senate had roused themselves to bring to bear on a *contio* in Rome the overwhelming physical presence of large numbers of conservative-minded citizens from Italy; or, to put the same step in different terms, they had for once taken to their logical and practical conclusion the potential effects of the extension of voting rights to all of Italy. Cicero recalls, for instance, how Pompey, in person, had issued appeals to all of Italy and had intervened in particular to evoke support in the newly founded *colonia* of Capua, in which he himself was holding a magistracy. But he had also spoken both before the Senate and before the people, to defend Cicero's record, and to implore their support for his return.[52]

The same sequence of events is recalled by Cicero in the *Pro Sestio* also, with some different details. Which features of an episode will be referred to or given special emphasis depends on the current purposes of the speaker. Taking a look at two different rhetorical accounts of the same events, by the same speaker, is therefore quite instructive, and offers

---

50. Cicero *Post red. in Sen.* 9/24.
51. Cicero *Post red. in Sen.* 10/25–26.
52. See Cicero *Post red. in Sen.* 11/29; cf. *Post red. ad Quir.* 7/16.

a salutary reminder that in seeking evidence about "what happened," we are participating in a debate among contemporaries as to how events ought to be understood. In the *Pro Sestio*, Cicero brings out how many of the *principes* were "produced" before the people to speak in his favor. It is also here that he makes his most loaded contrast between the normal, disreputable *contiones*, where those present had been paid to attend, and almost any other form of popular gathering. We should not fail to miss the boldness of Cicero's claim that the standard form of political meeting was precisely the only form of gathering that did *not* give expression to the true opinion of the people.

Cicero's text marking the contrast between the disreputable *contiones* of the last few years and those that Lentulus Spinther had held as consul needs to be quoted in full. He begins with the disreputable *contiones*.

> At the present moment, unless I am mistaken, the state is in such a condition that, if you remove from it the gangs of hired men, all seem likely to have the same opinion on the *res publica*. For there are three contexts in which the judgment and will of the *populus Romanus* on public affairs can be most clearly expressed: at a *contio*, at *comitia*, and when they come together for *ludi* and *gladia-tores*. What *contio* has there been over these years—at any rate one that was not hired but genuine—at which the consensus of the *populus Romanus* could be perceived? Many *[contiones]* on the subject of myself were held by that most criminal gladiator [Clo-dius], to which no decent person came, no person of integrity. No respectable person could bear to set eyes on that foul countenance or hear that raging voice. Those *contiones*, made up of depraved men, were inevitably turbulent.[53]

Cicero then turns to the quite different character of the *contiones* held by Lentulus Spinther.

> P. Lentulus as consul held a *contio* about that same person, myself. A gathering together of the *populus Romanus* was brought about, and all the *ordines*, all of Italy, stood together in that *contio*. He pleaded his case with the greatest gravity and fullness of expression,

---

53. Cicero *Sest.* 50/106. The argument seems to me to require that the word *non* should not be supplied: "Quae contio fuit per hos annos, quae quidem esset non conducta, sed vera, in qua populi Romani consensus perspici <non> posset?"

in so great a silence, with such approval on the part of all, that it seemed that nothing so *popularis* had ever fallen on the ears of the Roman people.[54]

Cicero then speaks of the other *principes* who came forward, or were "produced," to speak for his cause.

Cn. Pompeius was *productus* by him [Lentulus] and offered himself to the *populus Romanus* not only as the proposer of my restoration but even as a suppliant. His speech was grave and pleasing, as always in *contiones,* but I venture to assert that no opinion of his was ever marked by greater *auctoritas,* nor his eloquence by greater attractiveness. In how great a silence were the other *principes civitatis* heard when they spoke on my behalf![55]

Cicero says that he will not mention all of the speakers but will make one exception.

I make an exception at this point only of the *contio* delivered by that same *inimicus* of mine (the other consul, Metellus Nepos) about me, before the true *populus,* in the Campus Martius.[56]

It is clear, therefore, that the context for some, and probably all, of these *contiones* was the Campus Martius. It is therefore all but certain that they were delivered immediately before the people reassembled into their *centuriae* to vote. Once again it is clear that the notion that the voting of the Roman people took place without persuasion or debate, while formally correct, fails to take into account the fact that *contiones* could be delivered immediately before the voting process began. Although, in general, rival *contiones* could indeed be held, at which opposed views on prospective legislation could be, and were, expressed, and although persons "produced" before *contiones* by the presiding officeholder might express themselves in a way contrary to the overall tone of the meeting, we could reasonably still decline to characterize even these exchanges as open debate. Furthermore, as in the case in question, the vote for Cicero's return, a *contio* held immediately before the formation of the voting units

54. Cicero *Sest.* 50/107.
55. Cicero *Sest.* 50/107–8.
56. Cicero *Sest.* 50/108.

(in this case *centuriae*) would have been held by the officeholders putting forward the legislation. Its function would therefore have been, as in this case, persuasion and the expression of solidarity, rather than debate.

This rather rare example of the delivery before the crowd of a whole series of speeches in which the *principes* successfully expressed unanimous sentiments designed to lead the people in a particular direction is described even more concretely and explicitly by Cicero in the speech he delivered to the people after his return. Once again, different details are selected for emphasis. Cicero records here too that (after the consul) Pompey spoke first and was followed by others.

> At that same time and from that same place, you [the people] heard the leading men—the most honored and prominent men, the *principes civitatis,* all the ex-consuls, all the ex-praetors—say the same thing, so that it was established by the testimony of all that it had been through me alone that the *res publica* had been saved. So when P. Servilius, a most weighty man and most distinguished citizen, had said that it was by my efforts that the *res publica* had been handed on safe and sound to the magistrates who succeeded me, the others spoke in the same vein. But you heard at that time not only the authoritative opinion of a most distinguished man, L. Gellius, but also his testimony. For, since he had [in 63] almost caught wind of a move to affect the loyalty of the fleet that he commanded, with great consequent danger to himself, he said in your *contio* that if I had not been consul when I was, the *res publica* would have been completely destroyed.[57]

It is hardly surprising that Cicero takes the opportunity in the *Pro Sestio* to emphasize the contrast between the act of legislation that secured his return and others, with an aside implying that sometimes not enough people turned up to represent their *tribus:* "We often see many *leges* being passed. I leave aside those that are carried in such a way that barely five people are found to cast their vote [in each tribe], and those from a different *tribus.*"[58] It may well be true, in the case either of uncontroversial formal acts of legislation or of ones where the exercise of force frightened most voters away, that sometimes very small numbers of voters presented themselves. The significant aspect of the vote of the *comitia centuriata* in

---

57. Cicero *Post red. ad Quir.* 7/17.
58. Cicero *Sest.* 51/109. See p. 36 above.

57 is, however, not that contrast but the way in which, for once, the *principes civitatis* did indeed succeed in mobilizing support and presenting a united front—and thus, for a moment, living up to the image of the secure hegemony of the Senate over the people that modern commentators have imagined. It was achieved by the mobilizing of voters from all over Italy. If similar efforts to tap the potentialities of the new situation created by the enfranchisement of Italy after the Social War had been continued, who can now say what the effects might have been?

Even in this vote of 57, however, everything depended on persuasion— first the encouragement of people to come, then rhetorical persuasion addressed to them at the *contio*. Behind that, as Cicero's words also make quite clear, lay also the physical domination of the voting space, achieved by (for once) bringing large numbers of like-minded persons from elsewhere in Italy to Rome. Though this vote represented a major (and temporary) change in *political* direction, the underlying constitutional structure that it reflects was—just as much as in the case of any *popularis* vote—an expression of popular sovereignty.

The fragility of this brief hegemony achieved by the *principes* was demonstrated very clearly in the later months of 57, after Cicero's triumphal return. Disturbances may even have begun in July, if Asconius is right to attach to the *ludi Apollinares* a report of how a mob of lower-class persons burst into the theater (or rather, as it will have been in 57, a temporary theater) and caused all the spectators to flee. The motivation that he gives is the high price of corn *(annonae caritas),* and it may be that Asconius has mistaken the *ludi* concerned.[59] For very detailed contemporary accounts from Cicero reflect similar disturbances, for the same motive, at the *ludi Romani* in September. These episodes, to which we now turn, are very significant in various ways: in illustrating the vitality of Roman public life; in demonstrating the power of the *plebs urbana,* except in the very rare circumstances when conservative forces from Italy were organized; and in showing how the violent demands of the plebs had immediately advanced beyond the arrangement of a free monthly distribution of corn, to cover measures for the protection of the supply of corn for purchase in the market.

A series of letters from Cicero to Atticus enables us to follow the march of events in the autumn of 57 with considerable precision. It is relevant to note that these are private letters, not public speeches, and

59. See Asconius 48C. For the possible confusion, see the commentary by B.A. Marshall ad loc.

that they are recording events that Cicero found profoundly distasteful. It is ironic that the series begins with the letter in which, in the first part, Cicero describes the vote of the *comitia centuriata* in August, his own triumphal return, the enthusiastic crowd that greeted him in Rome, and his own speech in the Senate in early September. Then the mood and the context change abruptly.

> On those two days, when the price of corn was very high and people had rushed together, first to the theater and then to the Senate, and, instigated by Clodius, were shouting that the shortage of corn was my fault, and when during those days a meeting of the Senate was being held on the corn supply and, in the talk not just of the *plebs* but even of the *boni*, Pompey was being called on to take over responsibility for it—and he himself sought this—and the multitude was demanding of me by name that I should propose this [in the Senate], I did so and expressed my opinion in detailed terms. Although the *consulares,* other than Messalla and Afranius, were absent, claiming that they could not give their opinion in safety, a senatus consultum was passed following my opinion, to the effect that negotiations should be opened with Pompey to persuade him to take on this task and that a *lex* should be passed. When this senatus consultum was immediately read out, and when the mob, in their foolish newfangled style, had applauded by chanting my name, I held a *contio*. This was afforded me by all the magistrates who were present, except one praetor and two *tribuni plebis*.[60]

Nothing could illustrate more clearly how the Senate could find itself operating under direct popular pressure, and how the results of their deliberations could have to be announced immediately and be embodied in a *lex* to be passed by the people.

Cicero goes on to discuss different drafts of the proposed *lex,* which were put forward in the Senate by the consuls, on the one hand, and by one of the tribunes, on the other (the tribune's would have given Pompey greater funds and wider powers). For our purposes, the significance of this last report is simply to underline again the fundamental fact that the Senate was not a parliament; it could pass decrees, but it could not legislate. Drafting took place in the context of discussions there, and

---

60. See Cicero *Att.* 4.1.4–6 (73); the passage quoted is from 4.1.6. See also Cicero *Dom.* 3/5–12/31 and Dio's account of the same events (39.9).

whatever was eventually proposed in a *rogatio* before the people could not be emended in public debate; it could only be accepted or rejected there. But it was only by the people that legislation could be passed.

Cicero's next two letters to Atticus turn to the complex question of the legal and practical steps that were necessary if the site of his house was to be freed of the shrine to Libertas that Clodius had had placed there and if the house itself was to be rebuilt. The exchanges that Cicero describes in his letter to Atticus of early October again show a complex interplay between deliberations among privileged groups, on the one hand, and speeches to the crowd and their reactions, on the other.

First, a meeting of the pontifices declared that the dedication of the shrine had not been authorized by a vote of the *populus* or plebs and was consequently invalid. Then Clodius was given by the praetor, Appius Claudius Pulcher, the opportunity to address a *contio*. According to Cicero, he told them (falsely) that the pontifices' verdict had been in his favor and that Cicero was attempting to gain repossession of the site by force; he urged them to follow him and protect their Libertas. It does not seem that any action followed.

After further meetings of the Senate, a decree for the restoration of the neighboring portico of Catulus (and, by implication, of Cicero's house) was passed, and the consuls gave out the contract for this work, which involved the destruction of Clodius' new portico.[61] Some weeks later, Cicero returns to the story in a letter to Atticus written on November 23. Violence had now begun to play a central part. On November 3, an armed gang, operating on Clodius' orders, had attacked the workmen rebuilding the portico of Catulus, had torn it down when it was nearly up to roof level, and had set fire to Cicero's brother's house next door. What then followed shows a new feature in the evolution of political violence, its extension to draw in prominent private houses that were not affected (like Cicero's) by legal measures.

Cicero was attacked when going down the Sacra Via and retreated into a private house. Clodius then attempted to storm and burn the house of Milo on the Cermalus (the area on the northwest side of the Palatine and hence very near the Forum). An armed group then emerged from another house of Milo's situated on the slope of the Capitol and killed some of Clodius' followers.

Cicero's narrative then turns back to constitutional moves, which now

---

61. See Cicero *Att.* 4.2.1.–5 (74).

revolved around public steps to prevent the holding of the elections for aedile, at which Clodius was a candidate. Very significantly, the measures involved the posting up of written material (the proposal by Marcellinus as consul-designate that trials relating to all the issues concerned with Cicero's house should be held before there were any elections); Milo's announcement that on all days on which elections could be held, he would watch the heavens for unfavorable omens; and *contiones* delivered by the consul Metellus Nepos, by Appius Claudius Pulcher, and by Clodius himself. But the upshot was that unless an announcement of unfavorable omens could be made by Milo *in campo* (in the Campus Martius), the elections would be held.

In this context, therefore, we see the competition for the occupation of public space, characteristic of the Forum, being played out in the Campus. Milo occupied it with a large band of followers before dawn, and Clodius did not dare to appear. For the next day, the consul Metellus, who was evidently due to conduct the elections unless they could be prevented, asked Milo to declare the (unfavorable) omens to him in the Comitium, and Milo and his followers went there while it was still dark. The proposal (as Cicero does not need to make explicit) had evidently been a ruse. For, in fact, Metellus went straight toward the Campus, only to be followed hastily by Milo, who caught up with him and declared the unfavorable auspices. The elections could therefore not be held. At the moment when Cicero was writing, Milo's forces were established on the Campus.[62] This story perfectly illustrates the way in which the constitutional topography of the city and the archaic rules that still governed public action shaped the deployment of persuasion and naked force in the public arena. But once again we have to note that it was in the public arena, not behind closed doors, that the outcomes of political disputes were determined. It would in fact not be until January 56 that Clodius would finally achieve his election as one of the aediles of that year.

It was not only that the debates, opinions, and even decrees of the Senate could have effect, other than in quite limited areas, only if they could be embodied in a popular vote, but that the presence of the crowd could silence debate even within the Senate itself. This point is illustrated with painful clarity in Cicero's account of a meeting of the Senate in mid-December 57. The debate itself went entirely in directions that Cicero approved. The question of the Ager Campanus (hence going back to Cae-

---

62. See Cicero *Att.* 4.3.2–5 (75).

sar's legislation of 59) was even raised, to play a large part in the following year; others spoke about the need for setting up courts and about the political violence of the time. But then outside forces intervened.

> Next his [Clodius'] gangs suddenly raised a pretty loud shout from the Graecostasis and the steps [just outside the Curia]. They were incited, I think, against Q. Sextilius and the friends of Milo. When fear thus fell on us, suddenly, with great complaining on the part of all, we went off.[63]

The sheer brevity of the account and the lack either of any reference to a possible use of force to drive away Clodius' followers or of surprise that a meeting of the Senate might end in such a way make this letter very significant.

Other issues that would dominate the political life of the next year were also beginning to appear. The tribunes who entered office on December 10, 57, included C. Porcius Cato. A fragment from book 22 of the lost annals of an early imperial historian, Fenestella, perfectly captures the now established role that a tribune could hope, by rousing popular feeling, to play in foreign policy.

> So, when the *tribuni* had entered office, C. Cato, a turbulent and rash youth, and not ill-prepared for public speaking, began by repeated *contiones,* and with popular rumor in his favor, to devise *invidia* both against Ptolemaeus, who had already left the city, and against the consul Publius Lentulus [Spinther], who was now preparing to set out.[64]

The issue referred to was the decree of the Senate that Ptolemy Auletes, recognized as the legitimate king of Egypt in 59, but driven out by a revolt of his subjects in 58, should be restored to his throne by Lentulus Spinther when he took up the proconsulship of Cilicia. This issue rapidly became more complex and afforded the subject matter of many of the most vivid demonstrations of popular feeling attested for 56. Once again, we are confronted with the power of the people to override by a *lex* arrangements for provincial commands already made by the Senate. Nothing is in fact heard at this point of a *lex* proposed by C. Cato on this

---

63. Cicero *Q.f.* 2.1 (5).
64. Fenestella frag. 21 Peter.

subject, but Plutarch reports, in not entirely clear terms, that another tribune, Canidius, did propose a law, entrusting the task to Pompey, who was to go to Alexandria merely as a mediator, accompanied by two lictors but no army.[65] This bill seems to have been promulgated before the end of December 57, for a letter of Cicero, probably written in mid-January, seems to imply that legislation by Canidius and Cato was ready to be voted on.[66] This letter is one of a series written by Cicero to Spinther in early 56 to keep him abreast of political moves in Rome, which reveal that by this time a further factor had been introduced, namely, the claim that the Sibylline Books, when consulted, had indicated that no army should be used for this purpose.

This issue was only one of a series of complex issues that were played out in 56 in the Forum and that involved, as in the previous three years, the interplay of organized violence, popular opinion, oratory, the personal reputations of the major figures, and manipulation of the rules of Roman public life. In the case of the issue about Egypt, Cassius Dio provides an exceptionally clear account, which perfectly illustrates the way in which tribunician power was now used as a means of bringing before the people issues that were by tradition considered by the Senate. According to Dio it was the fact that at the very beginning of 56 lightning had struck the statue of Jupiter on the Mons Albanus which had led to consultation of the Sibylline Books by the relevant board of priests (the *quindecimviri sacris faciundis*). A passage in this text allegedly advised collaboration with the king of Egypt but not assistance to him with a large force. Previous arrangements were then rescinded, following the advice of C. Cato (at this stage, therefore, if Dio is correct, Cato put through a *lex* cancelling the senatorial decree of 57, so far as it related to Egypt). Dio then continues:

Such was the nature of the oracle; and it was made public through Cato. Now it was unlawful to announce to the populace any of the Sibylline verses, unless the Senate voted it; yet as soon as the sense of the verses, as usually happens, began to be talked about, he became afraid that it might be suppressed and so brought the priests before the populace and there compelled them to utter the oracle

65. Plutarch *Pomp.* 49.6.
66. See Cicero *Fam.* 1.4.1 (14). The suggestions made about chronology are far from certain.

before the Senate had taken any action at all in the matter. The more scruples they had against doing so, [the more insistent] was the multitude. Such, then, was the oracle, and it was translated into the Latin tongue and proclaimed.[67]

Further senatorial discussion now followed, and Pompey made public his willingness to act in Egypt without an army. Very significantly, Ptolemy's letter asking for this assistance was also read out at a *contio,* by another tribune, Aulus Plautius.[68]

This issue inevitably became entangled with others, and the interplay of different subjects of public dispute is the subject of perhaps the most vivid of all of Cicero's accounts of open-air political life, contained in a letter of his to his brother, Quintus, written in February 56. Clodius, now elected aedile, was prosecuting Milo for violence. C. Cato had promulgated a *lex* that would have gone beyond any previous bill proposed by him and would have abrogated Lentulus Spinther's command in Cilicia. Cicero describes the verbal exchanges and violent conflicts that attended the trial, which other evidence shows to have been a *iudicium populi* conducted before the thirty-five *tribus* (precisely the procedure that Cicero had once imagined using against Verres; see chap. 2).

On the eighth day before the ides of February, Milo attended [to stand trial]. Pompeius spoke [in his defense], or tried to. For as he stood up, the Clodian gangs *[operae]* raised a shout, and this was what he encountered throughout his whole speech, that he should be interrupted not only by shouting but by abuse and curses. When he reached the end of his speech—for in this instance he showed his strength, was not frightened off, and said everything, sometimes even being met with silence, when he had won through by *auctoritas*— when he reached the end of his speech, Clodius arose. He was greeted by such a clamor from our people (for it had been agreed that there would be a reply in kind) that he could not control his thoughts or his tongue or his countenance.[69]

---

67. Dio 39.12–16, Loeb trans. of 15.3–16.1.
68. See Dio 39.16.2.
69. Cicero *Q.f.* 2.3.2 (7). Note the commentary by W.W. How and A.C. Clark, *Cicero, Select Letters* (Oxford: Clarendon, 1926), no. 19, and Alexander, *Trials,* no. 266. See Cicero *Mil.* 15/40: "privato Milone et reo, ad populum accusante P. Clodio." See also Dio 39.18.

Clodius struggled on for two hours, being greeted with obscene verses relating to himself and his sister, Clodia. He then turned to blurring the distinction between a *iudicium populi* and a *contio*, by addressing questions to his followers and evoking responses from them.

> Furious and pallid, in the midst of the clamor, he took to asking his followers who it was who was killing the plebs by starvation: the gangs would answer, "Pompeius!" "Who wanted to go to Alexandria?" They would answer, "Pompeius!" "Whom did they want to go?" They would reply, "Crassus!"

The matter came to blows, and Cicero states explicitly that an assault was launched by "our" people, that the gangs fled, and that Clodius was driven off the Rostra.

As with all the complex events on which it will be necessary to touch, no attempt will be made here to follow out all the details or to explore the hints in contemporary or later sources as to personal motives, private plots, personal rivalries, or reported steps to gain control of groups who might appear in the Forum to influence events. All that is attempted here is to bring out the nature of the public exchanges in the Forum or other established locations, which were the object of more private political maneuverings, and which alone could lead to decisive results, in the form of legislation, a verdict in a trial, or elections to office. (Perhaps the only effective major decision that could be, and routinely was, taken by the Senate behind closed doors was the vote on the consular *provinciae* for the next—or in effect next-but-one—year, on which subject Cicero delivered his *De provincis consularibus* in the Senate in 56. But, as we have seen many times, this too could be overridden by a popular vote in the Forum.)

The nature of popular politics in the Forum in 56 is best illustrated, first, by Cicero's *De haruspicum responso* and, second, by a complex of evidence relating to the consular elections for 55. It is quite clear that these elections, in which Pompey and Crassus were in the end successful, were not perceived just as a matter of personal rivalries; on the contrary, their ominous significance for the future of the *res publica* was brought out very explicitly in public speeches to the people.

Cicero's *De haruspicum responso* was not itself delivered before a *contio* but was spoken in the Senate, perhaps in May 56, and after his successful defense of Sestius, in which, as we have seen earlier in this chapter, he gave expression to his fullest exposition of the conservative position. A public issue over portents and their interpretation had arisen because of an earthquake and other unusual signs, over whose significance the haruspices were consulted.[70] Their response was that divine wrath had been aroused because sacred sites were being used as human dwellings. Clodius naturally seized on this response to reopen in public the question of Cicero's house, now being rebuilt on the site where his shrine of Libertas had briefly stood. Even before that, however, at the *ludi Megalenses,* held in early April, a major disturbance had occurred, which Cicero describes vividly in his speech. Cicero takes this disturbance as having been the occasion that, according to the haruspices, had aroused divine anger, because some *ludi* had not been properly conducted.

> Which therefore are the *ludi* that they say were not properly con-
> ducted and were polluted? Those games of which the immortal gods
> themselves and that very Idaean Mother wished you above all, Cn.
> Lentulus, by the hands of whose great-great-grandfather she had
> been accepted in Rome [in 204], to be the spectator. But if you had
> not chosen to watch the Megalesia that day, I do not know if it
> would still be allowed for us to live and to deplore these events. For
> an innumerable force of slaves was stirred up, collected from all the
> *vici,* by this pious aedile [Clodius] and suddenly when a signal was
> given, burst onto the stage through all the arches and doorways.[71]

Without describing at all clearly what followed next, Cicero seems to imply that the firm leadership of the consul of 56, Cn. Cornelius Lentulus Marcellinus, prevented the *ludi* from being wholly disrupted and had thus contributed to the preservation of the *res publica.* What the real purpose of the irruption had been inevitably remains obscure. Nothing is explicitly said by Cicero to connect it (as with a similar episode in 57, mentioned earlier in this chapter) with the corn supply, though the abuse directed at Pompey makes clear that shortages were still a major issue.

Earlier in his speech, Cicero had given an account of the *contio* in which Clodius had expounded to the people his interpretation of the response of the haruspices and its relevance to the question of Cicero's house. Behind Cicero's sarcastic and satirical characterization of Clodius'

---

70. See J.O. Lenaghan, *A Commentary on Cicero's Oration De haruspicum responso* (The Hague: Mouton, 1969).

71. Cicero *Har. resp.* 11/22.

pretended role as the defender of Roman *religio*, we can nonetheless discern the outlines of one of many examples of detailed expositions of public affairs before the people.[72]

In his *contio*, Clodius had focused his interpretation of the response on the desanctification of the shrine of Libertas and on the new house of Cicero constructed there: "It was about the sacred rituals and ceremonies that he made his speech, senators—he, Clodius! P. Clodius, I repeat, complained that *sacra* and *religiones* were being neglected, violated, polluted!" He had not, however, confined himself to general expostulation.

> He recited *in contione* this recent *responsum* of the haruspices concerning the *fremitus* [an ominous noise of unknown origin that had been heard] in which there was written, along with many other things, the phrase that you have heard: "that places that are *sacra* and *religiosa* are being treated as if *profana*." To the same end, he said that my house had been consecrated by a most pious priest, P. Clodius.

In his speech, Cicero provides ample evidence that his house had been formally freed in 57 from the status of being *religiosa* and that the *responsum* had contained many other clauses. The functional significance of Clodius' *contio* remains, however: *contiones* addressed to the people could involve the quotation of written documents and the exposition of the speaker's interpretation of them.

Equally, as was always the case, the complex rules for the conduct of public business were themselves the subject of open debate. Cicero explicitly praises the consul Lentulus Marcellinus for arranging for days taken up with religious celebrations (*supplicationes,* or the repetition of the Latin Festival) to use up all the days on which the tribune C. Cato might have put forward *leges*, as might others (tribunes?) who had promulgated some scandalous proposals relating to Caesar. Cato is described as having made a public speech *(contionatus)* to make clear that he would veto the holding of all elections so long as he was deprived of the power to put proposals to the people.[73]

Of course, 56 was the year in which Caesar, during his command in Gaul, agreed with Pompey and Crassus to join forces again in the face of conservative opposition; one specific point of agreement was that Pom-

---

72. See Cicero *Har. resp.* 4/8–5/9.
73. See Cicero *Q.f.* 2.5.2–4 (4.4–6) (9).

pey and Crassus would be candidates for the consulship of 55. The prolonged electoral campaign, marked by large-scale violence, and prevented by C. Cato's tribunician vetoes from coming to a result until early in 55, was a turning point in the decline of the Republic and was clearly felt to be so by contemporaries. For a conception of the political struggles of the second half of 56, however, we are almost entirely dependent on later narratives; there are no speeches and hardly any letters of Cicero's from the later months of this year, and his letters and speeches from subsequent years happen to recall this period very little.

Dio's detailed narrative sees the crucial factor as an alliance between Crassus and Pompey, in rivalry rather than in concert with Caesar, and tells a story of open conflict, partly in the Forum and partly in the Senate, between Lentulus Marcellinus as consul, the two belatedly declared consular candidates, and C. Cato and Clodius. A few crucial episodes stand out—for instance, Marcellinus publicly questioning both Pompey and then Crassus as to whether they did indeed intend to be candidates.[74] What seems to be the same scene is reported by Plutarch, who adds that the exchange took place with "the many bidding them answer."[75] In other words, what lies behind these stories is a *contio,* or perhaps more than one, of a now familiar type, with an officeholder interrogating prominent persons in public, and with the crowd joining in.

Plutarch, who reports the agreement as also involving Caesar, who sent soldiers to lend their weight in the elections, also records that L. Domitius Ahenobarbus, as a rival candidate for the consulship, claimed that the issue was not merely the occupation of an office but the threat to liberty from potential tyrants.[76] Suetonius alternatively asserts that in the early part of the year, Domitius had openly threatened (in a *contio?*) that if he became consul he would achieve what he had failed to bring about as praetor (in 58) and remove Caesar's *provincia* from him. Rightly or wrongly, Suetonius sees this as the threat that had impelled Caesar to make a pact with Crassus and Pompey.[77] It is not worth trying to weigh these later reports. It is clear enough that they reflect a situation where, in this year at least, the elections were seen as a genuinely political issue, with grave potential consequences for the *res publica.* Lentulus Marcellinus himself, as consul, is reported as having made it starkly clear to the people what was at stake

---

74. See Dio 39.30.
75. Plutarch *Pomp.* 51.
76. Plutarch *Pomp.* 52.1.
77. Suetonius *Div. Iul.* 24.1.

and as having been greeted with a fervently positive response. This at least is what Valerius Maximus records:

> Cn. Lentulus Marcellinus, as consul, when in a *contio* he was complaining of the excessive *potentia* of Pompeius Magnus, and [when] the whole people had given clear voice to their assent, said, "Applaud, Citizens, applaud while it is still allowed! For soon you will not be free to do so with impunity."[78]

The history of the remaining six years of the Republic was to show that, while persuasion and open debate on matters of principle was still possible, political exchanges were to be affected ever more profoundly by the need for physical domination of public space; that the respectable people *(boni)* would never again succeed in rallying the effective support of the gentry of the Italian towns; and that popular sentiment in Rome would indeed contribute to the establishment of monarchic rule.

---

78. Val. Max. 6.2.6.

VII

Popular Politics in Decline, 55–50

With the election of Pompey and Crassus to the consulship of 55, a quite clear change can be detected in the tone, atmosphere, and procedures of Roman political life. One way to express this change might be to say that in this period the available evidence serves to represent a political world that is significantly closer to the model which has been imposed, wrongly, by moderns on the overall political character of the later Republic. The relevant features of it are the importance of the consulship as a strictly political office, whose holders regularly initiated legislation (contrast the picture in the 60s, as presented in chaps. 4 and 5); the influence in Rome of the holders of great provincial commands (Julius Caesar above all); intense electoral competition, involving pacts *(coitiones)* between candidates, bribery, and violence; the considerable prominence given to the exertion of personal political influence among members of the Senate, whether in the form of patronage deployed by Caesar from Gaul, bribery, or marriage alliances, made and broken; violence on the part of the crowd, or rather rival crowds, in the Forum; but relatively few reports of *contiones* directed to the advocacy or explication of matters of policy.

In part, the change of atmosphere represents simply a change in our angles of vision. As Cicero explains in a famous letter written to Lentulus Spinther in 54,[1] he had believed in the first half of 56 that a real reversal of the measures of 59 onward was now possible, only to be warned off by Pompey, in terms that are not expressed entirely clearly but seem to have involved the future prospects of Cicero's brother, Quintus. Cicero had at any rate given up his plans for reopening the question of Vatinius' tribunate in 59 or of the Ager Campanus (see chap. 6), and explains his retreat as having been out of a combination of respect for the public achievements of both Pompey and Cicero and of his personal obligations to them. For these reasons, along with distrust of the loyalty to himself of leading senators and a desire not to provoke further conflict, Cicero had

---

1. Cicero *Fam.* 1.9 (20).

despaired of restoring the *res publica* to its former state and had even agreed to act as Vatinius' advocate in court—the point on which Lentulus Spinther had written to seek an explanation. Thus in these years, down to 51, Cicero consciously retreated from active political involvement. Relatively few letters by him are preserved for the years 55–52, and they contain few of the detailed representations of scenes from popular politics such as we find in those of the later 60s and earlier 50s; where there are allusions to events in the Forum or the Campus Martius, they are often relatively brief and allusive. By contrast, both his *Ad familiares* and his letters to his brother, Quintus, give vivid testimony to the need to seek and keep the favor of Julius Caesar during the latters' proconsulate of Gaul.[2] Then, in 51, a change in the system for nominating provincial governors (discussed later in this chapter) meant that Cicero went off to serve as the proconsul of Cilicia, returning to Italy in late 50, only a short time before the end of the period with which this study is concerned.

From this whole period of six years, there are no surviving properly political speeches of Cicero, though there are three very important forensic speeches in defense of political figures. Two are from 54; the *Pro Plancio*, defending the legitimacy of Plancius' election in spring 55 to serve as aedile for the remainder of the year; and the *Pro Scauro*, preserved only in the fragments quoted in Asconius' commentary. The third is the supremely important *Pro Milone* of 52, the text of the speech that Cicero would have made when defending Milo on a charge of murdering Clodius, if the pressures of the occasion had not made it impossible for him to get it out.

As has been stressed many times, this study aims, above all, to bring out the representations of popular politics provided by contemporary sources, while also trying to clarify the context from which, in each case, these contemporary representations themselves derive, and therefore the persuasive purpose of the speaker or writer in constructing them as they are. The most important contemporary narrative source, Caesar's own *De bello Gallico*, certainly also had a persuasive purpose, directly relevant to political events in Rome. But by its nature it does not offer illuminating representations of specific events there. By contrast, while the story of the late Republic simply cannot be written without the aid of

2. See, e.g., Cicero *Fam.* 7.5–9 (26–30), 17 (31), 16 (32), 10–13 (33–36), 18 (37), 14 (38); *Q.f.* 2.14 (13) (18), 2.16 (15) (20), 3.1.8–13 (21), 6 (8), 3 (26). The best treatment of Caesar's exercise of influence in Rome during his proconsulate remains M. Gelzer, *Caesar* (Oxford: Blackwell, 1968), chap. 4.

the Greek narratives of the imperial period by Plutarch, Appian, and Cassius Dio, we have to be cautious in using them to reconstruct the real context and atmosphere of particular scenes. Those of Plutarch's *Lives* (of Pompey, Crassus, Caesar, Cicero, Cato the Younger, and Antonius) that cover the period tend, in any case, to stress the attitudes taken up by each individual, without always representing in any concrete way the context in which political opinions were expressed. Moreover, Dio's narrative for these years devotes a high proportion of its coverage to Caesar's wars in Gaul.

Later narratives can therefore do relatively little to make up for the thinness of the contemporary evidence. One exception has to be made, however, namely, the masterly narrative introduction by Asconius to his commentary on the *Pro Milone,* together with the further explanations and stretches of narrative that he provides in commenting on particular passages. This major piece of political narrative, probably written in the 50s A.D., seems never to have been given its due in studies either of Latin literature or specifically of historiography.3 Perhaps the plain, clear, and unadorned style of Asconius has led to the presumption that what he wrote cannot be regarded as "Literature" and therefore deserves no attention. Alternatively, it may be the mere fact that Asconius' works on Cicero's speeches are classified as commentaries which has led to their not being given any place in our conception of Roman or Latin historiography. Yet, in his presentation of the context of the *Pro Milone* above all, Asconius, looking back from a century later and from a greatly changed political context, achieves not merely a remarkable level of detailed factual reporting and explanation, but a vivid reevocation of a moment of crisis in political history. This later account, then, will be used extensively in what follows.

For the reasons given, our evidence for this period will not provide any extended representations of sequences of exchanges in the Forum—either over laws or in association with the elections—of a sort now familiar from the events of the later 60s and the first half of the 50s. Sufficient examples have already been given of forms of persuasion addressed to the people, of the organization of force to determine the outcome of popular voting, of popular reactions, and of the limited, but sometimes very significant, intervention of groups from areas of Italy outside Rome.

---

3. For instance, Asconius receives precisely two sentences in *The Cambridge History of Classical Literature*, vol. 2, *Latin Literature*, ed. E.J. Kenney (Cambridge: Cambridge University Press, 1982), 37.

For these years, therefore, where the evidence is itself episodic and defective, we can afford to be selective and to focus on a small number of well-attested episodes. Legislation, which necessarily and in all cases involved voting by the people in the Forum, remained extremely important in these years, which saw the continuation in 55 (but not after) of tribunician laws conferring provincial commands, as well as more general legislation relating to the rules governing provincial commands, the conditions of candidature for office, electioneering, and association for electoral purposes. In the last year of the period, 50, Scribonius Curio, as *tribunus plebis,* was to reclaim the established legislative role open to the tribunes and to play a major part in public debates over the position of Julius Caesar in relation to the *res publica.* I will look at a number of significant episodes, roughly in chronological sequence.

For the passing of the law proposed by a tribune, C. Trebonius, to confer provincial commands on Pompey and Crassus, as consuls of 55, we are, as is typical of this period, dependent on the detailed later narratives of Plutarch and Cassius Dio. As I have noted earlier, we know from Cicero's *De provinciis consularibus,* spoken in the Senate in 56, that the Senate had duly debated the question of *provinciae* for the prospective consuls of 55 and had presumably decreed what these *provinciae* were to be. But, in a way that was by now almost customary, their dispositions were overridden by tribunician legislation early in 55.

In Plutarch's account, Trebonius proposed first that one consul should have Spain and Africa and the other Syria and Egypt, both with the freedom to conduct military operations as they pleased. It perhaps hardly needs to be stressed again that, with the application of tribunician legislation to such questions, fundamental issues about the shape and military activity of the empire were being brought for decision before the crowd in the Forum. Cato alone, Plutarch says, spoke against the measure from the Rostra, was pulled from it, returned, and was finally led off to the *carcer.* But he continued to speak while being escorted there, and the reaction of the crowd convinced Trebonius to abandon this step. Subsequently, a tribune, Aquillius, who was opposed to the law, was shut in the Curia, and Cato was physically expelled from the Forum when he tried to declare that unfavorable auspices had been observed. So the law went through by the use of force.[4]

Cassius Dio, describing the same events, gives a more detailed and

4. See Plutarch *Cato Min.* 43.

circumstantial account, reflecting his much superior grasp of the Republican constitution and politics.5 In his narrative, the *provinciae* to be allocated were "Syria and the neighboring areas," on the one hand, and the two provinces of Spain, on the other, with the same freedom to wage war. There was opposition to these proposals, especially from Caesar's friends, and hostility was only partially quietened by the proposal for an extension of the period of Caesar's command also. But the proposals were still opposed publicly by two other tribunes, Gaius Ateius Capito and Publius Aquillius Gallus, aided by Cato and Favonius. Favonius was given a *contio* by Trebonius but allowed to speak for only one hour. Cato, as in Plutarch's account, then spoke at length, until, in the end, he was led off to the *carcer*.

It is in this context that, as we saw earlier (see chap. 2), Dio reports that the opportunity to speak was given only to private persons (that is, persons not currently in office), as opposed to officeholders. There must be some confusion here, for the tribunes opposed to the bill could of course have held their own *contiones*. At any rate, Dio describes how Aquillius Gallus, fearing exclusion from the Forum, occupied the Curia overnight but was foiled by being locked in by his adversaries, and thus forced to stay there for most of the day. The law was passed by the physical exclusion of opponents and by driving out by force those who declared unfavorable omens.

What Dio then describes exhibits in a remarkably vivid way the relevance of time and place to politics in the Forum. When those who had voted for the law on *provinciae* were already leaving, he says, Ateius held a *contio*, showed the people the injuries suffered by Aquillius Gallus, "and by making such remarks as might be expected, stirred them mightily." But at that point the consuls arrived with a large escort, intimidated the crowd still in the Forum, and put through a *lex* for the extension of Caesar's command (Dio says for three years, others for five). If this is true, the *lex* must of course already have been promulgated for a *trinundinum*. As the variations of detail show, neither Plutarch's nor Dio's account can wholly be relied on for the facts, and neither can have the status of a contemporary report by Cicero in a letter. It is beyond doubt, however, that the Syrian command of Crassus (which was to lead in 53 to his disastrous defeat by the Parthians at Carrhae), the Spanish command of Pompey, which was the basis of his position for the rest of the 50s, and the extension of Caesar's command

---

5. Dio 39.33–36.

were all secured by mass voting in the Forum, in the degraded circumstances that now obtained.

Scattered evidence shows clearly that the elections for both the praetorship and the aedileship of 55, both held after the year of office had actually begun, were similarly marked by manipulation and violence.[6] The election of the aediles, however, has a special interest as regards the workings of popular politics, because of the prosecution of one of the successful candidates, Cn. Plancius, in 54, and the speech made in his defense by Cicero. Cicero's *Pro Plancio,* like his *Pro Murena* of 62 (see chap. 5), is invaluable as an exposition of one view of what was normal and expected in Roman elections. The prosecution was brought by M. Iuventius Laterensis, the descendant of consuls on both sides, who came from the important *municipium* of Tusculum, to the south of Rome. Plancius, in contrast, came from a family of merely equestrian rank and from the *praefectura* of Atina, some 110 kilometers east of Rome. Laterensis' case rested on the claim that only resort to improper means could have upset the natural expectation that he would be elected and Plancius not. I have already noted earlier (see chap. 2) the paradoxical significance that Cicero attaches to the contrast between Tusculum, where the fact that a local man was standing for a relatively minor office in Rome attracted no interest, and the reaction not only in Atina but in the neighboring towns—Arpinum, Sora, Casinum, Aquinum, Venafrum, Allifae. Not only was Atina in particular a populous place, but it contained persons of rank within the social hierarchy of the Roman *res publica,* namely, *equites* and *tribuni aerarii.* People from this region had therefore been moved to make the journey to Rome to vote, whereas there had been no such reaction in Tusculum and the neighboring area (where some historic small towns, Cicero says, such as Labicum, Gabii, or Bovillae, were in any case almost deserted).[7]

The *Pro Plancio* is thus extremely important for its conception of what the (partial and ultimately abortive) involvement of Italian communities in the electoral process in Rome meant, or might have meant. But it is also very significant for the way in which the demands of his task in defending Plancius lead Cicero, first, to stress the essential unpredictability of Roman elections and, second, to come quite close to asserting the principle of popular sovereignty in a way that is not characteristic of his

---

6. See Val. Max. 4.6.4; Plutarch *Pomp.* 52–53; Dio 39.32.
7. Cicero *Planc.* 8/19–9/22, 19/47.

writings after the mid-60s. The judgment of the *populus* was notoriously poor, he says, and in any case their vote represented simply enthusiasm for one person or another, not any considered or valid judgment.[8] Cicero quotes many historical examples of persons whose character and services should have earned them election but who were rejected on at least one occasion. Whatever consideration was due to rank, it was the people's right to choose. If it were to be simply a matter of noting the rank of the families of the candidates—consular, praetorian, or equestrian—nothing would be left of the electoral process.

> Popular support will have been removed, voting extinguished; [there will be] no rivalries, no *libertas* on the part of the people in entrusting magistracies, no need to wait for the result of the votes. There will be no further results that come out against expectation, as so often happens, and from now on no variation in the elections. But if it frequently happens that we are surprised that some have been elected and others not, if the Campus and those waves of the *comitia,* like some vast and deep sea, boil up in such a way that, like a tide, they wash toward some and recede from others, are we, amid such a clash of loyalties and such an eruption of rashness, to demand some limit, prudence, and rationality?[9]

Even more explicitly, in an earlier passage of his speech, Cicero had given very clear expression to the principle of popular sovereignty. A man might feel disposed to say that he could not accept the *iudicium* of the *populus,* but many citizens of the greatest distinction and wisdom had had to accept it, and with good reason.

> For it is the nature of any free people, and above all of this ruling people, which is the master and conqueror of all races, that it has the power either to give or to take away by its votes whatever it wishes with regard to anyone it wishes. But it is our role, we who are tossed about in the storm and currents of the *populus,* to bear with restraint the wishes of the people, to soothe them when they are hostile to us, to hold on to them when we have won them over, and to placate them when they are aroused. If we do not think

---

8. Cicero *Planc.* 4/9–10.
9. Cicero *Planc.* 6/15.

honores of great account, we need not serve the people. If we seek *honores,* we must not weary of supplicating the people.[10]

Cicero's use of the word *supplicare* to characterize the attitudes required of a candidate in relation to the people is deliberate, and is reemphasized in the following passage, when he controverts the imputed assumption that Laterensis might have been able to rely on his distinguished birth to secure election. Indeed, Cicero imagines the *populus* itself addressing Laterensis and giving the reason for its choice: "I have not preferred Plancius to you, Laterensis, but since you are equally good men, have conferred my *beneficium* rather on him who sought it from me than on him who did not supplicate me for it so submissively."[11] The aedilician elections in 55 had in fact been started and then broken off once before, and on the earlier occasion it had already been clear that Plancius had a majority. If, therefore, Cicero says later in the speech, Laterensis had thought it in conformity with his *gravitas,* he could have metaphorically prostrated himself before the *comitia* in a humble and broken spirit—and then would surely have been elected.[12]

We have of course to remember that it is essential to Cicero's case to set aside all considerations of political coalitions, bribery, or violence and to represent the popular will as resulting in a *beneficium* freely conferred on those who presented themselves in the required style. This necessity leads him into what were for him (by now) uncharacteristic assertions of the sovereignty of the people. But whatever allowances we make for Cicero's oratorical stratagems, the fact remains that the speech does remind us of the extensive range of less prestigious offices that were open to popular election at what Cicero calls the *leviora comitia* [the less important elections][13] (cf. chap. 2). In that sense, it offers some of the best evidence for the (entirely correct) thesis of Hopkins and Burton on political succession in the Republic, namely, that elective office was more open to competition for the more junior positions.[14] For Cicero also records

---

10. Cicero *Planc.* 4/11.

11. Cicero *Planc.* 5/12: "Ego tibi, Laterensis, Plancium non anteposui; sed cum essetis aeque boni viri, meum beneficium ad eum potius detuli, qui a me contenderat, quam ad eum, qui me non nimis summisse supplicarat."

12. Cicero *Planc.* 20/49–50.

13. Cicero *Planc.* 3/7.

14. M.K. Hopkins and G.P. Burton, *Death and Renewal: Sociological Studies in Roman History,* vol. 2 (Cambridge: Cambridge University Press, 1983), chap. 2, "Political Succession in the Late Republic."

very specifically here that of the candidates for the aedileship on this occasion, only one (Laterensis himself) came from a consular family, one came from a praetorian family, and the rest (including Plancius) came from families of equestrian status.[15] Elective office, and hence a seat in the Senate, was in no way the preserve of a closed aristocracy. What remains true is that a famous name, and by implication an inherited standing as a potential general, was felt to be more relevant the further a man moved up the hierarchy of office, and it was most relevant of all for the consulship. As we have seen, it had been only the previous quarter-century which had seen the emergence of the "civilian" consul, whose term of office was spent in Rome, participating in political exchanges, rather than in the field commanding an army. Moreover, it was to be only in the last half of the 50s that legislation became predominantly something put forward by consuls.

The full-scale "politicization" of elective office, and with it a vastly increased level of violence as deployed in the competition for office, was one of the most marked features of these years. It is no coincidence that when Cicero was delivering his *Pro Plancio,* the civil war and the dictatorship of Caesar were less than five years ahead. The signs of the growing prominence and influence of leading individuals were also very visible, in the most material form, in the center of Rome, and they can very properly be taken to symbolize the rapid transformation of Roman political life and of power relations in Roman politics. The most spectacular event of the year 55 must have been Pompey's opening of the very first permanent stone-built theater in Rome, with a shrine of Venus Victrix placed above its *cavea,* extensive porticoes extending behind the *scaenae frons,* the Curia in which Caesar would be murdered, and statues of fourteen personified nations to remind the people of Pompey's victories. The details need not be repeated here.[16] It need only be noted that extensive and varied *ludi* were given by Pompey to mark the event; Cicero's hostile account of them serves to confirm the reports by later sources that they included a display of elephants that, contrary to expectation and intention, aroused pity rather than enjoyment among the audience.[17]

---

15. Cicero *Planc.* 6/15.

16. See Platner-Ashby, *Topographical Dictionary,* s.v. "Theatrum Pompei"; E. Frézouls, "La construction du *theatrum lapideum* et son contexte politique," in *Théâtre et spectacles dans l'Antiquité* (Colloque Strasbourg, 1981, Leiden: E.J. Brill, 1983), 193; L. Richardson, *A New Topographical Dictionary of Ancient Rome* (Baltimore: Johns Hopkins University Press, 1992), s.v. "Theatrum Pompeii."

17. See Cicero *Fam.* 8.1.1–3 (240); Dio 39.38.

By the next year, plans were already well advanced for Caesar, using the huge profits of his campaigns in Gaul, to alter the monumental framework of the center of Rome in a way that would impact far more emphatically on the workings of politics. A famous, and notoriously puzzling, letter of Cicero's from 54 reports that Aemilius Paulus was engaged on building or repairing what appear to be two different basilicas, one of them "in the middle of the Forum." More significantly, various friends of Caesar's, Cicero himself among them, were spending sixty million sesterces "in order that we should widen the Forum and extend it to the Atrium Libertatis."[18] It is surely not probable that this is a prospective reference to the eventual Forum Iulium, which had not yet been begun, and which would be constructed to the northwest of the Forum itself; its centerpiece, the temple of Venus Genetrix, was to be dedicated in 46, and the new Curia Iulia, aligned with one of its sidewalls, only in 29. It must be the Forum Romanum itself to which Cicero is referring, and there is very good reason, as Nicholas Purcell has argued, for attaching the name "Atrium Libertatis" to the prominent, multistory Republican building that still stands on the slope of the Capitol, at the west end of the Forum, and is usually called the "Tabularium."[19] There is no evidence that the Forum was indeed extended in the last years of the 50s. Nor is there any indication that work actually started then on the other Caesarian project that Cicero goes on to mention, that of constructing an enormous marble enclosure, the Saepta, for the *comitia tributa* (and also the *centuriata?*), on the Campus Martius. This construction was to be completed only in 26, after the definitive assumption of power by Augustus. The relevance of this letter is *not* therefore that the building projects of a political dynast had already begun to transform the ancient meeting places of the *populus Romanus* but that Cicero can mention these projects in so casual a way. A fundamental change in presuppositions about the relations of a prominent

18. Cicero *Att.* 4.16.8 (89). See E.M. Steinby, "Il lato orientale del Foro Romano: Proposte di lettura," *Arctos* 21 (1987): 139; T.P. Wiseman, "Rome and the Resplendent Aemilii," in *Tria Lustra: Essays and Notes Presented to John Pinsent, Founder and Editor of "Liverpool Classical Monthly," by Some of Its Contributors, on the Occasion of the 150th Issue* (Liverpool: Liverpool Classical Monthly, 1992), 181; LTUR 1, s.v. "Basilica Pauli."

19. So N. Purcell, *"Atrium Libertatis,"* PBSR 61 (1993): 125. For the complex initial building history of the Forum Iulium itself, see R.B. Ulrich, "Julius Caesar and the Creation of the Forum Iulium," AJA 97 (1993): 44; R. Westall, "The Forum Iulium as Representation of Imperator Caesar," *Röm. Mitt.* 103 (1996): 83.

individual, with military prestige and huge financial resources, to the people had taken place within a very few years.

For the moment, the Forum and its surrounding buildings retained their existing form and their historic associations. In this same year, Cato, holding jurisdiction as praetor, justified his appearing in summer with no tunic under his toga by pointing to the statues of Romulus and Tatius on the Capitol and of Camillus on the Rostra, which were *togatae* with no tunics.[20] Cicero, defending M. Aemilius Scaurus in the same year, made more conventional use of the visual environment. As we saw earlier (in chap. 2), he refers to the fact that Scaurus' maternal grandfather, L. Caecilius Metellus Delmaticus, consul of 119, had rebuilt the temple of Castor and Pollux: Cicero says that he seemed, therefore, to have placed those two gods there precisely to implore the safety of his grandson. As for the Curia, on the opposite side of the Forum, it would serve to recall the *principatus* of Scaurus' father, the consul of 115.[21] Scaurus himself, so Asconius records, was acquitted by the votes of sixty-two of the seventy *iudices*, after making an emotional appeal by which "he greatly moved the *iudices*," and after referring to the luxurious displays that he had laid on as aedile in 58, his favor with the populace, and the memory of his father's *auctoritas*.[22]

Much more significant for the future were the events that followed on the death of Caesar's daughter, Julia, who was also the wife of Pompey. Suetonius notes that Caesar gave a gladiatorial show and a dinner in her memory, "which none had done before."[23] Dio goes into more detail: he says that after the normal funeral oration in the Forum (in fact a novelty as regards women, going back only half a century), some unspecified persons took the body and buried it in the Campus Martius. Who was responsible and whether we are seeing here a spontaneous crowd reaction are not clear. What is significant is that Domitius Ahenobarbus, as consul of 54, spoke against this action and said (evidently in one or more *contiones*) that it was sacrilegious to carry out such a step without the authority of a law.[24] We can hardly expect to understand at all fully an episode that is reported only quite briefly in a later source. But it clearly reflects the presence of a conflict between the traditional religious rules of

20. See Asconius 29C.
21. Cicero is quoted in Asconius 27–28C.
22. Asconius 20C.
23. Suetonius *Div. Iul.* 26.2.
24. See Dio 39.64.

the Republic and the pressure to give a symbolic prominence to persons related to important leaders.

Nonetheless, the dominance of individuals was still far from complete, and there remained a need for persuasion, whose effects could not be guaranteed. We can see an ineffective use of persuasion in another episode retailed by Dio, the trials of A. Gabinius. First, he was tried for *maiestas,* after his return from Syria. Popular sentiment was violently hostile to him, and the people are reported as having rushed together to the *quaestio,* with the intention of tearing him to pieces. The narrative must be exaggerated, for there was in fact nothing to prevent a large crowd from doing that, if it seriously intended to. At any rate, bribery and private influence on the *iudices* (so Dio says) secured his acquittal; Cicero reports that the jurors voted thirty-eight for and thirty-two against. There was then a second trial on lesser charges, apparently *de pecuniis repetundis,* at which Cicero defended Gabinius. Dio seems to be thinking of this event as a *quaestio* also, talking of those chosen by lot to act as jurors. But he also describes how Pompey, as proconsul of the Hispaniae and hence formally debarred from entering the city, addressed the people at a *contio* in defense of Gabinius and also read out a letter from Caesar. Nonetheless Gabinius was condemned.[25]

Pompey's unsuccessful intervention before the people may have been intended merely to alter the context of popular hostility and to demonstrate his and Caesar's support. As has been stressed many times, in atmosphere and in rhetorical strategies there was by no means a complete contrast between *contiones,* on the one hand, and *quaestiones,* meeting in the same space and with a surrounding *corona* of spectators, on the other (in topographical terms, of course, this particular *contio* was an exception). But it may be that a *iudicium populi* was also held, or at least threatened (as in the case of Verres, discussed in chap. 2), or in fact that the second, successful prosecution was a *iudicium* in which charges were brought by the tribune C. Memmius. Cicero confirms that some of the tribunes of the year declared that they would take steps in relation to Gabinius; and Valerius Maximus claims that Memmius accused Gabinius, who was then exposed to condemnation by the votes of the *populus.*[26] The details thus remain obscure, despite many passing allusions in contemporary and later sources.

Clearer and more distinctive in the material from this year is the

---

25. See Dio 39.62–63 (cf. 55.4–6); Cicero *Att.* 4.18.1 (92).

26. Cicero *Q.f.* 2.12.3 (16); Val. Max. 8.1.3. See Alexander, *Trials,* no. 296.

extensive evidence in Cicero's letters for the complex factors affecting the prospects for the consular elections for 53. Older and more recent patterns perfectly mix in Cicero's report from July 54: Messalla had considerable support; Scaurus (mentioned earlier in this chapter) was being prosecuted but still hoped to be a candidate, aided by the popularity of his lavish aedileship in 58 and the memory of his father; Domitius Calvinus had powerful *amici* and had put on a successful gladiatorial show; Memmius was supported by Caesar's soldiers and had the *gratia* of Pompey.[27] By later in July, Cicero was reporting that bribery was rampant and that Caesar, Pompey, and the current consuls were backing different candidates.[28] Finally, in October, Cicero sent the famous letter in which he describes a scandalous pact between the two consuls and two of the candidates, Memmius and Domitius. The details need not be retailed, except to note that efforts by the Senate to bring order and propriety into the electoral process depended on the eventual passing of a *lex* through the *comitia*. When the Senate intended to set up a *iudicium* on its own, some of the potential *iudices* appealed to the tribunes and argued against being required to act without an order from the *populus*.[29] In that very limited sense, the workings of politics were still constrained by the basic rules of popular sovereignty. Looking more widely, it has to be accepted that, however much our view is constricted by the particular angles of vision of our sources, we are not confronted in these years with a record of open public debate on public issues, so conspicuous a feature of the previous decade.

By contrast, Cicero's letters from the same period addressed to his brother, Quintus, who was currently with Caesar in Gaul, vividly reflect the importance attached to Caesar's goodwill and the influence exerted by Caesar on the elections in Rome. The machinery of the *res publica* was still there, and potentially in function, but no reader could mistake the change in presumptions that marks Cicero's comments on the prospects for the elections, if indeed they would ever take place.

> All those who are seeking the consulate have been accused of electoral bribery: Domitius by Memmius; Memmius by Q. Acutius, a good and learned young man; Messalla by Q. Pompeius; and Scaurus by Triarius. A major issue is at stake, because it signifies the

---

27. Cicero *Att.* 4.16.6 (89)—the same letter as in n. 18 in this chapter.
28. Cicero *Att.* 4.15.7 (90).
29. See Cicero *Att.* 4.17.2–3, 5 (91).

destruction either of these individuals or of the laws. Efforts are being made to prevent the *iudicia* taking place. Things seem to be tending toward an interregnum. The consuls want to hold the elections, while the accused do not, above all Memmius, since he hopes that Caesar's arrival [in Cisalpine Gaul] will lead to his becoming consul; but his stock has sunk to a remarkable degree.[30]

In the event, it was not until July 53 that Cn. Domitius Calvinus and M. Valerius Messalla Rufus were elected as consuls for the year and entered office. Before this, we hear briefly from Plutarch of one of the tribunes, Lucilius Hirrus, urging the people to make Pompey dictator, which must mean that he delivered *contiones* on the subject; Cato appears to have attacked Lucilius, also presumably in *contiones,* and friends of Pompey declared that he did not seek a dictatorship.[31] We do then catch the pale reflection of a public debate. Some more detail is provided by Dio, who records that the tribune had first proposed to revise the ancient tradition of electing consular tribunes rather than consuls, and that he had only turned to advocating a dictatorship when that proposal found no support.[32]

Given the almost complete absence of contemporary evidence for the politics of this year, we may pass on to the most significant events of 52, but only after noting the one letter of Cicero's from 53 in which he discusses the electoral prospects of his favored candidate for the consulship of 52, Milo, and urges his addressee, Curio, to be active on Milo's behalf. Milo, Cicero thought, had the support of the *boni,* because of his advocacy of Cicero's cause during his tribunate in 57; that of the *multitudo* and *vulgus,* because of the *magnificentia* of the gladiatorial shows that he had put on and the *liberalitas* of his nature; the enthusiasm of the young and those who exercised influence over the voting, because of his outstanding *gratia* and *diligentia;* and the *suffragatio* of Cicero himself (of which his letter is an example).[33] In this context, Cicero does not refer to the violence between the organized gangs of at least two of the candidates, Milo and P. Plautius Hypsaeus, and he may have been writing before it broke out. A brief snapshot of this violence is provided

30. Cicero *Q.f.* 3.2.3 (22).

31. See Plutarch *Pomp.* 54.1–3. In fact, an allusion in Cicero *Fam.* 8.4.3 (81) shows that another tribune, Coelius Vinicianus, also made this proposal in public speeches.

32. Dio 41.45.

33. Cicero *Fam.* 2.6.3 (50).

instead by Asconius, commenting on a passage in Cicero's *Pro Milone* where he claims that Clodius had once nearly succeeded in killing him "near the Regia."[34] Asconius comments as follows.

> But he seems to me to be talking of that day in the consulship of Domitius and Messalla—the consuls of the year before that in which this speech was delivered—on which there was a fight in the Via Sacra between the gangs of Hypsaeus and Milo, [in which] many of the *Miloniani* unexpectedly fell. In my view, the fact that he is speaking of the risk that he ran on that day is suggested both by the location of the fight—for it is said to have been joined in the Sacra Via, on which is the Regia—and because the candidates were constantly accompanied by their *suffragatores,* Milo by Cicero and Hypsaeus by Clodius.[35]

Cicero's hopes for Milo's success were unfulfilled, and January 52 arrived with no consuls or praetors in office. At this point, the wholly exceptional combined evidence of Cicero's *Pro Milone,* Asconius' invaluable introduction to it (setting the scene), and Asconius' selective commentaries on particular passages provides uniquely concentrated evidence for the working of politics and, above all, for the interplay between the main actors and the crowd. Only the most crucial scenes will be picked out here. The precise sequence of events depends on the relationship between the powerful but brief narrative by Asconius that serves as his introduction, on the one hand, and the fuller accounts of certain episodes that appear in his notes on individual passages, on the other.[36]

The context for the famous clash between Milo and Clodius and their followers on January 18, in which Clodius was killed, was continuing rivalry for the consulship of that year—between Milo, Plautius Hypsaeus, and Q. Metellus Scipio—along with Clodius' candidature for the praetorship. It will be very clear how speeches addressed to the people *(contiones)* characterized these political events at every turn, beginning with two by different tribunes, both hostile to Milo, on the day of the murder, though evidently before news of it was known (49C). The two

---

34. Cicero *Mil.* 14/37.

35. Asconius 48C. Subsequent citations to Asconius' narrative will be given in parentheses in text.

36. I have followed the chronology set out by J.S. Ruebel in "The Trial of Milo in 52 B.C.: A Chronological Study," *TAPhA* 109 (1979): 23.

tribunes were Q. Pompeius Rufus and C. Sallustius Crispus, later to achieve fame as the historian Sallust. It is very typical of the individualistic nature of Roman elective office holding that of the ten tribunes of the year, these two and T. Munatius Plancus were supporters of Clodius, while two others, M. Caelius Rufus and Q. Manilius Cumanus, supported Milo.

After the murder, which occurred on the Via Appia south of Rome, Clodius' body was brought to the city and set down in his house, which was situated, like many other such houses, including the nearby one owned by Cicero, on the northern slopes of the Palatine and thus not far from the Forum.[37] A very large crowd "of the lowest plebs and slaves" gathered at the house (32C), and on the next morning (January 19) there was an even larger one. Plancus and Pompeius Rufus also appeared, and they persuaded the mob to carry the corpse down to the Forum and place it on the Rostra. From there, both tribunes addressed *contiones* to the crowd, who then bore the body into the Curia and cremated it, burning down with it the Curia itself and the neighboring Basilica Porcia.

In a way that was still unusual, the crowd now also attacked the house of M. Aemilius Lepidus, who was then *interrex* in the absence of consuls, and also Milo's house, only to be driven off with arrows (33C). At another point, Asconius records an attack on Lepidus' house two days after Clodius' murder, just when Lepidus had been elected *interrex;* Asconius attributes the attack to the followers of Scipio and Hypsaeus, and says that the house was sacked as a way of pressuring Lepidus into holding the elections for the consulate. According to this version of the event, a gang of Milo's supporters then appeared, and Lepidus was saved by the fact that the two groups began to fight each other (43C).

Milo himself, meanwhile, returned to Rome and resumed his canvassing, not forgetting to make a cash distribution to the voters. After some days, the tribune M. Caelius Rufus provided a *contio* for him, and Cicero also spoke on his behalf (33C). By now, the conception that election speeches were a normal part of the process should not seem strange. Both speakers argued that Clodius had ambushed Milo, rather than the other way around.

On January 23, Q. Pompeius Rufus, also a tribune, addressed the people about the murder of Clodius and claimed that Milo would try to kill Pompey: "It was Milo who provided the body for you to burn in the Curia; he will also provide that which you will inter on the Capitol" (50–

---

37. See *LTUR* 2, s.v. "Domus: P. Clodius Pulcher."

51C). Asconius goes on to say that in daily *contiones,* the three tribunes Pompeius, Sallustius and Munatius Plancus aroused hostility to Milo over the murder and "produced" Pompey before the *populus* to interrogate him over Milo's alleged plots.

In February, the Senate passed an emergency decree in the established form of a vote that the available magistrates, along with Pompey as a proconsul in the vicinity of the city, "should take steps to see that the *res publica* suffered no harm" (wrongly called the *senatus consultum ultimum*). Then, in the following month—one intercalated to regulate the calendar—and after Pompey had returned from conducting a levy, the Senate decreed that the current *interrex* should hold an election by which Pompey became sole consul. Proceedings then began in the Senate, on Pompey's proposal, for the enactment of *leges* to set up courts to try those guilty of public violence (34–36C). At the end of the intercalary month, the Senate passed a decree declaring that the death of Clodius, the burning of the Curia, and the assault on Lepidus' house had all been "against the *res publica.*" Asconius then records very explicitly that on the next day, Munatius Plancus held a *contio* to explain what had been done in the Senate: "what the Senate had intended to decree, and who had asked for a division, and who had interposed [his veto] and why" (44–45C). Nothing could more clearly indicate the exposure of the Senate, and of individual senators, to public awareness.

The *leges* to set up criminal proceedings were evidently promulgated in early March, and passed by the *comitia,* after the normal interval, at the end of the month. In the intervening period, Munatius and his allies were able to utilize the device of the *contio* to conduct a sort of semijudicial procedure of their own: Munatius "produced" an alleged witness to the murder, who claimed that he and his associates had been kidnapped and held prisoner in a villa of Milo's; and Munatius and Pompeius "produced" a minor elected official, a *triumvir capitalis,* and interrogated him as to whether he had arrested a slave of Milo's for murder. These two tribunes, along with Sallustius, were then thought to have made peace with Milo and Cicero, and they desisted (37C).

The form of Pompey's *lex* was such that another popular vote was required, for it laid down that a presiding judge *(quaesitor)* should be elected by the *suffragium populi* from among ex-consuls, and the relevant *comitia* were immediately held (38C). As for the complex details of the trial of Milo itself, we need note only that it took place, as was normal, in the open air in the Forum, and that it began on April 4 and lasted for several days. Asconius' account again provides a classic illustration of how exposed such proceedings inevitably were to popular pressures. It could indeed be said not merely that they were so exposed but that they were by their nature intended to be. The *iudices* were required to function under the gaze of the *populus Romanus* and in a sense as its representatives. Of course, this power to intervene in the proceedings could itself be controversial. Thus, when on the first day of the trial, Marcellus, one of the defenders, began to interrogate a witness, "he was frightened off by such a tumult on the part of the *Clodiana multitudo* that he feared for his life, and [he] was given refuge on the tribunal by Domitius [the *quaesitor*]." Pompey, who was keeping watch from the temple of Saturn on the slope of the Capitol, had to promise to "come down" (to the Forum) on the next day with an armed guard, or *praesidium* (40C).

Then, on the evening before the last day of the trial, Munatius held a *contio* to urge the people to be present in force the next day.

> When the *iudicium* had been dismissed about the tenth hour, T. Munatius urged the people *pro contione* that they should be present in numbers on the next day and should not let Milo escape but should make their *iudicium* and their anguish clear to those proceeding to cast their votes. On the next day, the last of the trial, the seventh day before the ides of April, the *tabernae* were closed throughout the city; Pompey placed guards in the Forum and around all the entrances to the Forum. He himself, as on the previous day, took his seat before the Aerarium [the temple of Saturn], surrounded by a picked band of soldiers. (40–41C)

When Cicero spoke for the defense, the shouts that met him from the "Clodiani" were such that he "did not speak with his customary *constantia*" (41–42C). Milo was condemned by thirty-eight votes to thirteen and went into a comfortable exile in Massilia.

The significance of this sequence of events is, first, its drastic effects on the topography of the northwest corner of the Forum, which after several decades of rebuilding and restructuring, the details of which are not easy to follow (see n. 19 in this chapter), was to reemerge in the 20s B.C. with the Basilica Porcia gone forever, the Curia transformed into the Curia Iulia and realigned to sit at right angles to the southern wall of the new Forum Iulium, and the Rostra moved southwestward to face the new Rostra that now stood at the east end of the Forum, in front of the temple of Divus Julius. The fire that consumed the Curia in 52 could quite reasonably be taken as a symbol of the fact that the political life of the Republic was now almost—though not quite—at an end. Second, the episode is significant simply for the fact that it is recorded in such detail in a narrative written a century later, under the empire, in a much changed world. Though the narratives of political events in the Republic offered by Plutarch and Dio are often of remarkable quality, they do not rise to the level of Asconius' either in precision or in the power to evoke the atmosphere of a moment of crisis. Even a much more highly regarded narrative like Sallust's *Bellum Catilinae,* written far closer to the events described and with much greater literary pretensions, is, as history, merely feeble, impressionistic, and rhetorical by comparison.

For the reasons explored earlier in this chapter, our access to the workings of the public political process during the rest of the year 52 and in 51 is very limited. Rather more light is shed only when we come to the tribunate of C. Scribonius Curio in 50 and to the complex negotiations, ultimately unsuccessful, over the respective positions of Pompey and Caesar in that year. It is not that there was no controversial legislation in this period; on the contrary, a significant number of *leges* are attested, which must necessarily have been debated in *contiones* and then voted on by the *comitia tributa.* What is striking, and certainly significant, is that these years (and indeed the whole five-year period after the consulship of Pompey and Crassus in 55) did not see the passing of any further *leges* either overriding the normal senatorial allocation of *provinciae* or conferring long-term commands. In other words, the political process did not generate any further competitors to rival Crassus (who had been killed in 53 at Carrhae), Pompey, who retained his proconsulship of the two Spanish provinces, or Caesar, who retained Gallia Cisalpina with Illyricum, combined with Gallia Transalpina. No further *extraordinariae potestates* were created by tribunician legislation.

To this general pattern, there are two exceptions, of different types. One is that Pompey's command in Spain was renewed for a further four years, along with an increased allocation of funds. The original command had of course been secured by tribunician legislation in 55 (see discussion earlier in this chapter). There is no contemporary evidence for the procedure in 52, but Plutarch and Appian describe this step as a vote by the Senate.[38] If this is correct, the most likely context is simply the normal senatorial vote

---

38. Plutarch *Caes.* 29.5, *Pomp.* 55.7; Appian *BC* 2.24/92. Cf. Dio 40.56.2 (which offers no indication of procedure).

de provinciis consularibus, accompanied by the usual vote of funds. As is well known, the relatively scanty evidence for politics in this period provides ample indication that the Senate repeatedly discussed the allocation of consular provinces, having closely in view the disputed question of when it would legally be possible to send a successor to Caesar in Gaul (precisely the possibility that Cicero had argued against in 56 in his *De provinciis consularibus,* as mentioned earlier in this chapter).[39]

The continuation of Pompey's command in Spain seems neither to have been the subject of tribunician legislation nor to have been challenged or overridden by it. But another measure relating to provincial commands, also very obscurely attested, had a profound effect on the outbreak of the civil war in early 49. This was the measure passed in 52 by which, in contradiction to the long-standing conception of office holding in Rome, a five-year interval was established between the holding of elective office in the city and the taking up of a proconsulship in a province. It was the allocation of *provinciae* under this rule, on the part of the Senate, that Caesar was able to characterize in early 49 by saying that "*provinciae* were decreed to *privati,*" that is, to persons not currently, or prospectively, holding elective office.[40] This phrase is part of his brilliant portrait, at the beginning of his *Bellum Civile,* of the regime in Rome as an oligarchy trampling on established procedures and long-standing popular rights. What measures had actually been passed and by what procedures is by no means clear. Dio records under 53 a senatorial decree laying down a five-year interval; the intention must have been that only after that period should ex-consuls and ex-praetors be subject to the lot *(sortitio)* for provinces.[41] Whether this issue lay within the Senate's powers, without a consequential *lex,* is obscure. At any rate, Dio also records, under 52, that Pompey, as sole consul, "validated" this senatus consultum, which surely does mean that he proposed a *lex.*[42] The effect, as Caesar prejudicially argues, was to loosen the connection between popular election and provincial governorships. Thus Cicero, who since his consulship of 63 had held no elective office and had governed no *provincia,* found himself proconsul of Cilicia in 51–50, while Bibulus,

---

39. See, e.g., Cicero *Fam.* 8.1.2 (77), 8.4.4 (81), 8.9.2 (82), 8.5.2 (83), 8.8.5–7 (84).

40. Caesar *BC* 1.6.5. Note the invaluable edition by the late J.M. Carter, *Julius Caesar: The Civil War, Books I and II* (Warminster: Aris and Phillips, 1991).

41. Dio 40.46.2.

42. Dio 40.56.1: τό τε δόγμα τὸ μικρὸν ἔμπροσθε γενόμενον, ὥστε τοὺς ἄρξαντας ἐν τῇ πόλει μὴ πρότερον ἐς τὰς ἔξω ἡγεμονίας, πρὶν πέντε ἔτη παρελθεῖν, κληροῦσθαι, ἐπεκύρωσεν.

Caesar's opponent as consul in 59, acquired the vital strategic role of proconsul of Syria in the same period.

Similarly, we do not have any reports of the public political context of the passing of the law proposed jointly by all ten tribunes of 52 to allow Caesar, apparently by name, to stand for office (as consul) in absence and therefore without giving up his provincial command or exposing himself to the danger of prosecution. But Caesar's self-justificatory account of his own actions in 49 relates how he went to Rome after his initial victories in Italy and laid before the Senate the record of the *iniuriae* done to him by his enemies.

> He showed them that he had sought no extraordinary *honor* but, once the established interval before the holding of a (second) consulate had elapsed, had been content with that which was open to all citizens. A law had been passed by the ten tribunes in the teeth of speeches against it by his enemies—Cato resisted with particular bitterness and had delayed things by using his old ploy of dragging out the days with speeches—to allow him [Caesar] to be a candidate in absence, while Pompey himself had been consul. If he [Pompey] had disapproved, why did he let the law go through? If he had approved, why did he prevent him from enjoying the *beneficium populi*?[43]

We do get some indirect hints here of public debates about this law, as well as a clear characterization of it as a *beneficium* conferred on Caesar by the people. The same conception is expressed by him also earlier in the first book of the *Bellum Civile*.

> He had been grieved because the *beneficium populi Romani* had been injuriously wrenched from him by his enemies, and, with six months of his *imperium* snatched away, he had been dragged back to Rome, he whose candidature in absence the *populus* had ordered could be accepted at the next elections.[44]

---

43. Caesar *BC* 1.32.2–3. Caesar's reference to political maneuvering in relation to this measure is, however, supported by allusions in Cicero, for instance, in *Att.* 7.1.4 (124), of 50 B.C., recording that Cicero had visited Caesar at Ravenna (winter 53/2 B.C.) and had agreed to help him as regards Caelius, evidently to secure his assent as one of the ten tribunes of 52. For other references, see Shackleton Bailey's note ad loc. As will be clear, I make no attempt to discuss here the long-established question of the terminal date of Caesar's command in Gaul.

44. Caesar *BC* 1.9.2.

Even if we do not accept Caesar's representation of this legislation or its aftermath as the whole truth, we can see that the ideology of popular sovereignty was a potent weapon in the early stages of the civil war. Even Cicero was to claim, looking back from the year 46, that once the *populus* had ordered this *beneficium,* he (Cicero) had thought that it should be allowed to stand.[45]

Precisely by being, on the one hand, a measure put forward by all ten tribunes, evidently with popular support and against the will of at least some prominent senators, and, on the other, a *privilegium* conferring an exceptional right on someone who was already in possession of vast cash resources and military power, the "law of the ten tribunes" can be taken as a clear symbol of the connection between popular politics and the approach of monarchy. But we can gain only a faint impression of the public debates that evidently attended its passing in 52. For the reasons indicated earlier, our knowledge of public debate and conflict in the rest of 52 and also in 51 remains slight and allusive, and adds nothing significant to the picture already drawn of the forms of debate, exchange, and conflict in the Forum.

As regards the year 50, though our evidence, with no speeches of Cicero preserved, is in no way comparable to that for the earlier 50s, it does allow some greater insight. We have indications of the way in which electoral conflict on a broad scale now affected even the filling of places in the college of augurs. Because these posts were held for life—and therefore in many years no vacancy would arise—we hear relatively little about such elections. But we do need to recall that the principle of popular election to priesthoods had been established by tribunician legislation in 104 and had apparently been subverted by Sulla and restored in 63 (see chap. 5). An important principle of popular sovereignty was therefore involved. The evidence for 50 demonstrates that, whether we would expect it or not, such elections could be vigorously contested. As Caelius reports to Cicero in August, there was heavy voting, mostly along lines dictated by the political divisions of the moment rather than by personal connection or obligation.[46] Even so, we would not necessarily have expected that Antonius' candidature for the augurate at this moment would have engaged the attention of Julius Caesar, who was now in the last stages of his proconsulate of Gaul. But, as we have already seen briefly (in

---

45. Cicero *Fam.* 6.6.5 (234).
46. Cicero *Fam.* 8.14.1 (97): "magna illa comitia fuerunt et plane studia ex partium sensu apparuerunt, perpauci necessitudinem secuti officium praestiterunt."

chap. 2), this moment provides important evidence for the potential voting role of the Roman citizens resident in Gallia Cisalpina, and hence in
Caesar's province.

The account provided by Hirtius, in the last book of the *De bello
Gallico*, of Caesar's motives for supporting Antonius, and of the connection between this issue and the prospective one of Caesar's own candidature in 49 for the consulship of 48, is of immense importance. For it
indicates how, at this moment at least, issues of personal success or
failure and the attainment or otherwise of office were intertwined with
broader questions of policy and of political loyalties.

> Caesar himself, when the winter quarters [for 50/49] had been ar-
> ranged, set out, contrary to his usual custom, by the most rapid
> stages possible, for "Italy" [Gallia Cisalpina], in order to appeal to
> the *municipia* and *coloniae* to which he had commended the can-
> didature of M. Antonius, his quaestor, for a priesthood. For he
> strove to exert his influence both gladly, on behalf of a man who
> was so closely bound to him, and whom he had a little earlier sent
> on ahead to campaign for office, and fiercely, against the machina-
> tions and power of the small group who sought, by securing the
> failure of Antonius, to shatter the *gratia* of Caesar as he left [the
> province]. Even though he had heard en route, before he reached
> Italy, that Antonius had been elected augur, he considered it a no
> less compelling reason to visit the *municipia* and *coloniae,* in order
> to thank them for having offered their support in large numbers and
> their loyalty to Antonius. At the same time, he would commend
> himself and his [prospective] *honor* as regarded the electoral cam-
> paign of the following year, in view of the fact that his opponents
> were insolently boasting that it was L. Lentulus and C. Marcellus
> who had been elected as the consuls [for 49], in order to rob Caesar
> of every *honor* and *dignitas,* and that the consulate had been
> snatched from Servius Galba, although he had been much stronger
> in *gratia* and votes, because he had been tied to Caesar by friendship
> and collaboration in his legateship.[47]

The importance of this observation by Hirtius, who was to be consul in
43, could hardly be exaggerated. First, it adds another voice to the very

---

47. [Caesar] *BG* 8.50.

short list of contemporaries from whom we hear anything about the values that prevailed in Roman politics (Caelius' letters to Cicero in Cilicia are of course another noteworthy example). Second, it emphasizes the individualistic and competitive nature of Roman office holding, while at the same time indicating the importance of both bonds of loyalty on the one hand and personal enmities on the other, as between holders, or potential holders, of elective office. Third, it reminds us that the most important elective office, the consulship, has to be seen in the context of a wider network of other elective offices—more than fifty annually, as we have seen (see chap. 2)—including those, like priesthoods, that were open for competition only occasionally. Finally, and most important of all, it reveals that an apparently unimportant and "unpolitical" post, such as an augurate, like (of course) the consulate itself, could be the object of canvassing even in those parts of Italy that were more remote from Rome. This canvassing was not necessarily an empty gesture. Hirtius' reference to Caesar's appreciation of the *frequentia* of supporters of Antonius from the *municipia* and *coloniae* of Gallia Cisalpina has a quite concrete meaning: significant numbers of them must have gone to Rome and voted. The expression need not be held to mean tens of thousands or even thousands. It may well indicate no more than a few hundred *legati* from the towns, along with some other private persons. The fact remains that Caesar is represented as seeing the confirmation of support for an associate of his in this area as having a real relevance to his own electoral prospects for the consulship of 48. If we are to understand the erratic and increasingly violence-ridden politics of the public spaces of Rome itself, we have to see participation there against the vastly wider background of the inhabitants of Italy who were entitled to vote and might on occasion do so.

Even for the crucial year 50, which we can hardly fail to see as the last in which the institutions of the *res publica* functioned in their traditional manner of open competition and conflict, our sources for events in Rome are remarkably thin and are heavily dominated by later biographical or historical narratives. Most of what little we can discern relates to the public role of one of the ten tribunes, Scribonius Curio (of his nine colleagues, or fellow holders of the office, only one can even be named). Otherwise, only toward the end of the calendar year, when the term of office of the next tribunes had begun on December 10, can we see some significant detail of how public debate and conflict worked.

Curio had not originally been seen as a supporter of Caesar, and very probably had indeed not been one. Whether, as later sources allege,

Caesar finally secured his support by bribery cannot be known. At any rate, in the early part of his tenure of office, Curio revived the traditional public and legislative role of the tribunate in emphatic style. Dio in fact claims that Curio was already in alliance with Caesar but deliberately concealed this fact, expressing public opposition to him, making speeches against him (Dio's words indicate that he is speaking of *contiones* addressed to the people), and introducing various erratic legislative proposals.[48] Once again the contemporary evidence, relatively slight though it is, shows that a program, or set of public positions, on the part of an incoming tribune, could be known even before he took office. In mid-November 51, after Curio's election, but some three weeks before he entered office, Caelius, writing to Cicero, was anticipating that he would be unfavorable to Caesar and favorable to Pompey, and also speaks concretely of the prospective legislative acts of Curio as including measures relating to the Ager Campanus.[49] We need not follow the sparsely reported details of various bills reportedly proposed by Curio. But it is necessary to emphasize that his activity included measures relating to the running of the empire: the allotment of provinces,[50] the voting of a triumph,[51] and even a *lex* by which the *regnum* of King Juba in North Africa would be "made public," that is, taken over as a province.[52] It cannot be stressed too strongly that, as had been the case for the last two decades, debates and votes in the Forum could determine the allocation of power, resources, and prestige within the imperial system, and might (as with Cyprus in 58; see chap. 6) decide the shape of the empire itself.

The role of the tribunate in determining external policy had hardly been a major feature of the workings of the *res publica* until the last years of the second century (see chap. 2). But its role in constitutional and social measures had been established for centuries. Nonetheless, such legislation had not been a very prominent aspect of the known tribunician activity of the later 50s, and Curio's stance represented a new initiative. At first, nothing much came of it, but in February there was a change. Both phases are represented in a letter of Caelius' to Cicero, written, as he explicitly states, at two separate moments, in between which the political scene had altered.

---

48. Dio 40.61.2: καὶ ἐδημηγόρει κατ' αὐτοῦ ἀφ' οὗ γε καὶ δημαρχεῖν ἤρξατο, καὶ ἐσηγεῖτο πολλὰ καὶ ἄτοπα.

49. Cicero *Fam.* 8.10.3–4 (87).

50. See Cicero *Att.* 6.2.6 (116).

51. See the quotation from Varro's *De vita populi romani* 4 in Nonius Marcellus *De compendiosa doctrina*, ed. W.M. Lindsay, 1:214–15.

52. See Caesar *BC* 2.25.4.

Caelius' report deserves quotation, not least because it illustrates how a change in the public posture of a single tribune could suddenly alter the political climate.

> As for our Curio, his *tribunatus* is frozen stiff. . . . If it were not for the fact that I [as aedile] am in dispute with the shopkeepers *[tabernarii]* and aqueduct suppliers *[aquarii]*, a torpor would have fallen over the whole *civitas*. . . . As for what I wrote above, to the effect that Curio is utterly frozen, now he has warmed up, for he is being most fervently criticized. For in a most frivolous way, because he did not succeed in getting an intercalary month, he has fled to the *populus* and has begun to speak on behalf of Caesar, and [he] has thrown around the idea of a *lex viaria* not unlike the *lex agraria* of Rullus, as well as a law on the food supply *[lex alimentaria]* that would put the aedile in charge of distribution. He had not yet done this when I wrote the first part of the letter.[53]

The reference is clearly to the altered content of the *contiones* delivered by Curio. It is striking how having "fled to the *populus*" and "begun to speak on behalf of Caesar" are almost equated, and how both are associated with steps that would effect economic relations and the food supply of the urban population. The significance of this public posture and of the tendency of the proposed legislation is clear, even though we do not know whether any of his proposals were ever promulgated as *rogationes* or voted on. The comparison that Caelius makes between Curio's *lex viaria* and the *lex agraria* of Rullus (see chap. 5) is best explained by Appian's report that Curio's proposal would have involved an extensive program of repairs to the roads, with a five-year commission for Curio himself.[54]

The public politics of the year rapidly became embroiled in a complex of interlocking issues: Curio's desire to push through his proposed legislation; proposals to block this legislation by using up some of the possible voting days on *supplicationes;* and, above all, the issue of whether there would be changes in the allocation of the consular provinces and, if so, from what date. Caelius describes the issues in a letter written apparently in April, in which he explores the position taken up by various individuals, without making clear whether they expressed their views only in the

53. Cicero *Fam.* 8.6.4–5 (88).
54. Appian *BC* 2.27/102.

Senate or also in the Forum.⁵⁵ Pompey, he says, now took the view that Caesar should leave his province by the beginning of November; Curio was resolutely opposed and had abandoned all of his program *(actiones)* to concentrate on this issue. His legislative proposals could of course not have come to anything without a popular vote.

The complex movements of opinion through the middle part of 50— over whether Caesar could be allowed the right to stand for the consulship in absence, whether and when he should be required to hand over his province, and whether Pompey should lay down his command at the same moment—need not be explored here in detail.⁵⁶ What is important for the question of the role of popular politics is that we have quite clear evidence of the appeals made to the people by Curio and of the support offered by mass meetings for the idea of a compromise. For instance, Plutarch reports that when Curio proposed in the Senate that both Caesar and Pompey should lay down their commands, all the senators except twenty-two voted in favor: "he therefore, his face lit up with the joy of victory, rushed out to the people, who greeted him with applause and pelted him with garlands and flowers."⁵⁷ Hirtius confirms that this proposal had been put to the Senate by Curio, without mentioning a specific vote or the reaction of the people.⁵⁸ According to Plutarch in his *Life* of Caesar, moreover, Caesar had written to Rome to make just this proposal, and Curio had laid it before the people on his behalf.⁵⁹ (Curio's procedure therefore exactly mirrors that of Clodius in 58, in reading out before a *contio* what was claimed to be a letter of Caesar's from Gaul; see chap. 6.) This proposal for compromise certainly was Caesar's position, or it had become so by early 49, as he claims in his *Bellum Civile*.⁶⁰

We do not in fact have enough concrete evidence for particular episodes to be able to say precisely what propositions were set out in *contiones* before the people in the closing months of 50. But Appian records that when the consuls, with no constitutional backing from either Senate or people, asked Pompey to undertake the defense of Italy against Caesar's forces, which were believed to be advancing, Curio complained of the illegality of this action before the people and advised them not to

55. Cicero *Fam.* 8.11.3 (91).

56. Note, e.g., Caelius' letters: Cicero *Fam.* 8.13.2 (94), from June 50; *Fam.* 8.14.2 (97), from August; *Att.* 7.3.2–5 (126), 7.4 (127), and 7.7 (130), from December.

57. Plutarch *Pomp.* 59.4–5.

58. [Caesar] *BG* 8.52.4.

59. Plutarch *Caes.* 30.1–2; see Appian *BC* 2.30/119.

60. Caesar *BC* 1.9.5.

obey if recruited by Pompey. But then, since the end of his term of office was approaching, fearing for his safety and despairing of achieving anything on Caesar's behalf, Curio set off in haste to Caesar.[61]

Dio describes the same events in more concrete detail, and ends his account as follows.

> Curio, in response to this, delivered before the people a lengthy denunciation both of Pompey and of the consuls and, since his term of office had come to an end, at once set off to join Caesar.[62]

These are the last words of the fortieth book of Dio's great eighty-book history of Rome, which told the whole story from the coming of Aeneas to his own second consulship in A.D. 229. It can hardly be accident that the first half of Dio's entire story ends with the flight of a tribune to join the future dictator, whose name was to be used for centuries by dynasties of "Caesares" who had no family connection with himself. This was indeed, as Dio implies, the great turning point in Roman history.

Yet, all the same, we are not quite finished with the politics even of the year 50 itself. For Curio's last day in office will have been December 9, and on December 10 a new college of ten tribunes assumed office, among them Marcus Antonius, who had been quaestor in 52 and had served under Caesar in Gaul; as we have seen earlier in this chapter, Caesar had intended to support Antonius' candidature for the augurate earlier in 50 (why Hirtius says nothing of his standing also for the tribunate is not clear). At any rate, he must have come to Rome from Gaul in the summer of 50, will have been unmistakably a Caesarian candidate, and had been elected. Plutarch indeed records that Curio, by using his popularity as an orator and deploying large funds sent by Caesar, had secured Antonius' election to both the tribunate and the augurate.[63] The implication is of course, once again, that such elections had a fully political character.

For Antonius' role on entering office, we do not, finally, have to depend only on later narratives. Cicero's letters to Atticus contain two long and important ones that discuss the political juncture that had been reached and look back on the years of irresolution that had gone before. Both letters are written from Formiae, one on about December 19, and

---

61. Appian *BC* 2.31/120–23.
62. Dio 40.66.5.
63. Plutarch *Ant.* 5.1; see C.B.R. Pelling, *Plutarch, Life of Antony* (Cambridge: Cambridge University Press, 1988), ad loc.

one on December 25 or 26. In the first, he looks back on the steps that had allowed Caesar to accumulate so much power and suggests that it is too late to fight and that Caesar must be allowed his legally conferred right to stand for the consulship in absence.[64]

In the second letter, he describes how he had met Pompey and had discussed the situation with him at Formiae. Pompey, he says, was convinced that if Caesar became consul, the Republican constitution would be destroyed; but Pompey also believed that if Caesar saw that there would be real resistance, he would keep his army and province and give up hope of the consulship for the next year. If he did choose to fight, he could be resisted.[65]

That was Pompey's assessment, which turned out to be false, for Italy did not rise up to resist Caesar; Pompey's view that Caesar's victory would mean the end of the Republic was, however, correct. But Pompey and Cicero also had news of political positions currently being taken up in Rome.

> But we had in our hands [the text of] a *contio* of Antonius held on the tenth day before the calends of January [December 21], in which there was a denunciation of Pompey since the time he wore the *toga pura,* a complaint over those who had been condemned, and threats of armed force.[66]

Pompey, Cicero says, had asked what could be expected of a victory of Caesar, if his unstable and impoverished former quaestor could utter such things. We might see a rather more general significance in this report. As I noted much earlier (in chap. 2), a written version of Antonius' speech had been delivered to Pompey and Cicero at Formiae within four or five days of delivery. We cannot of course tell whether what Pompey and Cicero read was a summary or a complete text taken down by shorthand and then written out. Nor do we know whether less-privileged persons in Italian towns had access to similar texts. It is clear that it was possible for written versions of *contiones* delivered in Rome to be disseminated not only in Rome but outside it. The distances involved are also significant. It is not a question, in this instance, of the extremes of Italy, either north or south; nonetheless, Formiae lies some

64. Cicero *Att.* 7.7 (130).
65. Cicero *Att.* 7.8.4. (131).
66. Cicero *Att.* 7.8.5 (131).

130 kilometers by road from Rome and hence at least two days' journey, perhaps more. Within that range of distance from the Forum, where Antonius will have spoken, there lived not only the two hundred thousand to three hundred thousand adult male voters who inhabited the city and its suburban zone (see chap. 2), but the population of a large part of central Italy. When it was felt to be necessary, as when the *principes* decided to summon help for the recall of Cicero in 57, communications could be sent out more widely, even as far south as Capua (see chap. 6). Indeed, at this very moment, the widespread reaction of Italian towns to the news of Pompey's illness in 50 served to give what turned out to be a quite false impression of the support against Caesar on which he and the consuls would be able to call.[67]

There was therefore a potential "Roman" political community in Italy, which was almost never in reality fully exploited or called into play. But Cicero's second letter just cited reminds us that there was also, by contrast, a real political community in Rome, in the Forum, made up of whoever happened to be there to hear the speeches that went on being made to the very end, even as power was about to pass to military force. The crowd in the Forum was the heir of the *populus* of that small city-state, with an urban center and a surrounding territory, which is what Rome had been four centuries earlier. It still, in some sense, "represented" the now vastly increased number of Roman citizens, and when it came to voting, it still exercised the constitutional power of the sovereign *populus Romanus*. That was a paradox and may seem an absurdity. But the voting power that was exercised by the crowd now had effects that were felt from Britain to the Euphrates. So questions of how we should interpret so strange a political system, and how we should understand the exercise of power and persuasion within it, deserve some further consideration.

---

67. This point is made in fine style by Plutarch at *Pomp.* 57.

VIII

The Crowd in Rome: What Sort of Democracy?

All through this brief study the importance of inherited structures has been emphasized again and again: the annually elected magistrates, above all the two consuls, who for centuries had been mainly *imperatores* and were now for a few decades primarily "politicians" in Rome; the ten tribunes, elected as representatives and protectors of the people, taking their seats each day outside the Curia; the ancient popular assemblies, the *comitia centuriata* and the *comitia tributa,* and the long-established urban landscape of the political center (the Curia and the Comitium, the wider Forum, the temple of Castor and Pollux); and the secondary voting space, outside the ritual boundary of the city, the Campus Martius, where the *comitia centuriata* met, as an electoral, judicial, and legislative assembly, and where since the 140s the *comitia tributa,* in its role as an electoral assembly, had come to meet also.

Both as regards its actual institutions, which still provided the structure of those of the imperial Republic of Cicero's time, and in the values that were attached to it by later generations, it is impossible to overstress the importance of the archaic nuclear city-state of the fifth and fourth centuries. Indeed, in the historical tradition, the origin of many of the fundamental institutions of the *res publica* is located further back in time, in the regal period. T.J. Cornell was therefore, in essence, wholly right to characterize the story of Rome as "the history of an anachronism."[1] Moreover, whether we think of the survival of actual institutions or of the attention paid to archaic features in the historiographical tradition, many aspects of the "anachronism" were to have an astonishingly long life. We have only to think of the consulate, which persisted in some form from the late sixth century B.C. to the seventh century A.D., or of the Curia, allegedly con-

---

1. See T.J. Cornell, "Rome: The History of an Anachronism," in A. Molho, K. Raaflaub, and J. Emlen, eds., *City-States in Classical Antiquity and Medieval Italy* (Ann Arbor: University of Michigan Press, 1991), 53.

structed by the king Tullus Hostilius on the edge of the Comitium, altered by Sulla, and burned down in 52 (as we saw in chap. 7), only to reemerge almost on the same spot but with a different alignment, as the Curia Iulia dedicated in 29, reconstructed by Diocletian, transformed into a church in the seventh century, and still standing today.[2]

Equally, we need hardly stress the fundamental importance of argument from historical precedent in the late Republic itself, of the antiquarian studies associated with the names of Varro, Atticus and Nepos, and their relevance to Livy and Vergil, or of the way in which a profound antiquarian learning focused on early Rome communicated itself to Greek writers of the imperial period, whether Dionysius in his *Antiquitates Romanae*,[3] Plutarch in his Roman biographies or his *Quaestiones Romanae*, or Cassius Dio. Indeed, Dio, in talking of the trial of Rabirius before the *comitia centuriata* in 63 (see chap. 5), brings out most clearly both the importance of this element in imperial historiography and the real longevity of archaic customs. He explains how the assembly could be terminated by taking down the flag flown on the Janiculum on the opposite side of the Tiber.

> Now this matter of the flag is as follows. In ancient times there were many enemies dwelling near the city, and the Romans, fearing that while they were holding an assembly by centuries foes might occupy the Janiculum and attack the city, decided that not all should vote at once, but that some men under arms should by turns always guard that position. So they guarded it as long as the assembly lasted, but when this was about to be adjourned, the flag was pulled down and the guards departed; for no further business could be transacted when the post was not guarded. This practice was observed only in the case of the centuriate assemblies, for these were held outside the walls, and all those who bore arms were obliged to gather for them. Even to this day, this is done as a matter of form.[4]

The significance of the preceding passage lies both in the revelation that the *comitia centuriata* still met in the first half of the third century (as Dio

---

2. See *LTUR* 1, s.v. "Curia."

3. See now the admirable study by E. Gabba, *Dionysius and the History of Archaic Rome* (Berkeley: University of California Press, 1991).

4. Dio 37.28.1–3, Loeb trans. with adjustments.

indeed also states elsewhere)⁵ and in the antiquarian learning it displays. In this respect, Dio's great history belongs with Latin works of the second and third centuries, such as Aulus Gellius' *Noctes Atticae* or the works of jurists: perhaps the most noteworthy example of juristic antiquarian learning is an extraordinarily neglected text, Pomponius' *Enchiridion,* a second-century analysis of the evolution of Roman institutions that is preserved in the *Digest.*⁶

The power of the image of the Republic, in the minds of people who lived under an emperor and whose homes might lie hundreds or even thousands of kilometers from the city, is an aspect of cultural history of immense importance. I note only one further example, the speech of thanks for the conferment of the consulship of A.D. 379 addressed by Ausonius, from Bordeaux, to the emperor Gratian, who came from Pannonia.

> For my part, as consul by your gift, Imperator Augustus, I have not had to endure the Saepta or the Campus, or the voting, or the points [recording the votes], or the ballot boxes. I have not had to press people's hands, nor, confused by the rush of persons greeting me, have I failed to reply with their right names to my friends or given them the wrong ones. I have not gone round the *tribus,* or flattered the *centuriae,* or had to tremble when the *classes* were called [to vote]. I have not made any deposit with a trustee or agreed anything with a *diribitor.* The *populus Romanus,* the *Martius Campus,* the *equester ordo,* the Rostra, the "sheepfold" [the Saepta], the Senate, the Curia—for me, Gratian alone was all these things.⁷

Ausonius manages to import a remarkable level of detail into his representation of a vanished world, whose central institution, the consulate, was now in the gift of the emperor. The passage, like others written in the imperial period, is both a parade of antiquarian learning and a recognition that the roots of the imperial system really did lie in the communal institutions of a city-state.

---

5. Dio 58.20.4.

6. *Digesta* 1.2.2.

7. Ausonius *Gratiarum Actio* 3/13, in R.P.H. Green, ed., *The Works of Ausonius* (Oxford: Clarendon, 1991), 148, referring to Taylor, *Voting Assemblies,* 34 (for *puncta*) and 55 (for *loculi*). The word translated "sheepfold" *(Ovilia)* in fact also refers to the Saepta.

The passage is also, however, a recognition that in that city-state there had been real political competition and a real need to court and please the voters. The "anachronism" was still, in the fourth century, a living presence to educated people, whatever their geographical origins. What Ausonius, like Dio a century and a half before, is speaking of is the *comitia centuriata,* Dio of its functioning as a court, Ausonius of its electoral role. For them, the exploration, or evocation, of some traditional features was sufficient. But if we go back to the late Republic or to the histories of Rome written in the Augustan period, the issue of the nature of the *comitia centuriata* has a much greater significance. Cicero in the *De re publica,* Livy in his history, and Dionysius in his *Antiquitates Romanae* interpret the structure of this assembly, in very explicit terms, as having been deliberately intended to express social gradations, to organize the voters in groups whose priority was determined by wealth, and thus to make the resultant voting an expression of social precedence, proportioned to the "stake in society" of the individual.

What is curious and requires to be stressed is that all three of these analyses of the *comitia centuriata* are themselves also expressions of Roman antiquarianism. For, as we have seen briefly much earlier (see chap. 2), they all devote themselves to analyzing the structure and functioning of this assembly as it was thought to have been when first instituted under the kings. Cicero's account is the earliest, and does not explicitly say, in the surviving sections of the text, that the system had been changed subsequently. Instead, he speaks of the priority and separation of the *equites,* and then of the five *classes,* each divided into *seniores* and *iuniores,* into which the population was distributed, in such a way "that the *suffragia* should be in the control not of the *multitudo* but of the rich." The lawgiver (Servius Tullius) "took care for the principle that must be observed in a *res publica,* that the greatest number should not have the greatest influence."[8] In reading these words, written in the later 50s, we should remember the immediate context, namely, Cicero's despair of, and partial withdrawal from, the contemporary *res publica,* as well as the more general truth that all such observations are reflections of contemporary debates, and constitute a sort of dialogue between an imagined past and the present.

We have to see in a rather different light the account of the census classes and the *comitia centuriata* included by Livy in his first book,

8. Cicero *De re pub.* 2.22/39–40.

probably written around the time of Actium. That what Livy wrote was *Roman* history is a remarkable fact (more remarkable than is generally allowed) to which I will come back later in this chapter. For the moment, it is enough to say that Livy's work is derivative (in a nonderogatory sense) from the historical scholarship and ideological debates of the late Republic, and takes over a conservative and pessimistic tone. In his account of the measures supposedly instituted by Servius Tullius, he states categorically that in the *comitia centuriata* of the archaic period, the eighteen *centuriae* of *equites* voted first, followed by the eighty *centuriae* of the *prima classis*. Then, if a majority had not already been achieved, it might on occasion be necessary for the *secunda classis* to vote also. The purpose, in Livy's account, was quite explicit and accords with that alleged by Cicero: "gradations were established, in order that no one should seem to be excluded from the vote, and [yet] that all the power should remain with the *primores civitatis*." Livy goes on to say that the contemporary system was different, but without indicating in what way.[9]

Finally, the account in Dionysius' *Antiquitates Romanae* is also derivative from late-Republican representations of the remote Roman past. He too presents an idealized picture, in much greater detail, of the division of the people by Servius Tullius into *classes* according to wealth and of the priority accorded to the 18 centuries of cavalrymen and the 80 of the first class—98 *classes* in all out of a total of 193. Here, too, the purpose is said to have been to give the appearance of equality while reserving the preponderance of power for the rich.

It is at the end of this long account that, as we saw earlier, Dionysius records briefly, and with no detail, that subsequently the *comitia centuriata* had been reformed so as to be "somewhat more democratic."[10] As we also saw earlier, one certain feature of the later-Republican *comitia* was that the *centuriae* of *equites* did not vote first (see chap. 2).

This long digression has been necessary to bring out various crucial features of our access to conceptions about the Roman *res publica*. First, in sources written in the classical period, explicit discussions of Roman institutions and of the values attached to them have a very strong tendency to be related to the remote past. In this case, two of our three "sources" for the *comitia centuriata* admit explicitly that the system they are recalling no longer functioned in the same way. Second, as we have seen over and over again in the oratory of the later Republic, all evocations of the remote past

9. Livy 1.43.
10. See Dionysius *Ant.* 4.16–21.

are purposeful, or argumentative. In short, they are interpretations carrying an ideological message.

Third, the same is true of the uses to which this supposed "evidence" is put in the modern world. Take, for instance, the generally excellent paper by T.J. Cornell cited earlier in this chapter (n. 1). Here, these late-Republican and Augustan representations of the census and the centuriate assembly, as they had been in the remote archaic past, are taken as fact, and are then generalized so as to function as keys to the whole Roman social system: "These rights and privileges of Roman citizens were carefully weighted in favor of the upper classes, in accordance with the principle of 'proportional' equality."[11]

That principle was indeed the one which all three of these writers saw as having been explicitly embodied in the *comitia centuriata*, when it was structured in a way that no longer applied in full (if it ever had) and certainly had not done so since at least the later third century. Therefore, even as regards the *comitia centuriata* themselves as they were in Cicero's time, and even before we ask in what contexts this particular assembly functioned, we have to consider what we know of it in its contemporary form.

It is here of course that we encounter the fatal weakness imposed by the structure of our evidence—the restriction of analytical and evaluative accounts to the re-creation of the past, as well as the absence of any equivalent of the present-tense analysis of fourth-century Athenian institutions in the Aristotelian *Athēnaiōn Politeia*. The functioning of the Roman *res publica* in the age of Cicero has to be reconstructed from passing allusions and from items of persuasive discourse, whether the versions of "speeches" inserted in narrative histories or the surviving texts representing, precisely or otherwise, actual examples of speeches delivered. In all of these sources, there is a constant argumentative tension, in which interpretation of the present and interpretation of the past interact with each other.

We must therefore be extremely careful in distinguishing, so far as we can, between the interpretative messages carried by our sources and the attempt—severely limited by the nature of the evidence—to work out how any one Roman institution was structured and how it functioned at any specific period. Beyond that, we need to know in what context, or contexts, it functioned. Only with these considerations in mind can we tell what its significance was for the nature of the system overall.

---

11. Cornell, art. cit. (n. 1 above), 53.

These general questions gain an increased relevance from the recent reexamination of the *comitia centuriata* of the late Republic, and their functioning as an electoral assembly, by Alexander Yakobson.[12] Without rehearsing all the details, many of which remain uncertain, some broad characteristics of the late-Republican centuriate assembly can be established. First, the *prima classis,* which now voted first, consisted of seventy *centuriae,* one of *iuniores* and one of *seniores* from each of the thirty-five *tribus.* Second, estimates of the wealth required for a person to belong to the *prima classis,* while varying between twenty-five thousand and one hundred thousand sesterces, tend to center on forty thousand to fifty thousand. If we were to deduce from Livy's account of the archaic *comitia centuriata* that the assembly of his own time gave, and was intended to give, power to the *primores civitatis,* we would quite simply be wrong. The minimum wealth required seems to have been at a level equivalent to about 10 percent of that required for *equites* and (at the most) 5 percent of that which would be required for senators under the Augustan system. In short, it is here, and not in the equestrian order, that we can locate the "Roman middle class."

Even if, therefore, the effective right of decision, as regards the matters normally voted on by the *comitia centuriata,* had been confined to the *prima classis,* we would be concerned not with an oligarchy of the rich but with a much broader, though constitutionally privileged, possessing class. How the adult male population of Roman citizens, of something approaching a million in all, was divided between the various *classes* seems impossible to determine.

It is also unclear both what the structure of the lower *classes* was, and whether a strict order of voting was always maintained. Even if it was, which certainly cannot be disproved, Yakobson's study shows, first, that electoral bribery (like other means of gaining popularity) was not aimed strictly at the members of the *prima classis* but at the population as a whole; and, second, that a number of passing allusions in our sources show that there were examples of electoral success or failure being determined by only a narrow majority of *centuriae,* and hence that effective choice in electoral voting *could* be distributed across the entire range of *classes.*[13]

---

12. A. Yakobson, "*Petitio et Largitio:* Popular Participation in the Centuriate Assembly of the Late Republic," *JRS* 82 (1992): 32 and esp. section 3, pp. 44–45, "The Structure and Functioning of the Centuriate Assembly."

13. See Yakobson, "*Petitio et Largitio,*" 46–47, and, e.g., Cicero *Brut.* 67/237 and Asconius 94C.

These considerations are not brought forward in any attempt to deny what is quite clear, that the structure of the *comitia centuriata* did give a systematic advantage to the possessing classes and was valued by traditionally minded persons precisely for that reason. It is also extremely significant, first, that, as we saw earlier (in chap. 5), Cicero makes clear in his speech of 63 in defense of Murena that any proposal to disturb the established order of voting would have met strong opposition from the *municipia*. Second, as we also saw in some detail (in chap. 6), it is relevant that on the only occasion when the *principes* in Rome successfully exerted themselves to exploit the support of the possessing classes in Italy, for the return of Cicero from exile in 57, they did so by bringing them to vote in the *comitia centuriata* in the Campus Martius.

This wholly exceptional occasion is significant also in another way, namely, that it is one of the very rare moments in the late Republic when the *comitia centuriata* are found voting on a *lex*. The function that the *comitia centuriata* regularly performed was solely that of meeting, at one season in each year, to elect consuls and praetors. Their (broadly) class-based structure would therefore properly be seen as the key to the whole nature of the Roman political system, only if we gave a corresponding importance to the results of the praetorian and consular elections, as against all other forms of decision making within the *res publica*. But the thesis which is put forward in this study is precisely that the most important type of collective decision in Rome was not electoral, but the voting of *leges*.

It is not only that voting on *leges* was normally the preserve of the other archaic form of assembly, the *comitia tributa*, but that proposals for *leges* were far more often put forward by tribunes than by consuls or praetors, and that the area of application of *leges* came more and more clearly to extend into strategic and military matters, and to the allocation of provincial commands—in other words to be the determining factor in the competition for power and prestige among officeholders.

It is here that we find a very strange feature of the basis on which the Roman *res publica* has been, and still is, analyzed, and one which, in a way which is not in the least accidental, unites ancient commentators and modern ones. Why is so little emphasis given to the fact that in the *comitia tributa* every citizen could vote on an equal basis, with no priority accorded to wealth or social status? The distinction between the two types of structure was of course clear. As Cicero puts it in his *De legibus*, "The *populus*, when arranged by *census, ordines,* and age-groups *[aetates]*, brings more consideration to its vote than when called together indiscriminately into *tribus*."[14]

In the late-Republican and Augustan accounts of the evolution of the *res publica,* the emergence (apparently in the fifth century) of an assembly divided by *tribus* and concerned, first, with election of plebeian officeholders, and eventually (at least by the earlier third century), with voting on *leges* is presented obscurely and allusively, and there is no occasion to discuss the details here.[15] Equally, the origins and rationale of the system of *tribus*—artificial subdivisions of the population on a basis of locality— can hardly now be reconstructed.[16] All that is essential is to recall that the number of *tribus* had grown until it reached the canonical number of thirty-five in 241, and had then stopped at that, as well as that, in the historical period, the allocation of every citizen to a *tribus* was essential to the structure not only of the *comitia tributa* but also of the *comitia centuriata.*

Two principles, neither of which is in the least self-evident or generally characteristic of historical societies, were thus at work. The first was that decisions (electoral and legislative) should be taken by majority voting, in which in principle every citizen could participate. Even the retrospective evaluations of the structure of the *comitia centuriata* discussed earlier in this chapter, while emphasizing the due priority accorded to the richer classes, acknowledge the right in principle for every citizen to participate. Neither of these structures, therefore, excluded any adult male, in principle, on grounds of poverty. Second, both of these systems as recorded, while involving the principle of the majority vote, did so in a way that deliberately subdivided the citizens, in such a way that the effects of their individual votes *(suffragia)* were mediated through a system of subgroups *(tribus* or *centuriae);* the result of the vote of each subgroup was determined by a simple majority, but the overall result of the voting was determined by the outcome of a series of subgroup votes, each counting as one and being declared sequentially. We have seen a classic instance of these two latter principles at work in the vote on the deposition from office of a tribune in 67 (see chap. 4): when the votes of seventeen out of thirty-five *tribus* had been declared and all had voted for deposition, the tribune withdrew his opposition to the law at issue.

---

14. Cicero *De leg.* 3.19/44.
15. See, e.g., R.M. Ogilvie, *A Commentary on Livy Books 1–5* (Oxford: Clarendon, 1965), 380–81, on Livy 2.58.1.
16. See the classic work of L.R. Taylor, *Voting Districts.*

The representations and evaluations of the past, and in particular of the evolution of institutions, which were written in Rome in the late Republic and the Augustan period might have discussed the principle of majority voting itself, or that of voting in subgroups. But in fact it does not appear that detailed considerations relating to either of these principles are to be found anywhere in our sources.[17] This absence has been of immense significance for modern conceptions of Roman politics and society. For while our ancient evidence affords no starting point for any appreciation of the principle of decision by the votes of all citizens, without disenfranchisement on grounds of poverty, it does provide three separate, strongly favorable, evaluations of the subordinate principle, applied in one form of assembly but not in the other, that priority in voting should be given to subgroups composed of richer citizens and that the groups voting earlier, each producing one collective vote, should be made up of smaller numbers than those voting (if at all) later.

It must be stressed once again, therefore, that this principle *is* a subordinate one that depends on the wider principle of the majority vote, that the assembly to which it applied had only very restricted functions in the late Republic, and that by far the more important political function, the passing of *leges,* most often on the proposition of tribunes, took place almost entirely in the *comitia tributa,* in which—within his own *tribus*—each citizen had an equal vote.

In the curiously brief, allusive, and inexplicit references in the main narrative sources that offer representations of the evolution of early Rome, there is no equivalent, as regards the *comitia tributa,* to the three detailed expositions of the class structure of the *comitia centuriata,* and there is consequently no exposition of the values of a voting system on egalitarian principles. Had there been any, it is worth asking whether modern conceptions of Roman politics might not have been very different. As it is, what we have is simply one representation by Dionysius of the idea of the patricians complaining of the claim by tribunes to the right to propose laws binding on the whole community.[18] That right had been conceded at least by the earlier third century, and in the late Republic it had been an established element in the *res publica* for more than two

---

17. For the most general available modern discussion, see E.S. Staveley, *Greek and Roman Voting and Elections* (London: Thames and Hudson, 1972). Note also J.A.O. Larsen, "The Origin and Significance of the Counting of Votes," *Class. Philol.* 44 (1949): 164.

18. Dionysius *Ant.* 10.4.

centuries. But, as we have seen (in chap. 2), precisely this power on the part of the tribunes to propose *leges* without prior senatorial approval had been removed as part of Sulla's legislation. Its restoration was demanded throughout the 70s; and when it was restored in 70, Cicero was able to observe, with every justification, that the short-lived *dominatio* of the Senate was now over (see chap. 3).

The passage in which Cicero makes this point is of some significance, both as offering, as others do, a partial and indirect view of what the ideology of popular *libertas,* which surely existed, will have been like;[19] and also in focusing on the powers and rights of the tribunes, rather than on those of the ordinary citizen as voter. All of our access, such as it is, to conceptions of popular political rights comes from literary works written by members of the educated, possessing classes; if we were to demand strict proof that political rights were important in the conceptions of the "man in the street" in Rome, we could not have it. For all our knowledge comes from representations by others.

The same problem arises, but in an even more troubling way, with the mass of Roman citizens who were now to be found throughout most of the Italian Peninsula (see chap. 2) and with the soldiers who were now recruited throughout Italy to serve in the Roman legions.[20] It would therefore be natural to begin with some skepticism when we read Julius Caesar's account of how, early in 49, he addressed the soldiers of Legion Thirteen in Gallia Cisalpina on the subject of the constitutional wrongs perpetrated by his enemies in Rome. The verb he uses is the same as applied to public speeches in Rome *(contionatur).*[21] In his speech, according to his own report, Caesar spoke of the wrongs done to him by his enemies, of Pompey's *invidia,* of the suppression by force of that tribunician right of *intercessio* that in earlier times had itself been won by force. Even Sulla, who had stripped the tribunate of all its other powers, had left the right of *intercessio* untouched. But Pompey had removed even those benefits that had been enjoyed before. The senatus consultum calling on the magistrates to see that the *res publica* came to no harm had earlier been used in the face of destructive laws or tribunician violence, in secessions of the people or

---

19. See Cicero *Verr.* 2.5.68/175. See chap. 3 above and above all, P.A. Brunt, *The Fall of the Roman Republic and Related Essays* (Oxford: Clarendon, 1988), chap. 8, "Libertas."

20. See esp. P.A. Brunt, "The Army and the Land in the Roman Revolution," *JRS* 52 (1962): 69. See his p. 85 for a table of the areas of Italy in which recruitment for the legions is attested. A revised version of the discussion appears in his *The Fall of the Roman Republic,* 240–41 (the table is on pp. 276–77).

21. Caesar *BC* 1.7.

when temples and prominent places had been occupied. But nothing of that sort had occurred now.

The soldiers of Legion Thirteen, so Caesar says, shouted in reply that they were ready to avenge the wrongs done to their imperator and to the tribunes. We cannot of course take this as an objective report. But a moment's reflection is required before we conclude that none of these issues could possibly be of any concern to young soldiers recruited in the Italian countryside, or in Gallia Cisalpina itself. For, if they were typically in their early twenties, they will have been on average just about the same age as Vergil, who was born in 70 in Mantua, and a few years older than Livy, who was born in 59 (or perhaps 64?) in Patavium, both places that were within Caesar's *provincia*. Yet it was to be to these two authors that later Romans, like ourselves, were to owe their fundamental conceptions of the content and meaning of Roman history.

How and by what steps persons born in these north Italian, still provincial, communities came to be imbued with so profound a sense of Roman history is a problem that can hardly be dealt with here. All that this comparison is intended to make clear is that we cannot assert that people from the older Roman citizen communities of Italy, or those whose citizenship was new and was a product of the Social War, were not involved with Roman tradition and did not participate in the conflicting values that marked Roman politics. As we have seen earlier (in chaps. 5 and 6), there is more evidence to indicate that voters coming from outside Rome would take up a conservative position than that they might act as a force for change.

If we are to understand the very strange and anomalous political system which the later Republic was, we have to distinguish between three different things: its formal structures; the social realities of participation or otherwise in those structures; and the exercise of power, persuasion, and force between those individuals and groups who did participate. As regards formal structures, the fundamental argument of this book is that our evidence will remain unintelligible unless we accept that the constitution of the Roman *res publica* made it a variety of democracy. Every adult male citizen, unless specifically disqualified, had a vote, and there was no formal exclusion of the poor. Freed slaves could also vote, and the repeated debates and conflicts about whether they could be registered and cast their votes in any of the thirty-five *tribus* or should be confined (as they were until the end) to the four *tribus urbanae* presuppose the more fundamental principle that they were citizens, and could vote.

The system within which they voted was characterized by the feature that all voting, without exception, took place within subgroups *(tribus* or *centuriae)*. Within each subgroup, the principle of the majority vote prevailed. The vote of each subgroup then counted as one, and the result (whether electoral, legislative, or judicial) was determined by the majority of group votes. In one of the voting structures, the *comitia centuriata,* a principle of stratification by wealth prevailed, according to which the richer citizens both belonged to *centuriae* with smaller numbers of individual members and were able to vote first, with voting being abandoned when a majority (of *centuriae)* had been reached. But it is a far more significant fact that in the other group voting structure, the *comitia tributa,* no form of social stratification applied, and each citizen's vote counted equally.

Finally, it should be stressed that the *res publica* was a direct democracy, not a representative one. Membership of the Senate, it is true, was an indirect result of election to public office. But, while the Senate had important deliberative and even decision-making and administrative functions, it was in no sense a representative body, was not a parliament, and could not legislate. The widespread notion that the Senate was the governing organ of the Roman Republic is not merely misleading, it is straightforwardly false.

The formal powers of the citizen as voter were divided into three categories. First, there was a residual role for the *comitia* to meet as criminal courts, a function largely, but not entirely, taken over in Cicero's time by *quaestiones* with a limited number of senatorial or equestrian jurors. Then there were elections, conducted by either the *comitia centuriata* or the *comitia tributa,* both of which now met for this purpose in the Campus Martius. Over fifty public offices were now filled annually by election, and by 63 direct popular election also applied, after repeated conflicts and changes, to vacancies in the "colleges" of priests and to the position of Pontifex Maximus.

The most fundamental of all the rights of the people was, however, the fact that they, and they alone, could legislate. Proposals for *leges* could be put before them only by a limited group of elected annual magistrates, namely, consuls, praetors, or tribunes. It was not obligatory, except in the decade following Sulla's reforms, for any such proposal to have been approved by the Senate. The *comitia centuriata* could pass *leges* but very rarely did so. The normal assembly for the passage of *leges* was the *comitia tributa,* and it was far more common for laws to be proposed to the assembly by one or more of the ten *tribuni plebis* of each year than by any other elected officeholders. The exclusive right of the assemblies to pass legislation is by far the strongest reason why, in purely formal terms, the Roman *res publica* has to be characterized as a democracy.

It has been necessary to rehearse once again these formal, structural features of the Roman constitution, because if they are ignored, the patterns of power, and the ways in which successive changes came about in the late Republic, become wholly unintelligible. But it is of course essential to separate the emphasis on these formal features from any assessment in sociological terms of actual patterns of participation.

Here, enough has been said already. It would be much more satisfactory if we could establish patterns of participation, from within the plebs of the city, among the (very numerous) inhabitants of the *suburbium,* or among those who might come from the districts of Italy, from Rhegium to the Po Valley. But as we have seen already (in chap. 2), we can do no better than to recall that all the communities of Italy up (probably) to the Po were now allocated to one or another of the thirty-five *tribus,* that there are hints of an awareness throughout Italy of major issues in urban politics, and that groups or individuals might make their way to Rome to vote in elections or on *leges.* We may note in passing, amid a range of wholly inadequate evidence that illustrates participation from outside Rome, Cicero's passing allusion in the *Pro Sestio* to a man who, to disguise himself, "seized the muleteer's cloak with which he had first come to Rome for the *comitia.*"[22]

It is purposeless to dwell further on the unanswerable question of the levels or significance of participation by citizens from outside Rome. We can, however, be sure that, as the literature of the late Republic and Augustan period shows, the culture of Italian communities could be marked by a commitment to Roman traditions and values that went far beyond mere formal citizenship; Cicero, Vergil, and Livy are all products of this great cultural change.

There could thus be participation and voting, in both elections and legislation, and Roman political life was conducted in full awareness that this was possible. More than that, we cannot say. But if I was correct to suggest earlier (in chap. 2) that those who migrated to Rome or its neighborhood were not systematically transferred by the censors from their existing *tribus rusticae* to *tribus urbanae,* then the three hundred

---

22. Cicero *Sest.* 38/82: "mulioniam paenulam arripuit, cum qua primum Romam ad comitia venerat."

thousand or so people (some one-third of the total citizen body) who lived near enough to Rome to participate in the monthly distributions of grain will have included "representatives" of all the *tribus.*

The *populus Romanus* was not a biological descent-group, but a political community defined by rights and duties (the latter consisting predominantly of military service in the legions), and it was formed above all by the progressive extension of Roman citizenship throughout Italy, and by the distinctive Roman custom of giving citizenship to freed slaves. Participation as a citizen was not limited by considerations of wealth or class (though the holding of elective office certainly was),[23] but it will have been far more profoundly affected by distance. The unaltered convention that the citizen could exercise his rights only in person, by voting in the Forum or the Campus Martius, gave an overwhelming predominance in the politics of the late Republic to those "representatives" of the wider *populus Romanus* who lived in and around the city.

It remains very important to our understanding of late-Republican political life that a vast population living at a distance from Rome had the formal right to vote, and might be persuaded, or think it in its interest, to come to Rome to vote. Given the multiple ties of obligation and mutual benefit that existed between the numerous citizen communities of Italy and officeholders in Rome, as well as the accelerating competition for position and power, the wholly unpredictable patterns of extra-urban involvement represented one of the significant destabilizing factors in the last years of the Republic. As we saw in chapter 7, it was possible to explain afterward why Plancius had gained so much support from Atina and neighboring communities when seeking the aedileship in 55, but it had not been possible to predict this beforehand. Equally, a really important level of Italian involvement was successfully organized from Rome to secure the vote for Cicero's return in 57 (see chap. 6), but the expected support for Pompey against Caesar's forces in early 49 simply failed to appear (see chap. 7).

It was this highly anomalous structure, the product of a long evolution which had given Roman Italy some of the characteristics of a nation-state, but no corresponding representative institutions, which allowed the

---

23. See esp. C. Nicolet, "Le cens sénatorial sous la République et sous Auguste," *JRS* 66 (1976): 20; idem, "Augustus, Government, and the Propertied Classes," in F. Millar and E. Segal, eds., *Caesar Augustus: Seven Aspects* (Oxford: Clarendon, 1984), 89, trans. in C. Nicolet, *Rendre à César: Économie et société dans la Rome antique* (Paris: Gallimard, 1988), 221.

sovereignty of the *populus Romanus* to be exercised by the crowd in the Forum, or in other words by whoever happened to be there, or had a motive for being there, or was persuaded or organized into presenting himself, whether to use his vote, or to deploy physical force. Within the city (large parts of which are in fact still very little known), we can dimly perceive the organization of groups in the separate *vici,* and the role of what Vanderbroeck has called "intermediate leaders." But there seems to be no way, in the present state of the evidence, to go beyond Vanderbroeck's excellent study of popular leadership in the Rome of the late Republic.[24] The political sociology of the city inevitably remains as obscure to us as does that of Italy as a whole.

What is certain at least about the relation between the *populus* and the Roman state is that, in many profound respects, there was no state. There were the annual elected officeholders, who certainly could not be described as forming a "government"; and there was the Senate, which met, when summoned by a consul, praetor, or tribune, either in the Curia or in one of a number of temples in the center of the city. But there was no body of state employees in the sense characteristic of a modern state, and there was no machinery of government that was conducted behind closed doors. For, in this sense, there were no public buildings, other than temples, the Regia at the west end of the Forum (whose role and function is extremely obscure), and, at the other end of the Forum, on the slope up to the Capitol, the large multilevel building that we have always called the "Tabularium" but that we ought almost certainly now to identify as the Atrium Libertatis (see chaps. 2 and 7). This building, like the archaic treasury, the temple of Saturn *(Aerarium Saturni),* does seem to have functioned as a depository for public documents. But we still should not see these or any other public buildings in Rome as the seats of an "administration" that could be conceived of separately from the wider civilian community. It cannot be stressed too much or too frequently that the business of the community was communal, and was almost entirely conducted in the open air, whether we are speaking of *contiones* or of legislative assemblies; of trials before the people or of *quaestiones* conducted under the *conspectus* of the people, all in the Forum; or of *contiones* and meetings of the *comitia centuriata* in the Campus Martius. It was not merely that there was no administration or civil service functioning in-

---

24. P.J.J. Vanderbroeck, *Popular Leadership and Collective Behavior in the Late Roman Republic (ca. 80–50 B.C.)* (Amsterdam: J.C. Gieben, 1987). For "intermediate leaders" see his pp. 52ff.

doors, out of the sight of the civilian population, but there were no government buildings that served as the seats of operation of the annually elected officeholders. They too fulfilled their functions in public, in the open air, taking their seats at established locations within the Forum area or speaking from the Rostra. It was only when they had entered the Curia, or whatever *templum* was serving the same function, that senators performed what was of course a constitutional public function, but which was not carried out in the open air and was not directly visible and audible to the crowd. Even here, as we have seen, the reactions of the crowd outside could easily be heard inside (see chap. 6); and reports on what had been said or what votes had been passed inside the Curia could be made immediately to the crowd in the Forum (see chap. 7). Nonetheless, the debates in the Senate, even if we avoid the error of conceiving of it as a parliament, and even though it could not legislate, remain a distinctive and anomalous feature of the Republican system—partly because membership was lifelong, and partly for the specific reason that its debates took place indoors.

The private houses of senators, characteristically situated not more than a few hundred meters from the Forum, acquired a semipublic function, in the reception of allies and dependents who came to participate in the daily *salutatio;* and the senators' progress from their houses to the Forum and then back again, before and after the conduct of public business, was an established part of public life, and was one of the most significant means for the demonstration of prestige, popularity, and political support. That being so, and with the increasing levels of conflict and public violence, it frequently occurred that when someone was going down the Sacra Via from his house to the Forum, clashes between his and a rival's supporters took place (see, e.g., chap. 3).

If we look at the Roman Republic in comparison to other preindustrial societies, it is wholly correct to observe that the absence of any organized police force, or of any body of state employees trained to keep order and exercise the state's monopoly of the use of force, is characteristic, and is therefore not something distinctive to Rome.[25] It does nonetheless need to be stressed that, just as more generally we should not see Roman political life in terms of an opposition between "government" and "people," or subjects, so we cannot see in the exchanges that took place in the open air

---

25. See esp. the valuable studies by W. Nippel, "Policing Rome," *JRS* 74 (1984): 20; *Aufruhr und "Polizei" in der römischen Republik* (Stuttgart: Klett-Cotta, 1988); *Public Order in Ancient Rome* (Cambridge: Cambridge University Press, 1995).

in Rome—above all, in the Forum—any conflict or opposition between the organized forces of law and order and the population at large. We may well wonder what social forces served to contain ordinary, low-level, nonpolitical violence. But in the political context what is quite clear is that mass violence, though more and more evident, was always channeled into very specific topographical contexts within the wider framework of the city, and was always directed to quite specific political objectives. Insofar as it was physical force which determined the outcome of political conflicts, that force did not arise from the deployment of its employees by the state, but from appeals to different segments of society to be present to protect their interests, or to serve the cause of their ideals. Such an appeal might be backed by a senatus consultum calling on the magistrates to "see to it that the *res publica* suffered no damage," or it might be issued by the two consuls, by one in conflict with the other, or by any officeholder (or sometimes by ex-officeholders, as by Clodius in 57; see chap. 6). In other words, the increasingly prevalent deployment of violence was a function of political conflict, and of political persuasion directed to the population, or to different groups within it, not of the operations of the state. It was a very significant innovation when in 52, during the sole consulship of Pompey, soldiers were deployed in Rome as a means of political control (see chap. 7).

However, even if the absence of the organized deployment of force by "the state" was something that Rome had in common with other preindustrial societies, other features of the structure of power at Rome are very distinctive. As a republic in which office was conferred by annual election, Rome will not have differed significantly from many Greek city-states of the classical and Hellenistic periods. No other republic, however, had ever controlled an empire on anything like the scale of Rome's or for so long a period. Decisions made in Rome now had effects over an incomparably wider area than those that derived, or ever had derived, from any Greek city-state; and conversely the profits of empire were systematically displayed and demonstrated to the people in Rome, and were increasingly spent there for the people's benefit.

But the most distinctive and significant features of the late-Republican political system are the focusing of nearly all forms of communal political activity on a traditional open space, the Forum, and the fact that whichever citizens were there, or had been persuaded into being there, "represented" the larger *populus Romanus*.

As we have seen throughout this study, our evidence provides only the slightest hints as to what forms of personal commitment, loyalty, or dependence, or what pressures or forms of persuasion, might function to induce citizens to be present, whether from the immediate vicinity of the Forum; from the wider zone of the city and its suburbs, where (as it seems) some three hundred thousand of the nine hundred thousand citizen inhabitants of Italy lived; or from communities further away. It is clear that in particular circumstances the involvement of people from outside Rome could indeed be induced and that we would be wrong to conclude that Italy after the Social War was in no sense a real political community. But all the evidence confirms what common sense would suggest, that such involvement was partial and episodic, and that the casting of votes in Rome could in no way be numerically representative of the wider citizen body.

Within Rome, it is clear that news of the raising of political issues affecting their own interests could induce an immediate buildup of the crowd in the Forum. Precisely this reaction is stated quite explicitly by Cicero, in addressing the *iudices* who formed a third of the jurors in the case in which he was speaking in defense of Rabirius Postumus in 54.

> If it were to be reported that *sententiae* were being uttered in the Senate to the effect that you [as *equites*] should be subject to these laws, you would think it necessary to rush together to the Curia. If a *lex* were being put through [on that matter], you would fly to the Rostra.[26]

Cicero's words make the vital distinction between discussion within the walls of the Senate (of which news might still leak out) and the actual passing of legislation by the *comitia tributa* in the Forum, even if for rhetorical purposes he ignores the necessary posting up of the text of the law over the previous *trinundinum*. For, to repeat a point made earlier (in chap. 1), the most essential characteristic that distinguished the crowd in the Forum was that it was not confined to spectating, witnessing, protesting, or disrupting the operations of government by mass violence. It itself was the sovereign body, and as such exercised the legislative powers of the *populus Romanus*.

It is also crucial to the nature of Roman political life that the power of the crowd to exercise its sovereign legislative functions was constricted

---

26. Cicero *Rab. Post.* 7/18.

neither by a fixed timetable of meetings nor by the designation of a meeting place that was separate from the normal political, social, and commercial center of the life of the city. As regards time, only something more than half the days in the year were designated as *comitiales* (days on which the *comitia* could vote); and various technical factors, from the announcement of a *iustitium* to the proclamation of *supplicationes* or the insertion of an intercalary month, could either reduce or extend the availability of days for legislation. But in essence legislation could be put through at any time after the expiry of the relevant *trinundinum*. As regards space, if the *comitia centuriata* had in fact been regularly summoned, either for trials like that of Rabirius in 63 (see chap. 5) or for legislation like that for the recall of Cicero in 57 (see chap. 6), then that would, by the nature of this assembly, have meant summoning the citizens to a designated location outside the ritual boundary of the city. But in most years, the Campus Martius was the scene only of the elections, both by the *comitia centuriata,* following archaic tradition, and now by the *comitia tributa* as well.

It is a modern myth that Roman elections were determined purely by the personal claims or perceived prestige of the candidates or by obligations binding voters in a relation of dependence to them; and it is quite clear that properly political considerations also played a part. In that sense, electoral speeches, both by candidates and by others on their behalf, did play a role in elections. Precisely for that reason, the process of *ambitus,* of going around and commending oneself or one's protégés to the people, normally took place, like other aspects of political activity, in the Forum. It is interesting to observe that once the *lex Domitia* of 104 had secured the right of popular election even as regards vacancies in the "colleges" of priests (see chap. 5), the law actually obliged anyone who wanted to nominate someone to do so by making a speech at a *contio.* As the author of the *Rhetorica ad Herennium* points out in the 80s, some people were legally debarred from speaking.

A *lex* forbids anyone who has been condemned for extortion [*de pecuniis repetundis*] from making a speech at a *contio.* But another *lex* makes it obligatory to nominate *in contione* anyone who seeks the place of a deceased augur.[27]

---

27. *Rhet. ad. Herenn.* 1.11/20.

The very fact that this provision was formally incorporated in a *lex* reflects the ideological force attached to the idea that anyone occupying a public position should be subject to the judgment of the people.

Nonetheless, while elections to public office were, or could be, influenced by considerations of politics and policy, the most important context of political debate should be seen as having been not elections but the passing of laws. But, as has been emphasized throughout this study, the *contiones* delivered in the Forum, aimed at persuading the people to pass *leges* or at dissuading them, have to be situated in the context of all the other public and communal activities that successively occupied the same space, from triumphal processions to gladiatorial *munera*, theatrical *ludi*, funeral orations, the allocation of public contracts by censors or consuls, or the taking of oaths. All these processes by their nature required an audience and needed the visible presence of a crowd that could be thought of as being, or representing, the *populus Romanus*, under whose *conspectus* they would take place. The same was of course true of the *quaestiones* made up of limited numbers of senatorial or equestrian *iudices*, which in this period had largely—but not entirely—replaced the *comitia* themselves as the vehicle for public trials. The vividly reported conflicts as to whether the *iudices* should be senators, *equites*, or (as was eventually agreed in 70) a mixture of the two with *tribuni aerarii* added (see chap. 3) tend not to bring into focus the more fundamental question of how it had come to be agreed in the second century that carefully selected upper-class *iudices* could indeed perform this function on behalf of the *populus*. But it is abundantly clear, as we have seen (in chap. 2), that here too every aspect of the working of the *quaestio* was required to be open to observation and judgment by spectators in the Forum, as was also the conduct and performance of the orators who addressed them.

In formal terms, the Roman orator had to train himself for three different audiences: Senate, *populus*, and *iudices*.[28] In reality, a speech addressed to the *iudices* seated in the Forum was addressed also to the *corona* of spectators who crowded, or might crowd, around the court. In that sense, a *quaestio* was a public show, which might well have to compete for attention with other *quaestiones* being conducted at the same time, in neighboring sections of the open-air arena of the Forum. Cicero, in his *Brutus*, gives a vivid description of the atmosphere of public expectation when a famous orator was about to perform.

---

28. See, e.g., Cicero *De or.* 3.55/211.

I would like an orator to have the good fortune that, when it is heard that he is about to speak, the places in the *subsellia* are occupied, the tribunal is full, the *scribae* can win favor by granting and conceding places, the *corona* [of spectators] is numerous, the *iudex* is attentive. When he who is to speak rises to his feet, the *corona* will give the sign for silence, and then there will be repeated expressions of agreement and admiration—laughter, when he wishes it, and, when he wishes, tears.[29]

But the forensic speech before a *quaestio* could be something more than an oratorical display, or a contribution to the public reputation of the orator. It could also carry a political message, or a loaded interpretation of episodes from Roman history. We have earlier seen Cicero in 65, when still in his relatively *popularis* phase, doing just this in the course of his defense of Cornelius (see chap. 4). In doing so, he was following an established tradition, and he himself, in his *De oratore*, represents the great orator Marcus Antonius as delivering a strongly *popularis* view of early Roman history while speaking in defense of Norbanus at a trial in the 90s.

I gathered together all types of civil discord, with their associated wrongs and dangers, and derived the speech from a survey of all the successive phases of our *res publica,* and concluded by saying that even though all instances of discord had always been an affliction, some nonetheless had been just and practically necessary. . . . Without dissension among the *nobiles,* the kings could not have been driven from this *civitas;* nor *tribuni plebis* created; nor the *consularis potestas* so often limited by *plebiscita;* nor the right of *provocatio,* that patron of the state and champion of *libertas,* granted to the *populus Romanus.*[30]

Any such characterization of early Roman history, much of it, as in this case, belonging to a distant past of which very little could really be known for certain, was of course a piece of persuasive discourse, or a one-sided contribution to a public debate. The same is true of what Cicero, speaking in his optimate voice in the course of his defense of Sestius in 56 (see chap. 6), says of the historic role of the Senate within the Republican system.

29. Cicero *Brut.* 84/290.
30. Cicero *De or.* 2.48/199.

This is the only way, believe me, to *laus* and *dignitas* and *honor*: to be praised and cherished by good men who are wise and of a naturally good disposition, and to know the organization of the *civitas* most wisely established by our ancestors. For they, when they could no longer tolerate the power of the kings, created annual magistrates, in such a way that they placed over the *res publica* the perpetual council of the Senate. . . . They set up the Senate as the guardian, supervisor, and champion of the *res publica*. They wished the magistrates to respect the *auctoritas* of this *ordo* and to be, so to speak, the servants of this most weighty council.[31]

It hardly needs to be pointed out that this oration too is an example of persuasion, or historical reinterpretation. Cicero could after all not have known, any more than could anyone else, what had been in the minds of leading Romans in the late sixth century. In any case, while all our sources assert that the consulate had been established then, it is not in the least clear whether a Senate with a defined membership and functions had even existed at that period.[32] In the last decades of the Republic, while the Senate was by now a long-established central institution, its dominance over the *res publica* was an aspiration, not a fact. For, as we have seen over and over again, measures approved by the Senate could not pass into law until voted on by the crowd out in the Forum; and even long-established strategic functions of the Senate, like the determination of the consular *provinciae*, could be overridden by a *lex* proposed directly to the people by a tribune.

That is not of course to say that political debate did not take place in the Senate; as Cicero's *De oratore* indicates, the political orator had to be capable of two different styles: briefer and less showy in the Senate, more forceful, impressive, and varied in a *contio*.[33] But, at all times, legislation could not be passed except by the sovereign people; and after the restoration of the full powers of the tribunes in 70, as Cicero himself had said, the *dominatio* of the senators was over.[34] That meant that, even more than ever before, it was the *contio* in the Forum which was the essential vehicle of persuasion and debate. Very rapidly, however, in the two decades after the restoration of tribunician powers, while debate conducted

---

31. Cicero *Sest.* 65/137.
32. See T.J. Cornell, *The Beginnings of Rome* (London: Routledge, 1995), 245–46.
33. Cicero *De or.* 2.82/333.
34. Cicero *Verr.* 2.5.68/175. See chap. 3 above.

via the medium of *contiones* remained central, the use of organized violence to control the traditional location of political and constitutional proceedings, the Forum, became ever more important. In terms of the violence and instability of the crowd, and the vulnerability of its voting procedures to physical pressures, Cicero was perhaps misguided when he looked with suspicion and contempt on the workings of the Greek city-states of his time. He does so most notably, once again, in a forensic speech, his *Pro Flacco,* delivered in the Forum in late 59, in which he provides an extended comparison between the voting procedures of Greek cities and those established at Rome. His immediate purpose was to discredit the votes *(psēphismata)* passed by the *ekklēsiai* of Greek cities in support of the accusation of Flaccus. But in the course of this effort, he expounds many important distinctions between the popular assembly in Rome and in Greek cities, as usual combining factual observations with loaded interpretations. It should be observed, particularly given the date of his speech, in the consulate of Caesar in 59, that his argument leads him to contrast the orderliness and discipline of the Roman assembly with the uncontrolled license allegedly characteristic of Greek ones.

He begins by characterizing Greek *psēphismata* as not following the delivery of authoritative speeches or being bound by the taking of oaths but being voted by a show of hands and by the shouts of an excited populace. But when he comes to compare Roman voting, a note of anxiety creeps in.

> O most excellent custom and discipline that we have inherited from our ancestors, if only we would hold onto it! But, I know not how, it is already slipping from our hands. For those most wise and most venerable men wished there to be no force in a *contio.* As for what the *plebs* might vote or the *populus* order, they wished the matter to be voted on or rejected, when the *contio* had been dismissed, when the different sections had been separated, when the *ordines, classes,* and age-groups had been rearranged by *tribus* and *centuriae,* when the proposers had been heard and the matter promulgated and made known over many days.[35]

This speech is perhaps as close as Cicero ever comes to providing a rationale for the very distinctive Roman custom of voting in groups

---

35. Cicero *Flacc.* 7/15.

determined by social rank (in the case of the *comitia centuriata*) and age. He does also, however, bring in three other relevant features: the promulgation of *leges* in advance; the persuasion of the people through *contiones;* and the formal separation between the *contio,* or mass meeting, and the *comitia,* with the people divided up into categories for voting purposes.

He does not make any specific allusion to the location where either the *contio* or the meeting of the *comitia* that followed took place, and he would not have needed to, since his audience would have known that it was where he himself was now speaking, in the Forum. He does, however, when he continues further, point implicitly to a very distinctive and important feature of the Roman public meeting. For he pours scorn on the rashness of the typical Greek *contio,* or meeting, conducted with people sitting down, and then proceeds to represent what the typical context for this type of meeting would be.

> When inexperienced men, unversed in and devoid of knowledge of any kind, had sat down together in the theater, they would undertake useless wars, would place seditious men in charge of their cities, and would expel the most deserving citizens from the community.[36]

In the following year Cicero himself would be expelled from the Roman *civitas,* following political pressures that did not at all correspond to his idealized picture of the orderly and controlled *contio* and *comitia* at Rome. In the year after that, as we have seen (in chap. 6), the *principes civitatis* did succeed in imposing on the city population the force of the presence of large numbers of respectable persons from Italy, who duly did meet in the Campus Martius, listen to orations from the *principes* themselves, and vote in orderly fashion for Cicero's return. But this effort to bring the results of the extension of the citizenship into real effect in Rome was never repeated. If it had been, there must have been a chance of producing something like the stable, socially deferential, conservative *res publica* that was Cicero's ideal.

The reality of the late 50s turned out to be quite otherwise. Again, it is a matter of pure speculation whether the model of the Hellenistic Greek *ekklēsia* that Cicero presents so contemptuously to his hearers might in fact have offered a less turbulent context for collective decision making

---

36. Cicero *Flacc.* 7/16.

than the Forum. As for voting by a simple majority, by a show of hands, Cicero might well have been right to imply that voting in groups (and, as he does not explicitly say, by each individual in order using a written voting tablet) might have been expected to produce the socially controlled environment to which he aspired. As I noted earlier, in the *De legibus* he puts into the mouth of his brother, Quintus, an expression of regret at the introduction of the secret ballot in the later second century, precisely on the grounds that it reduced the influence of the *principes* on the voters.[37]

In any case, whatever the potential advantages, from a conservative standpoint, of a system of voting in a complex set of subgroups (which are never really discussed in any ancient source and must remain obscure to us), it signally failed to produce the stable social and political order, dominated by the respectable men *(boni* or *optimates),* that Cicero sets out as his ideal in the *Pro Sestio.*

What, it may be asked, if Rome had had a designated location for assemblies, and if, like contemporary Greek cities, it had come to use its theater as the natural place where the citizens could meet, sit down, listen to speeches, and vote? One deterrent was of course the fact that until Pompey's great stone theater was opened in 55 there was no permanent theater in Rome. Whether the long hesitation about having one in fact owed something to fears about the possible introduction of a quite different context for public assemblies, we cannot tell. All that is certain is that, while the Senate sometimes used a meeting place provided as part of Pompey's theater complex, there is nothing whatever to suggest that the theater itself was ever used for political meetings in the few remaining years of the Republic. The potential, and under the empire the actual, political role of theaters as political meeting places was to be fulfilled only in the new, monarchical, context, as one of various locations where the ruler showed himself in person before his subjects. Both Lucan and Plutarch were to record later that in the night before his final defeat at Pharsalus, Pompey had a dream in which he appeared in his theater, and received the applause of the people.[38]

In any case, even under the empire, the *comitia* continued to meet for elections in the Campus Martius (where the massive enclosure for voting, the Saepta, planned by Julius Caesar, was finally dedicated by Agrippa in 26) and for legislation in the Forum. The conception of the voting assem-

37. Cicero *De leg.* 3.15–16/34–37. See chap. 2.
38. Lucan *Phars.* 7.7–8; Plutarch *Pomp.* 68.2.

bly in which participants could be seated on the concentric raised tiers of seats in a theater was never to have the slightest place in Rome.

If this idea had gained hold, it would of course in any case only have accentuated the gross disparity between the numbers who could, or ever did, participate and vote in Rome and the nine hundred thousand or so citizens to be found in Italy in Cicero's time. For the theater of Pompey, for instance, seems to have accommodated no more than some ten thousand spectators. There was of course one arena for public gatherings in Rome, the Circus Maximus, that could take a vastly greater crowd. Estimates vary between 150,000 and something over 200,000, and it remains to this day the largest-capacity sports arena ever created.[39] In theory, therefore, something like one Roman citizen in five or six *could* have participated in a public meeting there. Once again, however, it was only under the empire that a combination of the literal visibility of a single ruler, the use of heralds, and the carrying around of written messages gave the Circus a distinctive political role in mutual communications between the mass of the people and the emperor.[40]

The political life of the Republic, however, demanded above all the delivery of speeches, and hence the communication to the public of complex forms of information, argument, and persuasion by individual orators. In the first instance, therefore, the nature of the acts of communication and response that will have been involved will have been predetermined by the limits of audibility, in a system where no form of amplification, even a simple megaphone, ever seems to have been used by orators.

There is nonetheless good reason to believe that, on occasion, far greater numbers will have been present and participating than the restricted group who will have been able to hear and understand what was said by orators using the unaided human voice. The still relatively open space of the Forum, measuring some eighty by forty meters, was considerably larger than the Pnyx in Athens (some 3,200 m² as opposed to 2,400).[41] Moreover, we should not forget Cicero's evocative description of the scene in 67 when the Forum was packed and the neighboring

39. See J.H. Humphrey, *Roman Circuses: Arenas for Chariot Racing* (London: B.T. Batsford, 1986), chap. 3, esp. p. 126.

40. See, e.g., A.D.E. Cameron, *Bread and Circuses: The Roman Emperor and His People* (London: King's College London, 1974); F. Millar, *The Emperor in the Roman World*, 2d ed. (London: Duckworth, 1992), 368–69.

41. See the valuable paper by L. Thommen, "Les lieux de la plèbe et de ses tribuns dans la Rome républicaine," *Klio* 77 (1995): 355, esp. 366.

templa were covered with spectators in the period leading up to the voting of the *lex Gabinia*.[42] At a guess, therefore, we might suppose that up to around twenty thousand people could have been present in and around the Forum at moments of particular political involvement.

Physical presence was in any case not all that was at issue, for this study has listed many cases when the content of *contiones* delivered in the Forum is commented on by contemporaries who were not themselves present at the time, or where it subsequently entered the historical record. It can surely be accepted without difficulty that the actual delivery of a speech, literally heard in the first instance by perhaps only a few hundred people, was only the start of a secondary process of dissemination, of course liable to simplification or distortion. Rumor and reputation were fundamental factors in late-Republican politics.[43]

The central element in the political life of the late Republic, and the source from which rumor and the formation of public opinion started, was the appearance of the orator before the *populus* in the Forum. As we saw earlier, Polybius had caught the essence of this element, as of so much else, noting that ambitious young Romans typically "concerned themselves with legal cases and greetings, spending their time in the Forum, and through these means tried to recommend themselves to the many."[44] Polybius thus catches the vital necessity of visibility, a visibility that in the Republican context could be achieved only in the Forum. It was the Forum that mattered, because, as has been stressed many times over, it functioned as a public stage where there were always spectators, and where a multiplicity of different communal functions—among which jurisdiction had a central role—succeeded each other, or could be witnessed taking place simultaneously. It was there too that senators could be observed on their way to or from the Curia, that a young man, like Cicero in the year 90 (see chap. 2), could hear different speeches every day, and that the audience could be transformed into sovereign actors, empowered to legislate, by the formal process of separating into their *tribus* to vote.

From the point of view of the modern observer, what can be seen in

---

42. Cicero *Man.* 15/44. See chap. 4 above.

43. See esp. Z. Yavetz, "Existimatio, Fama, and the Ides of March," *HSCPh* 78 (1974): 35.

44. Polybius 31.29.8: οἱ λοιποὶ τῶν νέων περὶ τὰς κρίσεις καὶ τοὺς χαιρετισμοὺς ἐσπούδαζον, κατὰ τὴν ἀγορὰν ποιούμενοι τὴν διατριβήν, καὶ διὰ τούτων συνιστάνειν ἑαυτοὺς ἐπειρῶντο τοῖς πολλοῖς. Cf. chap. 2 above.

operation in Rome is precisely not a "face-to-face" society, for the scale and geographical distribution of Roman citizenship was now not that of a nuclear city-state, but of a nation-state; but it was still an archaic face-to-face political system, in which a single open space, at the heart of a large city, provided the arena for a wide range of communal functions and was the stage on which political discourse was uttered. We may, as has been the dominant mode in the twentieth century, imagine that we know of structures of social and political dependence which lay behind the political debates which took place in the Forum, and which determined the results of electoral and legislative voting. But until some evidence for the determination of political outcomes by these hypothetical structures is produced, it would be better to focus our attention on the images with which our sources actually present us. If we do that, we will see the Forum not only as the stage for the delivery of political discourse but as the long-established public space in which the *conspectus populi Romani* could develop into active response and dialogue and into physical competition for the domination of the area. The fact that such a domination was important was a function of the more fundamental fact that laws in the Roman *res publica* could be enacted only by the votes of the people. In that limited sense, in its modes of persuasion (by the delivery of speeches to those who turned up) and in its modes of legislation (by direct popular voting), the system of the Roman *res publica* was indeed democratic. The strength of the popular strain in Roman political tradition was not only its emphasis on the right of the tribunes, from their bench in front of the Curia, to bring help *(auxilium)* to citizens and to propose legislation to them, but the insistence that public functions should take place before the gaze of the people. Its weakness, as the story of the late Republic makes abundantly clear, was that the long-inherited insistence on visible action and audible speech in the Forum meant that it was a product of chance, circumstances or organization by interested groups that determined which persons—always a tiny minority—would in fact be present in the Forum to perform the function of "representing" the whole *populus Romanus*.

Nonetheless, however hesitant we may be to allow the name of democracy to a system whose structural weaknesses and contradictions were so profound, it remains the central argument put forward in this study that any valid assessment of the Roman Republic must take account of the power of the crowd. The same proposition could be advanced in different terms, namely, that we should be asking, like Cicero, precisely what it was that distinguished the Roman Republic, as a political system, from a Greek city-state. Cicero, it is quite clear, was acutely aware of the disturbing implications of this question. Far from blandly assuming that the crowd in Rome was safely under the control of its betters, he recognized it as a powerful and dangerous force that all the influence of inherited institutions could restrain only with difficulty. This at least is the view which he expresses in another section of his *Pro Flacco.*

> At this point be sure to recall yet again what the rashness of the multitude is like, what the fickleness typical of Greeks is like, how great is the power of a seditious oration at a *contio.* Here, in this most weighty and moderate political community, where the Forum is full of *iudicia,* full of magistrates, full of the best men and citizens, where the Curia, as the avenger of rashness and the controller of loyalty, looks out on and invests the Rostra—nonetheless, how great are the waves that you can see being whipped up at *contiones!*[45]

In stressing the power of oratory, in acknowledging the force of the crowd, in asking how far the institutions visible in the Forum could serve to restrain popular feelings, and in raising the question of what in reality distinguished Rome from a Greek democracy, Cicero was touching on fundamental problems about the nature of Roman politics. These are questions which still demand an answer from us.

---

45. Cicero *Flacc.* 24/57.

Subject Index

Numerals in italics indicate years B.C.

administration, political: absence of, in modern sense, 212–13

Aedes Castoris. See Castor and Pollux

Aerarium Saturni as depository for public documents, 212

aristocracy, applicability of term, to Rome, 4–6

Asconius: on the context of the *Pro Milone,* 169; on violent rivalry for the consulship of *52,* 181; on voting by the *tribus,* 81–82

assemblies: comparison of Roman and Greek popular assemblies, 220–21; distinction between functions of *comitia tributa* and *centuriata,* 24. See also *comitia centuriata; comitia tributa*

Bibulus (M. Calpurnius Bibulus): *contiones* and *edicta* of, 130–31; as consul in *59,* 126; imprisonment of, in the *carcer,* 129–30; prevented from taking oath, 135–36

biographies, imperial: individualistic nature of, 95, 169; Plutarch's *Lives,* 169

Bona Dea, rites of, 118

bribery, electoral: 68–69, 120; Cato the Younger accuses Gabinius of, in *59,* 135; in consular elections of *53,* 179; in the late Republic, 203; by Milo in *52,* 182

Caesar (C. Julius Caesar): death of his daughter Julia, 177; extension of his *provinciae* in *55* secured by physical control of votes, 172; on his family history, 75; and the First Triumvirate, 123; imprisons Cato the Younger in the *carcer* over issue of the *lex agraria,* 126, 131; is given Cisalpina, Illyricum, and Gallia Transalpina as a result of the *lex Vatinia,* 132–33; proconsulate of Gaul, 168; his return to Rome in *49* represented as defense of *intercessio,* 187–88, 207; supports Antonius for augurate in *49,* 189

Campus Martius: competition for dominance of, 158; as site of *comitia* meetings, 16, 197; as venue for *contiones* and voting, 150, 153

carcer, 39; as site of public executions, 111

Cassius Dio: on the *comitia centuriata,* 190; on the issue of consular *provinciae* in *55,* 170–71

Castor and Pollux, temple of: as base for physical dominance of Forum, 41, 137; function as speakers' platform, 41; location of, in Forum, 41; steps of, removed by Clodius, 136–37

Cato the Younger (M. Porcius Cato): accuses Gabinius of electoral bribery in *59,* 135; imprisoned in the

Cato the Younger (*continued*)
  carcer after opposing a *lex agraria*
  of *59*, 126, 131; physically expelled
  from the Forum after opposing proposals concerning *provinciae* for
  Pompey and Crassus in *55*, 170
census: of *188*, 21; of *70*, 27–28; functioning after *70*, 28
Cicero (M. Tullius Cicero): acts as advocate for Cornelius in *65*, 88–92; on
  ballot law *(lex tabellaria)*, 26–27,
  222; compares contemporary politics with historical precedents, 88–
  92; compares Roman and Greek popular assemblies, 220–21; *contiones*
  of, 95–97; destruction of his *domus*,
  141; on election defeat of Servius
  Sulpicius, 17; on electoral bribery,
  68, 179–80; on his exile of *58*, 139–
  40; on the planned revolution of *63*,
  108–11; on political presence of *populus* in the Forum, 57, 61, 70–71,
  173; on popular sovereignty, 172–
  73; as proconsul of Cilicia, 168; on
  his prospective prosecution of Verres
  and election to aedileship, 14, 60,
  71–72; on the prosecution of Milo
  by Clodius, 161–62; *Pro Sestio*,
  147–48; return from exile, 150–51
Circus Flaminius, function of, 116
Circus Maximus, role and size of, 223
clientela, role of, 7–8
Clodius (P. Clodius Pulcher): gathers
  weapons and supporters at the temple of Castor and removes its steps,
  136–37; murder of, in *52*, 181–82;
  opposes Cicero's return from exile,
  138–39; as tribune for *58*, 134–35
comitia centuriata: its existence into
  the third century A.D., 198; its function as an electoral assembly, 203–
  4; structure and role of, 6, 16–18,
  197–99, 202–4
comitia tributa: as sovereign body of
  the *res publica*, 92; structure and
  role of, 15, 19, 197, 204

comitium as constitutional center, 39–
  41
commentariolum petitionis, 33
consul: increased politicization of consulship in *59*, 124, 175; political context of consulship, 190; longevity of
  the consulate, 197; role of, 18–19
contiones. See speeches
corn: free monthly distributions of,
  138; public demonstrations against
  high prices of, 44, 60, 155
Cornelius (C. Cornelius) accused of
  maiestas in *65* and acquitted, 82–
  83, 88–92
curia: burnt down in *52* during crema-
  tion of Clodius' body, 182; existence of a Curia on same site to present day, 198; as location for Senate
  meetings, 39
Curio (Scribonius Curio): leaves Rome
  to join Caesar, 194; proposes *lex
  viaria* and *lex alimentaria* in *50*,
  192; as tribune, 190–91

democracy: applicability of term, to
  Rome, 11, 205, 208–9, 225–26;
  and Cicero's political rise, 74; and
  the *comitia tributa*, 204
Dionysius of Halicarnassus on *suburbium* of Rome, 31
domus as retreat from crowd violence,
  44

East: political effects of the conquests
  of the *60s*, 121
elections: consular elections for *63*
  and *62*, 98–101; for *53*, 179; for
  praetorship and aedileship marked
  by violence in *55*, 172
executions as public rituals, 110–11

Forum: intended extension of, 176;
  need for physical control of, 84,
  112–14, 125; organized efforts to
  dominate, 136; plan of, *Plate II*, 40;
  as public space from *80–50*, 39–

44; and the role of written material, 45; size and capacity of, 223–24; as venue for diverse public activities, 44, 147; as venue for election campaigning, 19, 25, 216
freedom of speech, applicability of term, to Rome, 46–47

Gabinius (A. Gabinius): is accused of electoral bribery by Cato the Younger in 59, 135; consul in 58, 134–35; tribune in 67, 79–82
gradus Aurelii, lack of archaeological evidence for, in Forum, 43

history, early Roman: Cato the Younger invokes Romulus on the Capitol by appearing togatus with no tunic, 177; Cicero defends M. Aemilius Scaurus by reference to earlier rebuilding of the temple of Castor and Pollux by Scaurus' grandfather, 43, 177; historical evidence affected by successive reinterpretations of, 94, 200; use of historical imagery and precedents in political speeches, 88–92

Italy: applicability of term nation-state, 34, 211; its involvement in political process at Rome, 29–34, 149, 172–73, 190, 208, 210–11, 215

laws (leges): leges agrariae, 101–2, 123–24, 131; leges tabellariae, 26; lex Gabinia giving Pompey extensive military forces, 80; lex viaria and lex alimentaria proposed by Curio, 192; passing of, 209
leges. See laws
libertini, registration of, 23–24, 85
Livy: on granting of voting rights to cives sine suffragio, 21; on voting in the comitia centuriata, 201
lot (sortitio): for provinciae, 186; use of, 3, 143

Lucullus (L. Lucullus): consul in 74, 76; replacement of Lucullus by Q. Marcius Rex, 78

Milo: prosecution of, by Clodius in 56, 161–62; prosecution of, for murder of Clodius in 52, 183–84

nobilis, 4
nundinae, rationale behind institution of, 20

oligarchy, (in)applicability of term, to Rome, 186, 203

patricii, absence of modern study of, 4
plebs urbana, political dominance of, in Rome, 101–2, 104, 155
Plutarch on the issue of consular provinciae in 55, 170
Polybius on Roman politeia, 24
Pompey (Cn. Pompeius Magnus): conquest of Syria, 117; destruction of his domus, 141; election to consulship for 55, 167; election to consulship for 70, 64–65; given military command against Mithridates, 85–86; opening of theatrum Pompeii, 175; proposed as dictator by Hirrus in 53, 180
populus: interaction between populus and state officials, 111, 113, 127–28, 176–77, 212; literacy of, 131; political influence of, in the Forum, 56–57, 83–85, 87, 95, 224; political involvement of, 13–15, 35, 211
praetor, role of, 18–19
provinciae: of Gallia Cisalpina, Illyricum, and Gallia Transalpina, 133; legislation affecting provincial commands, 170; measure taken in 52 establishing five-year interval between an elective office and provincial governorship, 186

quaestiones, location of, in Forum, 41

res publica: and the execution of citizens, 108, 110; expansion of, 21; functioning of, 120, 202; internal structure of, 92; necessity of publicity in, 115
revenues, tribute. *See* tribute revenues
rostra, 41

Sallust (C. Sallustius Crispus): *Bellum Catilinae,* 94–95; on *tribunicia potestas,* 59
Senate: constitutional weakness demonstrated by Bona Dea affair, 118–19; entry to, 5, 175; limits of powers of, 7, 71–72, 209, 219; passes decree against public violence surrounding death of Clodius, 183; and *salutatio,* 213; selection of *legati* passed to *populus,* 133; votes to end Cicero's exile, influenced by physical presence of voters, 151
Social War, 27
speeches *(contiones):* distinction between forensic and political, 13, 218; electoral, 216; evidence from, 9–10; political content of, 59–60, 164; political influence of, 126; prevented by physical intervention, 135; speeches to *iudices* as vehicle for political debate, 91; uniqueness of Cicero's, as surviving examples, 95–96
suburbium of Rome, 31
suffragia. See votes
Sulla (L. Cornelius Sulla): provisions and effects of his legislations, 53–54; on his reforms of the 80s, 49–50

tribunes, structure and function of, 197
tribuni plebis: effect of restoration in the case of L. Lucullus, 79; restoration of legislative powers in 70, 66

tribunicia potestas: and management of the eastern empire, 76–79; restoration of, 59, 66
tribus, 19, 205; Asconius's description of voting procedures, 81–82; division and increase in number of, 20–21; voting rights of, 35–36
tribute revenues, public display of, for political influence, 117

Vatinius passes *lex* in 59 giving Cisalpina and Illyricum to Caesar, 132–33
Verres: Cicero on prospective prosecution of, in 69, 13–15; Cicero's prosecution of in 70, 70–72
vici: absence of evidence for social and political structure of, 136; definition of, 32–33
violence, crowd: against M. Calpurnius Bibulus in 59; following murder of Clodius in 52, 182; as a means to affect legislation, 83–85, 125, 136, 214; stone throwing at consul in 67, 83
violence, organized, 136–37; against Q. Fabricius and his followers, 149; between gangs supporting consular candidates Milo and P. Plautius Hypsaeus in 53, 180–81; Clodius mounts attack on workmen rebuilding *domus* of Cicero, 157; *lex* on *provinciae* of 55 is passed by forceful exclusion of opponents, including Cato the Younger, 171
voters, 36–38; constitutional rights of, 92–96; literacy of, 130; registration of, in *tribus,* 23–24, 85; social and geographical distribution of, 37–38
votes, voting, 205–6, 209; absence of evidence for procedures in early Republic, 20; control of voting by physical force, 138; voting in the *comitia centuriata* of the late Republic, 203–4

Index of Literary Sources

Appian
  BC
    1.121/561: 64
    1.55/2.41: 53
    1.59/266: 53
    2.24/92: 185
    2.27/102: 192
    2.30/119: 193
    2.31/120–23: 194
Asconius
  20C: 177
  27C–28C: 43, 177
  29C: 177
  31C: 31
  45C: 35, 85
  46–47C: 141
  48C: 155, 181
  52C: 36
  57–81C: 88
  58C: 83
  59–60C: 88
  61C: 90
  64–65C: 35, 84
  66–72C: 89
  67C: 60
  71C: 47
  72C: 82
  74–76C: 84, 89, 90
  78C: 60, 90
  79–80C: 91
  84C: 56
  87C: 98
  94C: 203
Aulus Gellius, NA, 13.3.5: 67
Ausonius, Gratiarum Actio, 3/13:
  199

Caesar
  BC
    1.6.5: 186
    1.7: 207
    1.7.2: 54
    1.9.2: 187
    1.9.5: 193
    1.32.2–3: 187
    1.51.1: 54
    2.25.4: 191
  BG
    8.50: 189
    8.52.4: 193
Cassius Dio
  36.2.2: 77
  36.15.1: 78
  36.17.2: 78
  36.23–36: 81
  36.38: 84
  36.42.1–3: 85
  36.42.2: 35
  37.21.4: 105
  37.25.3: 97
  37.26–27: 106
  37.27.3–37.28.3: 16
  37.28.1–3: 198
  37.31.1: 91
  37.37.1: 106
  37.43.1–4: 114
  37.49–50: 121
  38.3: 126
  38.4.2–3: 127
  38.4.4–5.5: 127
  38.6.1–3: 128
  38.6.4–6: 128
  38.6.6: 128

Cassius Dio (*continued*)
  38.12.3: 136
  38.13: 138
  39.9: 156
  39.12–16: 161
  39.16.2: 161
  39.18: 161
  39.30: 165
  39.32: 172
  39.33–36: 171
  39.38: 175
  39.62–63: 178
  39.64: 177
  40.46.2: 186
  40.56.1: 186
  40.56.2: 185
  40.61.2: 191
  40.66.5: 194
  41.45: 180
  43.43: 105
  58.20.4: 199
Cicero, M. Tullius
  Att.
    1.1.2 (10): 29, 98
    1.14.1–2 (14): 116
    1.14.2–5 (14): 118
    1.16 (16): 119
    1.19.4 (19): 122
    2.1.3 (21): 96
    2.3.3–4 (23): 123
    2.16.1 (36): 131
    2.18.1 (38): 132
    2.18.2 (38): 132
    2.19.3–4 (39): 132
    2.20.4 (40): 130
    2.21.3–5 (41): 130
    2.24.3 (44): 134
    3.12.1 (57): 140
    3.15.6 (60): 140
    3.23.1–4 (68): 146
    4.1.4–6 (73): 156
    4.2.1–5 (74): 157
    4.3.2–5 (75): 158
    4.15.7 (90): 179
    4.16.6 (89): 179

    4.16.8 (89): 42, 176
    4.17.2–3 (91): 179
    4.17.5 (91): 179
    4.18.1 (92): 178
    6.2.6 (116): 191
    7.1.4 (124): 187
    7.3.2–5 (126): 193
    7.4 (127): 193
    7.7 (130): 193, 195
    7.8.4 (131): 195
    7.8.5 (131): 195
  Brut.
    33–34/127–28: 50
    60/216–17: 60
    67/237: 203
    84/290: 218
    89/305: 47
  Cat.
    3.8–9/20–21: 110
    4.7–8/14–16: 111
  Clu.
    13/38–39: 56
    28/77: 61
    34/93: 43, 57, 61
    37/103: 62
    40/110: 54, 62
    49/136–38: 62
  De amicitia
    26/97: 47
  De leg. ag.
    1.3/7: 38
    2.1/1: 102
    2.5–6/13–14: 103
    2.5/13: 45
    2.7/18: 104
    2.26–27/70–71: 104
    2.37/101: 105
  De leg.
    2.2/5: 28
    3.4/11: 103
    3.9/22: 54
    3.11/26: 66
    3.15–16/34–37: 222
    3.15–16/34–35: 26
    3.19/44: 205

De off.
  2.12/58: 60
  2.16/57: 60
  2.16–17/57–59: 74
De or.
  1.9/38: 24
  2.48/199: 218
  2.82/333: 219
  3.55/211: 217
De re pub.
  2.22./39–40: 16, 200
Div. in Caec.
  3/8–9: 70
  16/50: 41
Dom.
  3/5–12/31: 156
  9/21–22: 144
  15/40: 145
  21/54: 137
  28/75: 37
  30/79: 18
  33/89–90: 38
  42/110: 140
Fam.
  1.4.1 (14): 160
  1.9 (20): 167
  2.6.3 (50): 180
  5.2.6–8 (2): 113
  6.6.5 (234) 188
  7.5–9 (26–30): 168
  8.1.2 (77): 186
  8.1.1–3 (240): 175
  8.4.3 (81): 180
  8.4.4 (81): 186
  8.5.2 (83): 186
  8.6.4–5 (88): 192
  8.8.5–7 (84): 186
  8.9.2 (82): 186
  8.10.3–4 (87): 191
  8.11.3 (91): 193
  8.13.2 (94): 193
  8.14.1 (97): 188
  8.14.2 (97): 193
  10–13 (33–36): 168
  14 (38): 168

  16 (32): 168
  17 (31): 168
  18 (37): 168
Flacc.
  7/15: 220
  7/16: 221
  24/57: 226
Har. resp.
  4/8–5/9: 164
  11/22: 163
  23/48: 145
Man.
  9/26: 79
  15/44: 82, 224
  17/52: 80, 86
  19/56: 86
  20/59: 81
  23/68: 86
Mil.
  8/22: 85
  14/37: 181
  32/87: 36
  33/89: 36
Mur.
  11/24: 100
  17/38: 19
  18/38: 100
  19/40: 74
  20/42: 29, 100
  23/47: 17
  24/49–16/53: 100
  38/81: 112
Phil.
  1.3/8: 29
  9.7/15–16: 45
  12.11/27: 53
Pis.
  1/3: 74
  2–3/4–7: 96, 113
  15/36: 37
  215: 97
Planc.
  3/7: 174
  4/9–10: 173
  4/11: 174

Cicero, M. Tullius (*continued*)
  Planc. (*continued*)
    5/12: 174
    6/15: 173, 175
    8–9/19–23: 30
    8/19–9/22: 172
    19/47: 172
    20/49–50: 174
    29/69: 56, 64
  Post red. ad Quir.
    7/16: 151
    7/17: 154
    8/18: 37
  Post red. in Sen.
    2/4: 146
    5/12: 139
    6/13: 139
    7/18: 143
    9/24: 151
    10/25–26: 151
    11/27–28: 37
    11/29: 151
    13/32: 139
  Q.f.
    1.2.15 (2): 135
    2.1 (5): 159
    2.3.2 (7): 161
    2.3.4 (7): 30
    2.5.2–4 (9): 164
    2.12.3 (16): 178
    2.14 (13, 18): 168
    2.16 (15, 20): 168
    3.1.8–13 (21): 168
    3 (26): 168
    3.2.3 (22): 180
    6 (8): 168

  Rab. perd.
    3/8: 107
    4/11: 107
    7/20: 107
    12/35: 108
  Rab. Post.
    7/18: 215

  Sest.
    8/18: 135
    10/24: 143
    12/28: 139
    15/34: 35, 137
    17/39–40: 139
    19/43: 138
    25/55–26/56: 138
    28/60: 144
    29/62: 114
    33/72–35/77: 149
    36/78: 149
    37/79–39/84: 150
    38/82: 210
    43/93: 80
    50/106: 152
    50/107–8: 153
    51/109: 36, 154
    53/113: 128
    58/124: 148
    59/125–26: 148
    60/128: 37
    65/137: 219
  Sull.
    23/65: 105
  Vat.
    9/21: 129
    10/24: 134
    11/28: 44
    14/33–34: 142
    15/36: 133
    17/40: 141
  Verr.
    1.1/2: 71
    1.7/18–19: 68
    1.8–9/22–26: 68
    1.10/31: 65
    1.15/44: 66
    1.15/45: 65
    1.16/47: 71
    1.18/54: 27
    1.60/155: 54
    2.1.1/1, 5/12: 71
    2.1.5./12–14: 16
    2.1.42/122: 63

2.1.46/119: 57
2.1.49/129: 71
2.2.41/100: 63
2.2.55/138: 69
2.2.71/174: 70
2.3.70/163: 63
2.3.75/173: 63
2.3.96/223: 69
2.5.14/36–37: 74
2.5.21/52: 63
2.5.55/143–44: 72
2.5.68/175: 67, 207, 219
2.5.69/177–78: 70
2.5.72/186: 42

Com. pet., 8/30: 34

Digesta, 1.2.2: 199
Dionysius of Halicarnassus
   Ant.
      4.13.3–4: 31
      4.16–21: 201
      4.20–21: 16
      4.21.3: 17
      4.24.5: 36
      10.4: 206
      10.41.1: 46

Fenestella, 21/22: 159

Granius Licinianus, 33.14: 58

Herodotus, 1.167: 20

Livy
   1.43: 16, 201
   2.58.1: 205
   25.2.8: 32
   31.50.6–7: 46
   38.36: 22
   45.15.3–7: 23
   45.15.4: 36
   45.36.1–6: 46

Per.
   77: 35
   89: 54
Lucan, *Phars.*, 7.7–8: 222

Macrobius, *Sat.*, 1.16.34: 20

Orosius, 6.6.4: 117

Pliny
   NH
      6.30/117: 97
      7.27/99: 117
      15.1/2: 60
      18.4/16: 60
      33.16/53: 76
      35.7/23: 25
Plutarch
   Ant.
      5.1: 194
   Caes.
      5.1–2: 75
      6.1–4: 76
      15: 114
      29.5: 185
      30.1–2: 193
   Camillus
      22: 21
   Cato Min.
      26.2: 114
      27–29: 114
      43: 170
   Cic.
      8.1: 74
      13: 97
      22: 111
   Crass.
      12: 64
      12.2–3: 65
      12.3–4: 66
   Luc.
      5.4: 61
      33.5: 79
      37: 32, 87

Plutarch (*continued*)
  Pomp.
    21.3–5: 64
    22: 66
    23: 66
    25: 81
    30: 86
    45: 117
    47: 127
    49.6: 160
    51: 165
    52.1: 165
    52–53: 172
    54.1: 117
    54.1–3: 180
    55.7: 185
    57: 196
    59.4–5: 193
    68.2: 222
Polybius
  6.14: 24
  6.16.4–5: 24
  6.53.1–6.53.3: 6
  31.29.8: 25, 224

Rhet. ad Herenn., 1.11/20: 216

Sallust
  Bell. Jug.
    40.1–2: 50
    73: 52
  Cat.
    3.8.1–2: 73
    21.3: 98
    24.1: 98
    26–27: 99
    29: 108
    37–39: 109

    43: 109
    48: 109
  Hist.
    1.55 M = 1.48 McG.: 58
    2.45 M = 2.42 McG.: 44
    3.48.8–12 M = 3.34 McG.: 59
    3.48.19–20 M = 3.34.17–20
      McG.: 63
    5.13 M = 5.11 McG.: 79
    5.14 M = 5.12 McG.: 78
Suetonius
  Div. Aug.
    46: 33
  Div. Iul.
    5.1: 67
    6: 75
    9: 130
    10: 75, 130
    11: 76
    15–16: 114
    19.2: 123
    20.4: 126
    24.1: 165
    26.2: 177
    41.3: 32
    49: 130

Val Max
  2.7.1: 115
  4.6.4: 172
  5.2.7: 56
  6.2.6: 166
  8.1.3: 178
  9.12.7: 41
Valerius Maximus, 5.9.2: 9
Vell. Pat.
  2.18.3: 53
  2.40.4: 105